**net•s Assessment** **National Educational Technology Standards for Students**

Resources for Student Assessment

M. G. (PEGGY) KELLY

JON HABER

International Society for Technology in Education
EUGENE, OREGON

National Educational Technology Standards for Students
Resources for Student Assessment

M. G. (Peggy) Kelly and Jon Haber

DIRECTOR OF PUBLISHING
Jean Marie Hall

ACQUISITIONS AND DEVELOPMENT EDITOR
Scott Harter

PRODUCTION EDITOR
Tracy Cozzens

PRODUCTION COORDINATOR
Amy Miller

COPY EDITOR
Nancy Olson

LAYOUT AND PRODUCTION
Tracy Cozzens and Kim McGovern

COVER DESIGN
Kim McGovern

International Society for Technology in Education (ISTE)
480 Charnelton Street
Eugene, OR 97401-2626
Order Desk: 1.800.336.5191
Order Fax: 1.541.302.3778
Customer Service: orders@iste.org
Book Publishing: books@iste.org
Rights and Permissions: permissions@iste.org
World Wide Web: www.iste.org

First Edition
ISBN 1-56484-220-7

ABOUT ISTE

The International Society for Technology in Education (ISTE) is a nonprofit professional organization with a worldwide membership of leaders in education technology. We are dedicated to promoting appropriate uses of information technology to support and improve learning, teaching, and administration in PK–12 education and teacher education. As part of that mission, ISTE provides high-quality and timely information, services, and materials, such as this book.

ISTE's Seal of Alignment Program

As classrooms become more student centered and students become more tech savvy, educators must apply new strategies for both curriculum development and implementation and the assessment of learning outcomes. As the trusted source for information on education technology, ISTE believes in recognizing exemplary programs and products through its peer-reviewed ISTE Seal of Alignment Program (**www.iste.org/nets/seal**). This program recognizes curriculum and assessment resources that have successfully aligned themselves with one or more components of the National Educational Technology Standards (NETS) for Students, Teachers, and Administrators.

The NETS-aligned assessment resources outlined in this book can help school leaders identify assessment solutions that meet their state and local needs. Current assessment partners include Certiport (a sponsor of this book; **www. certiport.com**), International Computer Driving License (**www.icdlus.com**), Learning.com (**www.learning.com/tla**), Microsoft (**www. iste.org/resources/asmt/msiste/**), and PBS TeacherLine (**http://www.pbs.org/teacherline/**).

ISTE's Book Publishing Program

ISTE Book Publishing works with experienced educators to develop and produce classroom-tested books and courseware. Every manuscript and product we select for publication is peer reviewed and professionally edited. We look for content that emphasizes the use of technology where it can make a difference—making the teacher's job easier; saving time; motivating students; helping students who have unique learning styles, abilities, or backgrounds; and creating learning environments that would be impossible without technology. We believe technology can improve the effectiveness of teaching while making learning exciting and fun. We value your feedback on this book and other ISTE products. E-mail us at **books@iste.org**.

ISTE thanks Certiport, SkillCheck, and Thomson Course Technology for their sponsorship of *NETS•S: Resources for Student Assessment*. Their support of this work and of ISTE's larger mission is deeply appreciated, and speaks highly of their commitment to advancing effective uses of technology in education.

Visit ISTE on the Web

ISTE is home of the National Educational Technology Standards (NETS) Project, the National Educational Computing Conference (NECC), and the National Center for Preparing Tomorrow's Teachers to Use Technology (NCPT[3]). To learn more about ISTE or request a print catalog of our books, visit our Web site at **www.iste.org**, which provides

- current education technology standards for PK–12 students, teachers, and administrators,
- a bookstore with online ordering and membership discount options,
- *Learning & Leading with Technology* magazine and the *Journal of Research on Technology in Education,*
- *ISTE Update,* online membership newsletter,
- teacher resources,
- discussion groups,
- professional development services, including national conference information,
- research projects,
- member services.

ABOUT CERTIPORT

CERTIPORT®
Achieve • Distinguish • Advance

Certiport is pleased to partner with ISTE to provide assessment solutions for ISTE's National Educational Technology Standards for Students (NETS•S) and Teachers (NETS•T), and is a proud sponsor of *NETS•S: Resources for Student Assessment.*

As an ISTE 100 Member, Certiport has collaborated with ISTE to align its Internet and Computing Core Certification (IC³) to the NETS. IC³ is the world's first validated, standards-based, vendor-independent training and certification program for basic computing and Internet knowledge and skills. It's the only global certification program in support of the NETS on the market today.

In addition to endorsement by ISTE, the IC³ standard has been ratified and endorsed by national and international qualification bodies, standards organizations, and such academic institutions as the American Council on Education; ACT; the Computer Technology Industry Association; the Global Digital Literacy Council; the Oxford, Cambridge & Royal Society for Arts in Britain; the National Infocomm Competency Centre in Singapore; and the New Zealand Qualifications Authority. More than 3,000 training and testing centers in 64 countries worldwide have adopted the IC³ program for digital literacy at school and in the workplace.

Without question, the global reach of IC³ complements and supports the international adoption of the NETS. In its review of the IC³ program, ISTE determined that IC³ clearly supports implementation of the NETS•S and NETS•T in specific, carefully reviewed, and documented ways. It substantially prepares students and teachers to effectively use technology as prescribed by these standards.

In order to realize the global promise and potential of the NETS, Certiport is committed to helping ISTE make available a full and effective range of assessment tools such as IC³. For more information on Certiport, its relationship with ISTE, and support for the NETS, visit **www.certiport.com**.

NETS•S ALIGNMENT
Meets: 1A, 1B, 2A, 2B, 2C, 3A, 4A, 5A
Supports: 5C

NETS•T ALIGNMENT
Meets: I.A., II.C., V.C., V.D., VI.D.
Supports: I.B., IV.B., V.A., VI. A.

ABOUT SKILLCHECK

SkillCheck

SkillCheck is a leading provider of performance-based assessment solutions, offering more than 18 years of experience developing and delivering testing on information and communication technologies (ICT) and other skills to education and industry.

As a partner and developer of the Internet and Computing Core Certification (IC^3), Skill-Check has worked closely with ISTE to ensure that the goals of this globally emerging certification are in alignment with the NETS. SkillCheck has worked with the NETS leadership team to provide options for ISTE's NETS•T Candidate Readiness Benchmark and to ensure that the IC^3 certification program is informed by the latest thinking in education technology.

With the passage of the No Child Left Behind Act and other federal, state, and local initiatives, testing has become increasingly important to educators at all levels. SkillCheck is committed to providing flexible, high-quality automated assessments that can be used to measure learning retention, academic readiness, and success in K–12, 2-year and 4-year colleges, and vocational programs.

SkillCheck's innovative testing solutions and expertise in test development, validation, and deployment have empowered educational institutions around the world with high-quality, performance-based testing solutions and easy-to-use test-making tools that can add value to any educational curriculum. Its expertise in large-scale automated testing has been informed by years of working closely with some of the largest and most successful businesses in the world on pre-employment and post-training assessments.

To learn more about resources SkillCheck has available for educators, visit **www.skillcheck.com/education**.

ABOUT THOMSON COURSE TECHNOLOGY

Thomson Course Technology is dedicated to helping people teach and learn with technology. As a proud sponsor of *NETS•S: Resources for Student Assessment,* its goals are aligned with ISTE's mission to provide "leadership and service to improve teaching and learning by advancing the effective use of technology in K–12 education and teacher education."

Since 1989, Thomson Course Technology has published innovative texts and creative electronic learning solutions to help educators teach, students learn, and individuals expand their understanding of emergent and current technologies. Its goal is to produce dynamic products in all technology-related disciplines, as well as instructional resource materials and powerful technology-based assessment and learning solutions that surpass customer needs and expectations.

The No Child Left Behind Act is redefining Thomson Course Technology's mission in the K–12 world, just as it is challenging technology-using educators at every level to lend their expertise to the ongoing debate about exactly what "technology literacy" is and how it should be assessed. Thomson's market-leading software SAM (Skills Assessment Manager) is a testing and training tool that measures and reinforces Microsoft Office, Internet, Microsoft Windows, and other key technology concepts. Through SAM, districts can provide teachers with a customizable, flexible solution for training and assessing students' knowledge of and proficiency in basic technology skills and concepts. Districts can also use the tool to assess teachers' knowledge and skill in integrating technology into the classroom.

Over the years, Thomson Course Technology has evolved its own goals from supporting technology literacy efforts to enabling true technology fluency. Being literate means you can read; being fluent means you truly understand and can communicate. One lesson learned from developing products such as SAM is the value of courseware that looks on the surface like an assessment tool but in reality helps both teachers and students progressively refine and adjust how they teach and what they learn. Because no one has yet defined precisely the right way to reach all students and give them the basic technology skills they need, such midcourse corrections make teaching tools truly useful.

Thomson Course Technology is confident you will find the information provided in this book helpful in navigating the evolving educational landscape, and looks forward to an ongoing dialogue with you. To find out more about Thomson Course Technology, please visit **www.course.com/school**.

ABOUT THE AUTHORS

M. G. (Peggy) Kelly, Ed.D., has 16 years of experience teaching in the public schools in kindergarten through eighth grade and has coordinated a parent cooperative preschool. She has taught at the university level for more than 20 years. She is the co-director of ISTE's National Educational Technology Standards (NETS) Project and has directed the development of the standards publications. Dr. Kelly is a past president of ISTE, served on the National Educational Computing Conference (NECC) Board, and chaired NECC in 1998. At California State University San Marcos, she taught courses in mathematics for education and educational technology and supervised student teachers. She is currently associate dean of the College of Education and continues to work on collaborative projects with the public schools.

Jon Haber is president of SkillCheck, Inc., a test development firm in Burlington, Massachusetts, that specializes in performance-based assessment for the education, training, and employment industries. He founded SkillCheck in 1988 and has worked with companies such as Manpower, Inc., to create assessment solutions to ensure computer literacy for hundreds of thousands of temporary and permanent employees worldwide. Under his leadership, SkillCheck developed the Internet and Computing Core Certification (IC³) in concert with members of the ISTE NETS leadership team and other specialists in education technology around the world to define computer and Internet literacy standards that can be measured using an industry-standard professional IT certification. SkillCheck has also worked with numerous U.S. schools and districts to create specialized assessment solutions.

Contributing Authors

Lajeane Thomas chairs the ISTE Accreditation and Standards Committee. She is also director of the NETS Project and a professor of curriculum, instruction, and leadership at Louisiana Tech University in Ruston. She has served on the National Educational Computing Conference (NECC) Board and on the ISTE Board, and is a past ISTE president. She currently holds a position on the Specialty Area Studies Board of the National Council for Accreditation of Teacher Education (NCATE) and, as ISTE's representative to NCATE, has led the effort to establish education technology standards for accreditation of teacher preparation programs. At NECC 1997 in Seattle, she received the ISTE Outstanding Technology Leader in Education Award.

James Sweet is senior vice president of Digital Education Architects (www.educationarchitects.com), a consulting practice that provides creative vision, technological expertise, and collaborative leadership to help schools create personalized learning environments for digital generation students. He has served as senior program associate in the North Central Regional Educational Laboratory at Learning Point Associates and as director of online learning for Chicago Public Schools. He has presented at ISTE's National Educational Computing Conference (NECC), the Consortium for School Networking, the Association for Supervision and Curriculum Development, and the American Educational Research Association.

Talbot Bielefeldt is director of ISTE's Research and Evaluation Department and administrator of the Center for Applied Research in Educational Technology. He has served as program evaluator on numerous educational initiatives, including U.S. Technology Innovation Challenge Grants, Preparing Tomorrow's Teachers to Use Technology (PT[3]), and Enhancing Education Through Technology. In addition, he has participated in studies of technology planning, laptop computing, teacher preparation, and online learning for a variety of private foundations, state agencies, and school districts. He holds a master's degree in educational policy and management from the University of Oregon.

CONTENTS

Contents

Appendices

PREFACE

In this era of accountability, it's sometimes said, "You get what you test." While that phrase may seem almost punitive in inferring that assessment drives the curriculum, enough work has taken place over the last several years to demonstrate the benefits, as well as the challenges, of integrating assessment into classroom experiences.

We have all seen or heard stories of how overemphasizing standardized test preparation can work to the detriment of good teaching practices. On the other hand, we have also seen or experienced the benefits of using the clearly defined, objective-driven goals of assessment to inform the curriculum and the professional development of teachers. Assessment also lets educators, administrators, and researchers make decisions based on a picture of classrooms, schools, and districts informed by data. *NETS•S: Resources for Student Assessment* sets the stage for you, as an educator, to create a well-defined assessment program focused on assessing student development of technology knowledge, skills, and application.

Given our current globalized, technology-driven economy, the ability of students and educators to master and use technology to enhance learning across the curriculum is becoming increasingly critical.

Although we continue to espouse the importance of technology, the infusion of technology into education continues to lag behind our expectations. While most schools are reported to have Internet access, the access at the classroom level isn't always as pervasive as necessary. We must continue to work to increase the use and effectiveness of technology in the classroom for teaching and learning. As a testimony to the national level of commitment, nearly all states have adopted technology standards for education, most of them based on the International Society for Technology in Education's (ISTE) National Educational Technology Standards for Students (NETS•S), the NETS for Teachers (NETS•T), and the NETS for Administrators (NETS•A). Effective assessment strategies can help us look at the results of our work in a critical way as a means to improve our teaching and implementation strategies.

But, at the same time these goals are being met, we're recognizing that access to equipment and the adoption of state-level education technology standards—important as they are—do not by themselves ensure positive academic outcomes. Initiatives such as the Partnership for 21st Century Skills (www.21stcenturyskills.org), as well as similar projects on the state, national, and international levels, are highlighting important lessons regarding the implementation and use of education technology.

Among the most notable:

- Technology literacy consists of both "hard" skills and "soft" skills. Hard skills are the mastery of today's technology tools. Soft skills are the higher-order thinking skills required to apply these technologies effectively in real-world settings and for real-world purposes.

- Technology can be taught as a stand-alone subject. However, integrating technology into the curriculum by employing education technologies to support content area learning leads to greater student achievement in both hard and soft technology skills.

- Assessment—measuring the level of student technology knowledge, skill development, and ability to apply the skills—is a critical part of determining whether education technology is being successfully implemented in the classroom.

NETS•S: Resources for Student Assessment is designed to provide educators and other stakeholders with the resources needed to make informed choices about how best to assess student technology achievement as defined by the NETS•S. These resources include

- a review of the National Education Technology Standards and the NETS Essential Conditions required to successfully implement an education technology program that includes a well-defined assessment strategy.

- a review of the grade-level performance indicators and a collection of rubrics that translate the high-level goals of the NETS•S into measurable objectives that can be assessed using a variety of techniques.

- a primer on assessment basics and information about different forms of assessment, from familiar multiple-choice tests to technology-rich performance assessments.

- examples and case studies that demonstrate how technology assessments have been successfully implemented at the school, district, state, and national levels.

Just as technology can be infused into the teaching and learning of any academic subject, so too can assessment and education be combined in ways that enhance both student performance and the timely, accurate measurement of that performance. At the same time, the advanced tools currently being developed to assess student technology abilities represent an innovation in testing methodologies that can be applied across all academic disciplines.

The Big Picture of Technology Assessment

Our task is to provide an education for the kinds of kids we have, not the kinds of kids we used to have, or want to have, or the kids of our dreams.

—K. P. GERLACH

Part 1 of this book provides you with both an overview of ISTE's National Educational Technology Standards for Students (NETS•S) and the educational policy context that's driving technology assessment.

It also addresses the fundamental questions that must be answered before a school, district, or state can develop an effective system to assess student attainment of the NETS•S. Answers to the following questions will help you be accountable to the public while remaining sensitive to the complexities of working with children in the classroom.

WHAT?

What do stakeholders—teachers, administrators, district staff, school board members, parents, students, and the community at large—really want to know about education technology? Do they want to

- measure basic computer literacy?
- measure students' ability to use technology as a research and learning tool?
- measure students' performance using all NETS•S performance indicators?

WHY?

Why is an assessment or set of assessments being developed? The rationale should be clearly defined. Is it to

- inform professional development for teachers?
- update and strengthen graduation requirements for students?
- track student achievement in meeting standards over time?
- report to the board of education on the effectiveness of technology expenditures and their influence on learning outcomes?
- examine the impact of teachers' professional development in technology?

HOW?

How will evidence of meeting the NETS•S be collected? Will it include individual student data or a group sample? Will it take the form of test scores or a portfolio of student work samples? Consider the questions

- If a self-reported survey is the assessment instrument of choice, how will it be administered and how will the data be collected?
- If quantitative data are needed to measure student achievement, how will that data be gathered consistently to ensure accurate analysis of the data can occur?
- How can a teacher's own classroom observations serve as the basis for an assessment? If they can, how will teachers have the time, tools, and training to make such observations accurately and consistently?
- If comparisons of individual students or groups of students over time is the goal, how will the data be collected, stored, and compared? Will the data need to be aggregated and disaggregated to look at specific populations or subgroups?

WHO?

Who are the primary consumers of this information? Once that's determined, ask

- In what format and at what level of detail do these consumers want the information?

- How will the data be communicated in a way that meets both the purposes of the consumers and the purposes of the assessment?

Part 1 will provide educators at every level with the basic information they need to frame these questions and then begin to answer them within the context of local environments.

CHAPTER SNAPSHOTS

CHAPTER 1
Assessing the Technology Literacy of K–12 Students

This chapter begins by reviewing the educational policy context that's influencing current student technology assessment initiatives. The chapter also introduces the NETS•S and its performance profiles. The narrative includes a discussion of the relationship between the NETS•S and the accompanying NETS for Teachers (NETS•T) and NETS for Administrators (NETS•A). Guidance is provided for how you may want to use the contents of this book and organize your reading.

CHAPTER 2
Rubrics for the NETS for Students

What does "meeting the standards" mean? This chapter includes a matrix of the NETS•S assessment rubrics for Grades 6 through 8, showing the progression of benchmark targets for technology use for Grades 6, 7, and 8. In addition, the chapter sets the stage for part 2 by describing how the matrix can be used to develop benchmark assessments for each of the four grade ranges (PK–2, 3–5, 6–8, and 9–12).

CHAPTER 1

Assessing the Technology Literacy of K–12 Students

The popular wisdom is that kids in classrooms today are far more comfortable with technology than are most of their parents and teachers. Stories of plugged-in kids surfing the Web, text-messaging friends, posting to blogs, and playing multiuser games—often at the same time—can make us forget that not all K–12 students enjoy the same access to these technologies and resources. The fact that many students surf the Internet and chat online every day does not necessarily mean they have the technology skills they need to succeed in the 21st century. How can we go beyond these popular images and anecdotes to accurately measure students' ability to use technology effectively for learning?

Around the world, several countries have already taken steps at the national level to ensure that information and communication technologies (ICT) are a fundamental component of elementary and secondary education, in the same category as literacy, math, science, and social studies. To compete in the global 21st-century economy, therefore, all American students will find it increasingly necessary to develop basic technology competencies that will, in turn, support critical thinking, problem solving, and other higher-order thinking skills. As such, it's crucial to develop valid and reliable ways to assess student technology competence.

Given that over the past several years assessment projects at the state level have focused on language arts and mathematics skills, assessing technology has generally been thought of in the context of the role which it plays as a *medium* for assessing student performance with regard to academic content standards. From this perspective, technology is the electronic bubble sheet, the computer-delivered test, the automated grader, the e-portfolio. Only recently has technology become the *subject* of assessment at the district, state, and national level. The purpose of this book is to provide a set of resources, strategies, and options for assessing the entire range of technology skills that students need for success in their education and careers.

Some of these resources directly support assessment projects within the classroom by modeling stand-alone technology assessments as well as assessments that integrate technology and content area learning. Other resources support large-scale assessment projects that go beyond the classroom; these projects are designed to gather the types of quantitative data needed either for determining accountability for the successful implementation of education technology or for scientifically based research purposes. This broad scope allows this book to address everyone with a stake in student technology literacy and assessment—whether you're a classroom teacher, school or district administrator, parent, community member, or policy maker—with the aim of giving you the tools you need to assess how well your students are meeting the ISTE NETS•S.

CATALYSTS FOR ASSESSMENT

In the last century, Sputnik galvanized the American scientific and political establishment to focus attention on the need for more effective and creative science education in U.S. schools. In today's global economy—with highly paid technical jobs increasingly moving overseas—political, business, and education leaders in the U.S. are focusing on the role of technology in education.

This increased attention has led to some positive outcomes, such as the investment to provide most U.S. schools with Internet access. Statistics available through Quality Education Data and the U.S. Department of Education point to continuing increases in technology expenditures: "The Technology Purchasing Forecast…predicts that school district total technology budgets for the 2004–2005 school year will total $7.06 billion, including both E-rate and district spending" (Quality Education Data, 2004). Along with this increase in spending have come improvements in student and teacher access to technology, as well as calls for increased accountability.

These accountability issues loom heavily over public schools. In the case of education technology, accountability issues take two basic forms:

- demonstrating that the investments made in education technology are leading directly to increased student learning (often measured by academic test scores), and

- demonstrating that increased access to technology is leading to increased student understanding of today's most essential ICT tools and the skills needed to use them.

At the same time that politicians and parents are demanding higher levels of accountability from schools, students are increasingly expecting teachers to provide them with an engaging, multisensory learning environment that's more like the interactive environments they're familiar with in video games and the Internet. It has been repeatedly demonstrated that technology effectively used in a learning situation can increase student motivation and engagement, and improve conceptual understanding of complex concepts. But how do we know if students are really acquiring the skills they need to take advantage of these new learning technologies? Parents and community members are looking to schools to provide evidence that these skills are being taught and that students are applying them to increase their learning.

In an era when public school expenditures and school performance are subject to intense scrutiny, these questions persist:

- Are students really learning to use the available technologies?

- What evidence do we have that students know basic technology skills and concepts?

- Are students using technology to learn complex academic content that cannot be taught any other way?

- How is all this technology supporting the development of higher-order thinking skills?

The resources collected in this book will help you examine these big-picture questions from a more informed perspective. They'll help you make decisions about how you want to assess your students' technology competence. As you think about developing a comprehensive technology assessment plan, you'll want to rely on what's already well-known about effective student assessment practices: having multiple measures, assessing over time, and assessing within the normal classroom context.

Before adding one more accountability measure to the ever-increasing pile of assessments, consider how technology differs from other content areas. It's not just a subject in and of itself; education technology is also a complicated and intricate curriculum delivery method. When integrated successfully, it supports the meeting of other content area standards and helps create a learning environment in which complex, creative, problem-solving thinking can take place.

FEDERAL EDUCATION POLICY AND ASSESSMENT

The role of the federal government in U.S. public education is quite limited when compared with the role of central governing authorities in other countries. While central governments in Great Britain, France, China, and many other countries have the ability to prescribe a national curriculum, including initiatives addressing ICT, with only a few exceptions education in the United States is a state-level responsibility. Curriculum development and approval in our country belongs to individual states.

One method the federal government has at its disposal for influencing state educational content and policy nationwide is targeted, legislated funding. The No Child Left Behind Act of 2001 (NCLB), a law that ties federal funding to the achievement of specific educational goals, is an example of how federal legislation can become a de facto mandate to be implemented at the state level.

Eighth-Grade Technology Literacy Requirement

Technology plays a key role in NCLB legislation, as the following excerpt shows.

No Child Left Behind Act of 2001
Title II, Part D, Enhancing Education Through Technology

PRIMARY GOAL: The primary goal of this part [of the NCLB act] is to improve student academic achievement through the use of technology in elementary and secondary schools.

ADDITIONAL GOALS: The additional goals of this part are the following:

- To assist every student in crossing the digital divide by ensuring that every student is technologically literate by the time he or she finishes the eighth grade, regardless of the student's race, ethnicity, gender, family income, geographic location, or disability.

- To encourage the effective integration of technology resources and systems with teacher training and curriculum development to establish research-based instructional methods that can be widely implemented as best practices by state educational agencies and local educational agencies (No Child Left Behind Act of 2001).

It's this 8th-grade technology literacy requirement that has spurred the most interest in assessing student achievement of the ISTE NETS•S. While *technology literacy* has varying definitions, the placement of this benchmark at the 8th-grade level is clear. Therefore, the rubrics in chapter 2 and appendix B include specific measures of student technology proficiency at the 8th-grade level as well as performance benchmarks for the 2nd-, 5th-, and 12th-grade levels. Teachers can use these 8th-grade rubrics to define a set of foundational skills upon which to build a technology preparation program for students entering high school.

In addition to establishing the broad goal of student technology literacy by the eighth grade, NCLB legislation requires that states, school districts, and individual schools provide scientifically based evidence to demonstrate the success of their programs. The question then arises: What constitutes scientifically-based evidence as far as student technology assessment is concerned? Many of the resources in this book are designed to help you answer that question within the context of your local environment (state or district, or both).

The Influence of NCLB on Technology Funding

Funding for education technology has never enjoyed a stable revenue stream at either the state or federal level. While teachers and schools have become masters at seeking external funding for education technology, this lack of consistent support will continue to be a challenge for those trying to implement long-range assessment plans (Cradler & Cradler, 2002).

NCLB includes an important provision—grants—for funneling money into education technology (see box on next page). These Enhancing Education Through Technology grants, also referred to as E^2T^2 or EETT grants, are provided by the federal government to individual states. Up to now, the states have then distributed the funds to school districts by using formula allocation and grant competition. This has enabled states and districts to use their own discretion in allocating federal funds for education technology. Due to recent cuts in EETT funding at the federal level, however, the process for distributing these funds is in a state of flux. Federal guidelines do, however, mandate that NCLB grant funds must be spent within the parameters defined by the following six priority areas:

1. accountability
2. literacy
3. a focus on "what works"
4. professional development
5. education technology
6. parent involvement

In addition to being one of the six priority areas, education technology plays a key role in the implementation of the other five areas, all of which are focused on improving student achievement (see next page).

Recent state and federal education initiatives, such as the No Child Left Behind Act of 2001, stress over and over the need for standards as a basis both for better teaching and for accurate assessment. It was within this context that ISTE first published the NETS•S in 1998. These standards have since been adopted or adapted by 49 of the 50 states. The ISTE NETS Project provides you with comprehensive standards and guidelines with which to examine student progress toward technology literacy. Before we can understand how these standards can be used as a basis for assessment, however, it's important to first understand how these standards have been framed and organized.

HOW TECHNOLOGY CAN WORK WELL IN SCHOOLS

No Child Left Behind (NCLB) focuses on how teachers and students can use technology.

Previous federal programs focused on increasing access to more technology. In an effort to improve student achievement through the use of technology, U.S. Secretary of Education Rod Paige announced a new Enhancing Education Through Technology (Ed Tech) initiative.

The goals of Ed Tech grants are to:

- Improve student academic achievement through the use of technology in elementary schools and secondary schools.

- Assist students to become technologically literate by the time they finish the eighth grade.

- Ensure that teachers are able to integrate technology into the curriculum to improve student achievement.

Technology must enhance learning.

- It's not enough simply to have a computer and an Internet connection in the classroom if they are not made part of the learning process.

- Technology is a tool like any other, and the value does not come from having access to it, but rather how it is used.

- Ed Tech grants will improve the quality of education by developing new ways to apply this tool to teaching and learning.

It expands options and provides better information on education.

- Several components of No Child Left Behind allow schools to purchase technology resources to support program goals. The result is technology aligned with specific goals tied to state academic standards.

- Online tests deliver reports on student progress instantaneously instead of weeks later. When designed well, curriculum software can engage students in solid academic curriculum like never before.

Excerpted from *Proven Methods: The Facts About...21st-Century Technology.*

AN OVERVIEW OF THE ISTE NETS FOR STUDENTS

The ISTE NETS for Students, or NETS•S, was expressly designed to define the knowledge and skills all students need to be fully prepared for the 21st-century learning environment and workforce. The six broad categories of standards and the bulleted standards within each category that make up the NETS•S are shown on the following page. Figure 1.1 lists detailed performance profiles based on these standards for each of the four grade ranges (PK–2, 3–5, 6–8, 9–12).

National Educational Technology Standards for Students (NETS•S)

1. **Basic operations and concepts**
   - Students demonstrate a sound understanding of the nature and operation of technology systems.
   - Students are proficient in the use of technology.

2. **Social, ethical, and human issues**
   - Students understand the ethical, cultural, and societal issues related to technology.
   - Students practice responsible use of technology systems, information, and software.
   - Students develop positive attitudes toward technology uses that support lifelong learning, collaboration, personal pursuits, and productivity.

3. **Technology productivity tools**
   - Students use technology tools to enhance learning, increase productivity, and promote creativity.
   - Students use productivity tools to collaborate in constructing technology-enhanced models, preparing publications, and producing other creative works.

4. **Technology communications tools**
   - Students use telecommunications to collaborate, publish, and interact with peers, experts, and other audiences.
   - Students use a variety of media and formats to communicate information and ideas effectively to multiple audiences.

5. **Technology research tools**
   - Students use technology to locate, evaluate, and collect information from a variety of sources.
   - Students use technology tools to process data and report results.
   - Students evaluate and select new information resources and technological innovations based on the appropriateness to specific tasks.

6. **Technology problem-solving and decision-making tools**
   - Students use technology resources for solving problems and making informed decisions.
   - Students employ technology in the development of strategies for solving problems in the real world.

FIGURE 1.1
Profiles Aligned with the NETS•S

Profiles for Technology-Literate Students

All students should have opportunities to demonstrate the following performances. Numbers in parentheses following each performance indicator refer to the standards category to which the performance is linked. See page 13 for a list of the standards.

GRADES PK–2
Prior to completion of Grade 2 students will:

1. Use input devices (e.g., mouse, keyboard, remote control) and output devices (e.g., monitor, printer) to successfully operate computers, VCRs, audiotapes, and other technologies. (1)
2. Use a variety of media and technology resources for directed and independent learning activities. (1, 3)
3. Communicate about technology using developmentally appropriate and accurate terminology. (1)
4. Use developmentally appropriate multimedia resources (e.g., interactive books, educational software, elementary multimedia encyclopedias) to support learning. (1)
5. Work cooperatively and collaboratively with peers, family members, and others when using technology in the classroom. (2)
6. Demonstrate positive social and ethical behaviors when using technology. (2)
7. Practice responsible use of technology systems and software. (2)
8. Create developmentally appropriate multimedia products, with support from teachers, family members, or student partners. (3)
9. Use technology resources (e.g., puzzles, logical thinking programs, writing tools, digital cameras, drawing tools) for problem solving, communication, and illustration of thoughts, ideas, and stories. (3, 4, 5, 6)
10. Gather information and communicate with others using telecommunications, with support from teachers, family members, or student partners. (4)

GRADES 3–5
Prior to completion of Grade 5 students will:

1. Use keyboards and other common input and output devices (including adaptive devices when necessary) efficiently and effectively. (1)
2. Discuss common uses of technology in daily life and the advantages and disadvantages those uses provide. (1, 2)
3. Discuss basic issues related to responsible use of technology and information and describe personal consequences of inappropriate use. (2)
4. Use general purpose productivity tools and peripherals to support personal productivity, remediate skill deficits, and facilitate learning throughout the curriculum. (3)
5. Use technology tools (e.g., multimedia authoring, presentation, Web tools, digital cameras, and scanners) for individual and collaborative writing, communication, and publishing activities to create knowledge products for audiences inside and outside the classroom. (3, 4)
6. Use telecommunications efficiently and effectively to access remote information, communicate with others in support of direct and independent learning, and pursue personal interests. (4)
7. Use telecommunications and online resources (e.g., e-mail, online discussions, Web environments) to participate in collaborative problem-solving activities for the purpose of developing solutions or products for audiences inside and outside the classroom. (4, 5)
8. Use technology resources (e.g., calculators, data collection probes, videos, educational software) for problem-solving, self-directed learning, and extended learning activities. (5, 6)
9. Determine when technology is useful and select the appropriate tool(s) and technology resources to address a variety of tasks and problems. (5, 6)
10. Evaluate the accuracy, relevance, appropriateness, comprehensiveness, and bias of electronic information sources. (6)

continued

FIGURE 1.1 *continued*

Profiles Aligned with the NETS•S

GRADES 6–8

Prior to completion of Grade 8 students will:

1. Apply strategies for identifying and solving routine hardware and software problems that occur during everyday use. (1)
2. Demonstrate knowledge of current changes in information technologies and the effect those changes have on the workplace and society. (2)
3. Exhibit legal and ethical behaviors when using information and technology, and discuss consequences of misuse. (2)
4. Use content-specific tools, software, and simulations (e.g., environmental probes, graphing calculators, exploratory environments, Web tools) to support learning and research. (3, 5)
5. Apply productivity/multimedia tools and peripherals to support personal productivity, group collaboration, and learning throughout the curriculum. (3, 6)
6. Design, develop, publish, and present products (e.g., Web pages, videotapes) using technology resources that demonstrate and communicate curriculum concepts to audiences inside and outside the classroom. (4, 5, 6)
7. Collaborate with peers, experts, and others using telecommunications and collaborative tools to investigate curriculum-related problems, issues, and information, and to develop solutions or products for audiences inside and outside the classroom. (4, 5)
8. Select and use appropriate tools and technology resources to accomplish a variety of tasks and solve problems. (5, 6)
9. Demonstrate an understanding of concepts underlying hardware, software, and connectivity, and of practical applications to learning and problem solving. (1, 6)
10. Research and evaluate the accuracy, relevance, appropriateness, comprehensiveness, and bias of electronic information sources concerning real-world problems. (2, 5, 6)

GRADES 9–12

Prior to completion of Grade 12 students will:

1. Identify capabilities and limitations of contemporary and emerging technology resources and assess the potential of these systems and services to address personal, lifelong learning, and workplace needs. (2)
2. Make informed choices among technology systems, resources, and services. (1,2)
3. Analyze advantages and disadvantages of widespread use of and reliance on technology in the workplace and in society as a whole. (2)
4. Demonstrate and advocate for legal and ethical behavior among peers, family, and community regarding the use of technology and information. (2)
5. Use technology tools and resources for managing and communicating personal/professional information (e.g., finances, schedules, addresses, purchases, correspondence). (3, 4)
6. Evaluate technology-based options, including distance and distributed education, for lifelong learning. (5)
7. Routinely and efficiently use online information resources to meet needs for collaboration, research, publications, communications, and productivity. (4, 5, 6)
8. Select and apply technology tools for research, information analysis, problem solving, and decision making in content learning. (4, 5)
9. Investigate and apply expert systems, intelligent agents, and simulations in real-world situations. (3, 5, 6)
10. Collaborate with peers, experts, and others to contribute a content-related knowledge base by using technology to compile, synthesize, produce, and disseminate information, models, and other creative works. (4, 5, 6)

Essential Conditions for Implementing the NETS•S

The complex national consensus process used to generate the NETS•S also generated a series of implementation concerns. Many leaders noted that just having a list of standards supported by a limited number of engaging, technology-rich learning activity models was unlikely to guarantee success in *implementing* the standards. Simply identifying what students should be able to *do* with technology does not necessarily mean that teachers and students would *use* technology more effectively for learning.

Contributors and stakeholders, both inside and outside education, responded to the development of the standards. They eventually identified a set of specific essential conditions necessary for educators at all levels to effectively use technology for learning, teaching, and education management. It was determined that physical, human, financial, and policy dimensions greatly affect both the success of technology use in schools and the ability of teachers to support students in meeting the standards. Therefore, to facilitate student achievement of the NETS•S, the consensus was that the following *NETS Essential Conditions* must also be present for the effective use of technology:

- **Vision**, with support and leadership from the education system
- **Educators** skilled in the use of technology
- **Professional development** to provide educators with education to support technology use in teaching and learning
- **Content standards** and curriculum resources
- **Student-centered** approaches to learning
- **Assessment** of the effectiveness of technology for learning
- **Access** to contemporary technologies, software, and telecommunications networks
- **Technical assistance** for maintaining and using technology resources
- **Community partners** who provide expertise, support, and real-life interactions
- **Ongoing financial support** for sustained technology use
- **Policies and standards** supporting new learning environments

Determining to what degree education systems are meeting these Essential Conditions is crucial to the development of a comprehensive assessment program evaluating how well students are meeting the NETS•S. The final chapter in this book will return to these Essential Conditions and address how each is crucial to supporting effective use of technology in education.

NETS for Teachers and Administrators

The NETS•S were published in 1998 and were the first in a series of technology standards documents. The initial reaction of the general education community was a combination of support and reflective questioning: If these standards are expected of students, then how are teachers going to be able to teach to these standards? What should teachers and administrators know and be able to do to ensure that students can meet the standards?

CONNECTING CURRICULUM AND TECHNOLOGY

The ISTE publication *National Educational Technology Standards for Students: Connecting Curriculum and Technology* (ISTE, 2000a) provides numerous examples of how technology can be used to support the attainment of content area standards.

Capitalizing on the idea that both teaching and assessing the NETS•S should be done in the context of standards-based lessons, *Connecting Curriculum and Technology* provides lesson ideas for use both in classrooms where the organization of the school or grade level is around curriculum areas and in classrooms where multidisciplinary instruction is divided into major content areas.

Lesson ideas are for each of the four grade ranges and model how teachers can teach and assess multiple sets of standards at the same time.

The dialogue that followed provided the foundation for two additional sets of standards: the NETS for Teachers (ISTE, 2000b) and the NETS for Administrators (ISTE, 2002). See appendix C for a complete listing of the NETS•T and the NETS•A.

One common thread throughout all the NETS is a focus on student learning: defining what is to be learned (NETS•S); planning, teaching, and assessing technology use in the classroom (NETS•T); and supporting that teaching, learning, and assessment (NETS•A).

Each set of standards takes a pragmatic approach to supporting student achievement in technology while at the same time acknowledging the complex professional requirements for teachers and administrators. The arrows in Figure 1.2 show the fundamental interconnections between the three sets of NETS.

It's the interconnection between the sets of standards that supports a coherent education technology plan within a school district or community. To foster student success, technology assessment planners should examine all three sets of standards in the context of what needs to be measured. While this book focuses on assessing achievement of the student standards, collecting and evaluating data pertaining to other elements of an educational program involving teachers and administrators may form an important part of an overall assessment plan. See also *National Educational Technology Standards for Teachers: Resources for Assessment* (ISTE, 2003).

FIGURE 1.2
Alignment of the NETS•S, NETS•T, and NETS•A

Note: Teachers should be able to meet all the NETS•S.

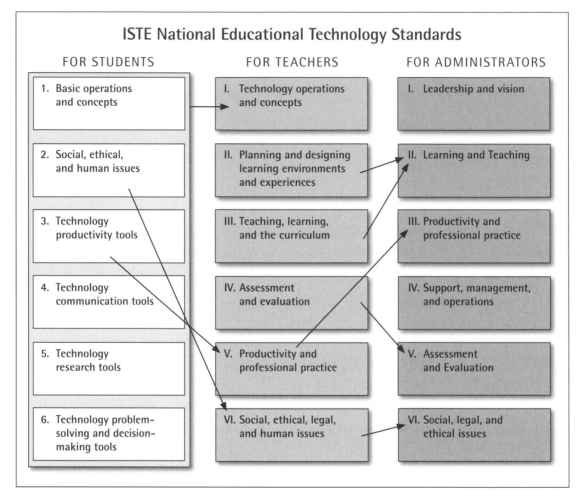

BUILDING A NETS•S ASSESSMENT

The NETS•S and its grade-range performance indicators provide a foundation upon which to build an assessment, or set of assessments, to determine student technology literacy. The chapters that follow provide numerous examples of how the standards can be used as the basis for an assessment program.

Just as academic curricula must consist of objectives that are teachable, assessment standards must consist of objectives that can be measured. Chapter 2 introduces a set of rubrics that build on the NETS•S grade-range performance indicators to provide assessment developers the means to match components of an assessment, such as test questions or classroom observations captured on a checklist, with specific NETS standards and performance indicators.

While the assessment options and methods discussed in this book vary widely, assessments in general fall into one of two categories:

- **Formative assessments** provide information about students' progress as their understanding develops. In the case of technology assessments, an online student response system that automatically generates a customized curriculum or tutorial for individual learning is a type of formative assessment. A student portfolio can be used as a formative assessment by documenting the student's progress in using technology during a school year, including student work, reflections, and feedback from teachers and peers.

- **Summative assessments** typically assess a student's knowledge or performance at benchmarks during the school year or at specific grade-level benchmarks. Final exams, culminating reports, or portfolios that students assemble to demonstrate mastery of a topic are examples of summative assessments.

The specific goals of your assessment program will determine the type of assessment you'll want to develop or purchase.

The NETS•S provides the conceptual framework for addressing technology assessment content; the rest of this book provides you with assessment-building resources and examples of tools and techniques to create assessments that meet educational goals. These include:

- Examples of how the educational guidelines of the NETS•S can be turned into measurable assessment objectives through the use of rubrics. The rubrics in chapter 2 map the grade-range performance indicators of the NETS•S to specific measurable outcomes.

- Examples of curriculum-embedded performance assessments (found in chapters 3 through 6). You'll discover ways teachers can integrate technology assessment into the assessment of academic content across the curriculum.

- Information on the principles and practices of professional test development (chapter 7) followed by detailed information for different assessment types. These include linear tests (chapter 8), self-reporting surveys (chapter 9), assessments based on student and classroom observation (chapter 10), portfolio assessments (chapter 11), and automated assessments delivered by computer (chapter 12). Taken together, these chapters serve as a primer for testing techniques, methods, and practices, providing important background for creating or evaluating any assessment project.

- Case studies demonstrating how some of the principles and methods described in chapters 7 through 12 have been used to create student technology assessments delivered at the district, state, and national level (chapters 13 through 15).

- A discussion of the practical considerations related to implementing a technology assessment program (chapter 16), followed by a final discussion of the NETS Essential Conditions needed for an assessment program—or any education technology program—to succeed (chapter 17).

Technology Assessment in an Academic Context

If we in the education community are to have any hope of accounting for the effects that technology spending has had on learning, it's imperative that we first be clear regarding

- what students should know about technology,

- what they should be able to do with it, and

- how that knowledge should be demonstrated.

Research on teaching and learning becomes muddled when the learning experience is focused on teaching students how to use the technology itself rather than on how to use the technology for learning. Is the *objective* learning to use the technology—or using technology to learn? Embedding the teaching and assessment of technology skills in a standard academic curriculum involves both awareness of the NETS•S and developmentally appropriate instruction.

It's important to remember that no single test or data source will capture all aspects of a student's competency in technology, just as no single assessment in language arts will produce a complete picture of a student's achievement in reading, writing, listening, speaking, and so forth. Because technology is ever-changing and always used in a particular context, the best technology assessment plans will incorporate multiple sources of data.

Technology assessments can, and should, be intertwined with existing academic assessment measures whenever possible. Certain basic technology skills, such as keyboarding, word processing, and searching the Internet, may be assessable in isolation, but assessing higher-level technology skills—for example, using digital research tools, applying technology to solve complex problems, and making decisions based on electronic data—requires the development of engaging, discipline-based testing scenarios in which the academic outcome is also assessed.

Assessment of student technology use should be completed within the larger context of evaluating overall academic achievement. As many researchers have pointed out, "technology cannot be treated as a single independent variable...student achievement is gauged not only by how well students perform on standardized tests but also by students' ability to use higher-order thinking skills" (North Central Regional Education Laboratory, 1999).

Before we start looking more closely at the strategies that teachers, schools, and districts are using today to piece together this assessment puzzle, it's useful to reiterate some of the questions that we started with:

- What do we want to know?

- Why do we want to know it?

Your answers to these questions will drive all other decisions and dictate what kinds of evidence of accountability will be deemed acceptable. Ultimately, it's up to our students to attain the competencies they need to succeed in higher education or the world of work. An effective technology assessment plan, however, can provide us with the data and evidence we need to help our students reach their goals.

HOW TO USE THIS BOOK

This book is intended for a number of audiences.

Classroom Teachers

As a teacher, in many ways you have the most experience developing and implementing assessments. During the course of a semester, you may create many quizzes, research projects, or essay assignments, as well as midterm and final exams. You may also regularly observe and assess student performance in class or on a particular project. Each of these activities is a form of assessment informed by the standards and objectives being assessed, your knowledge of the field, and your instructional experience. You're also frequently the first to implement innovative methods of assessment, such as a computerized assessment system or a portfolio project used to assess a student's progress in meeting the standards.

When a school or district makes plans to implement an assessment program based on the NETS•S, it's crucial that your experience be tapped. You're a critical resource for developing rubrics and new tests, or evaluating third-party commercial assessment options. You bear the burden of teaching to an agreed-on academic standard, such as a state-level technology standard. You also may be asked to implement a particular assessment in your classroom, such as a standardized technology test. Because of all this, it's important that you understand the variety of forms assessment can take.

As a teacher, *NETS•S: Resources for Student Assessment* can help you make decisions about how you want to assess your students' technology competency. In addition to providing both an introduction to best practices in test development and an introduction to a wide variety of test types—from paper-and-pencil multiple-choice tests, to surveys, portfolios, and performance-based skills assessments delivered on the computer—this book includes several practical examples of classroom-based assessment projects that have been successfully implemented at the 2nd-, 5th-, 8th-, and 12th-grade levels (see part 2).

In addition, this book will help you become informed consumers and advocates of sound assessment practices in your school and district. You know firsthand the difficulty of teaching to content area standards while at the same time trying to build technology competency. With the increasing focus on site-based decision making and the use of teacher-leaders to fill gaps in professional development and supporting administrative positions, you may have more influence on assessment decision making than you think. This book will get you up to speed fast.

What if an automated, standardized technology skills test is being proposed for your district? Chapter 7, which covers assessment basics, and chapter 12, which discusses automated assessments, will provide you with the information you need to critically analyze the proposed test. Similarly, if you're being asked to evaluate a survey that will be used to assess technology skill or technology use in your classroom, the information in chapter 9 will help you determine whether the survey will effectively meet your needs and the needs of the school and community. Also, the detailed rubrics in appendix B are useful for evaluating student digital products, reports, and presentations.

Library Media Specialists

As a library media specialist, you know that your role is to support the classroom learning experience. However, a recent survey reported in the *School Library Journal* (Brewer & Milam, 2005) shows that 95 percent of library media specialists provide students with instruction in technology. It's also no accident that information literacy—the academic discipline which inspired the research goals of the NETS•S—grew out of work in the library field (National Forum on Information Literacy, 2005).

Given your crucial role in helping students and teachers access and use the latest technology tools, you may be the key person in your school for assessing student knowledge, skills, and dispositions in the use of technology. Your instructional environment and circumstances differ from that of a classroom teacher, which may require you to think differently about issues of test deployment and implementation. In addition, your experience with helping students and teachers find and evaluate information from online resources will give you an important perspective on what should be covered by a technology assessment.

This book is designed to provide you with options for examining the NETS•S. While you may not create, give, or grade tests like a classroom teacher does, an understanding of assessment fundamentals will help you better understand the needs of teachers and students. Information about the types of assessments available, as well as questions to pose when evaluating an assessment project, will support you in being a valuable member of the school assessment and decision-making teams.

School Administrators

School administrators have the opportunity to see what is and isn't happening in the classroom and should be prepared to be curriculum and technology advocates for the school. Ample evidence shows that without leadership at the school level, effective technology use and coordinated technical support for teachers don't tend to happen. As an administrator, you're likely to have a few teachers who have embraced the opportunities and challenges of integrating technology into the classroom. These teachers build creative, standards-based lessons incorporating the use of technology without encouragement from the administration. However, without your leadership, the school won't have a cohesive plan for technology integration, and students won't have equal access to technology-rich experiences that help them meet the standards.

You may find yourself engaged in a delicate dance between district needs and the resource requirements of teachers and students at your school. Could a proposed district-wide technology assessment project benefit from input from your school's education technology champions? Are programs being recommended at the school, district, or state level taking into account your teachers' needs for clearly articulated educational standards or test implementation guidelines? As an administrator, you may be in the best position to balance an assessment program's competing goals, such as the state or district need to provide data for professional development of teachers versus parents' desires to know how their children are doing. By presenting all aspects of academic test development and implementation, this book can help you make an informed decision when choosing among alternatives.

This book provides a basis for working with a team of teachers to design an assessment program that makes sense for all stakeholders. Looking at what other districts and schools have done with linear assessments, portfolios, observation checklists, and surveys can inform your team's decision making.

District and State Administrators

It's the responsibility of district and state administrators to take a composite view of assessment in the district or state. As an administrator at this level, you must respond to the needs of the community—as well as political pressures—to provide appropriate and useful data for decision making. Since schools are expected to prepare students either for postsecondary education or immediate entry into the work world, it's the administrator's responsibility to ensure that learning outcomes are meeting student and community needs.

Looking internally, you must also be conscious of the increasing responsibilities placed on teachers. When considering assessment options, it's important to look for a solution that's both scalable for the district or state and capable of implementation by classroom teachers, or whoever will be responsible for administering the assessment to students. Understanding the principles of test development and the essential conditions for implementing an effective assessment program will help you ask better questions and make better decisions.

The case studies and examples in parts 3 and 4 of this book will help you understand many development, deployment, and scaling considerations. When vendors approach the district or state with Web- or computer-based test options, you'll need to be ready with the right questions. While an assessment expert on staff is ideal, that level of expertise isn't always available. Being armed with the right information can help support effective decision making for large-scale assessment programs.

Teacher Educators and Staff Developers

If you're a teacher educator or staff developer, you're often in the position of working with teacher candidates and teacher-leaders. This book provides a framework for looking at ways in which the NETS•S can be evaluated in a variety of contexts. Discussing the strengths and weaknesses of each assessment option, creating student assessment plans for specific scenarios or situations, and critiquing assessment plans are all valuable exercises for prospective teacher-leaders.

It's presumed that teachers who are trying to master skills covered in the NETS•T have already demonstrated achievement of the skills in the NETS•S. Thus, any assessment program applicable to the NETS•S can be modified to fit prospective teachers entering a course of study. Detailed discussion of the resources available to teacher educators for assessing student teachers' technology preparation can be found in *National Educational Technology Standards for Teachers: Resources for Assessment* (ISTE, 2003).

Whether working with current teaching staff in their own course of study using the NETS•S or NETS•T, or helping student teachers understand the types of technology assessments they may be asked to implement once they reach the classroom, you will be involved in assessment discussions at the classroom, school, district, and state levels again and again. A strong understanding of assessment design and how particular assessments have been created and implemented in a variety of environments will give you the tools you need to effectively plan and design professional development opportunities for teachers.

Educational Researchers

Assessing student achievement as it's defined by the NETS•S can play an important part in program evaluation. As a researcher, the techniques outlined in part 3 can help you design appropriate evaluation tools. What role NETS•S student assessments may have in a program evaluation will depend on the goals of the program. Most education technology interventions follow some variation of the logical three-stage structure given below:

> If we provide new resources (such as technology, curriculum, and professional development) then . . .

> > …teachers' practices and/or students' learning environments will change, which may lead to …

> > > …changes in student outcomes, such as improved school behavior and academic achievement.

Depending on the nature of the research being conducted, assessments based on NETS•S could be used as measurement tools for any of these stages. In a high school business class, for example, general technology skills might be the main student outcome of interest for the study. In that case, the appropriate assessment could be one that measures student performance on a standard set of tasks using a range of productivity applications, or it might consist of a rubric-based analysis of student products.

Benchmarking, measuring performance and outcomes, and quantifying student performance and classroom behavior are the cornerstones of educational research. The wide variety of resources in this book that document standard assessment techniques, common assessment methods, and current testing technology can form an important part of any educational research program.

Parents and Community Members

If you're a parent or community member, you can use this book to gain insight into the types of data that can be obtained to measure student attainment of the NETS•S. You can also learn how to be better consumers of data and advocate for contextually appropriate technology assessments. Parts 2 and 3 provide information both about the types of tests and test items most familiar to you and about alternative assessment options that may become increasingly important in the coming years.

In this age of accountability, data relating to student or school performance are more available to parents and other members of the community than ever before. At the same time, these data, whether sent home directly to parents or publicized in the newspaper, are often difficult to understand without first understanding the assessment tools and techniques used to generate the data.

For parents interested in how their children and schools are being evaluated, or parents or educational activists interested in improving the quality of education through effective uses of technology, this book can provide valuable resources to help you understand the principles and practices of assessment that are being used to account for student learning.

References

Brewer, S., & Milam, P. (June 1, 2005). SLJ's technology survey. *School Library Journal.* Retrieved June 15, 2005, from: www.slj.com

Cradler, J., & Cradler, R. (2002). NCLB poses challenges: New federal programs suggest an expanded role for technology. *Learning & Leading with Technology, 30*(2), 46–49, 56–57.

ISTE. (2000a). *National educational technology standards for students: Connecting curriculum and technology.* Eugene, OR: Author.

ISTE. (2000b). *National educational technology standards for teachers.* Eugene, OR: Author. Available at: http://cnets.iste.org/teachers/s_stands.html

ISTE. (2002). *National educational technology standards for administrators.* Eugene, OR: Author. Available at: http://cnets.iste.org/tssa/s_stands.html

ISTE. (2003). *National educational technology standards for teachers: Resources for assessment.* Eugene, OR: Author.

National Forum on Information Literacy. (2005). *Forum overview.* Retrieved August 1, 2005, from www.infolit.org

No Child Left Behind Act of 2001. Pub. L. No. 107-110, 115 Stat. 1425. (2002). Retrieved October 31, 2002, from www.ed.gov/legislation/ESEA02

North Central Regional Education Laboratory. (1999). *Critical issues: Using technology to improve student achievement.* Retrieved January 2, 2005, from: http://www.ncrel.org/sdrs/areas/issues/methods/technlgy/te800.htm

Proven Methods: The Facts About...21st-Century Technology. Retrieved August 1, 2005, http://www.ed.gov/nclb/methods/whatworks/21centtech.html

Quality Education Data. (2004). *2004–2005 technology purchasing forecast* (10th ed.). Denver, CO: Scholastic.

CHAPTER 2

Rubrics for
the NETS for Students

In researching what schools, districts, and states were doing to evaluate the NETS for Students (NETS•S), it was interesting, but not surprising, to discover that many organizations are struggling with the same issue: *how to better define the performance expectations implicit in the standards and performance indicators and make them stated objectives specific enough to be used as the basis for an assessment program*. The discovery of this problem was an important step toward the evolution of an assessment program for student technology achievement as defined by the NETS•S.

The NETS•S were originally created as educational standards, focusing on what needed to be taught. As such, educators have used the NETS•S to define and explore better ways to teach and use technology in the classroom. The NETS•S has also been invaluable in defining curricular approaches to advancing ICT literacy nationwide, having been adopted or adapted by 49 of our 50 states. However, as states and districts have sought ways to assess student achievement of the NETS•S, they've encountered a familiar problem: educational standards and assessment standards aren't necessarily the same thing. Educational standards that guide curriculum development focus on what can be taught. Assessment standards, on the other hand, must focus on what can be measured.

But what does measuring success in meeting those standards look like? For instance, what does meeting the standards mean in the primary grades, and how does that differ from meeting the standards in Grade 5 or Grade 8 or Grade 12? How do teachers know the activities and assessments they're currently using in middle school will enable their students to meet the standards at the eighth-grade benchmark specified by the No Child Left Behind Act (NCLB)? How can educational and assessment activities be sequenced so that students will gain competency over time and successfully attain each of the grade-range benchmarks in turn?

NETS•S ASSESSMENT MODEL

The book *National Educational Technology Standards for Teachers: Resources for Assessment* (ISTE, 2003) introduced the NETS•T Assessment Model. The model is designed to illustrate how teacher educators, professional development staff, and administrators can measure teachers' technology competency using a sustainable, scalable assessment program that aligns with a career-long professional development plan. This plan was based on a series of benchmarks that defined a teacher's technology competency at various points in the teacher's career, with guidelines for assessing competency at each of those well-defined benchmarks.

The NETS•S Assessment Model provides a similar organizational structure, but with a focus on assessing the technology competency of students. It defines levels of student achievement at benchmark points aligned with the NETS•S grade-range performance indicators: PK through Grade 2 (primary), Grades 3 through 5 (intermediate), Grades 6 through 8 (middle school), and Grades 9 through 12 (high school). This model, meant as a starting point for developing an assessment project on NETS•S, is outlined in Figure 2.1.

The NETS•S Assessment Model supports assessing achievement of the four grade-range performance indicators by further defining the standards and performance indicators to create objectives specific enough to be assessed. For example, the important eighth-grade NCLB goal to "assist every student in crossing the digital divide by ensuring that every student is technologically literate by the time he or she finishes the eighth grade" can be supported by the technology literacy proficiency benchmark defined in this model.

Having rigorously defined the benchmarks, the best tools to organize assessment standards and measure student performance are *assessment rubrics* and *developmental rubrics*. Their design and use is described in the next section.

THE DESIGN AND USE OF RUBRICS

Many of the resources provided in this book make extensive use of rubrics. Rubrics generally take the form of tables and are used most frequently to provide trained assessors with scoring guidelines to grade subjective assessments. Chapter 7 describes how rubrics are used by professional testing companies to consistently score large numbers of student-written essays for use in standardized academic exams such as the AP, SAT, and ACT.

FIGURE 2.1

NETS•S Assessment Model

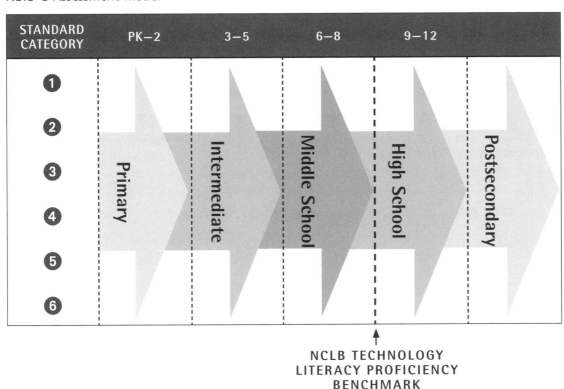

Developers of standards and assessments in education technology have used rubrics in a variety of creative ways, most notably in developing educationally appropriate and integrated assessment projects based on curriculum projects or performance tasks.

Several types of rubrics are used in this book. Traditional *assessment rubrics*—that is, tables or tools used to measure student attainment of specific performance indicators—are included in the descriptions of various assessment projects, such as the classroom assessments detailed in chapters 3 through 6 and the portfolio assessments discussed in chapter 11.

Another type of rubric, the *developmental rubric,* strives to capture the stages of technology skill development across age or grade levels. The NETS•S Developmental Rubric for Grades PK–12 (Figure 2.2) is an example of a developmental rubric applied to the NETS•S Assessment Model. To a certain extent, this rubric simply organizes the NETS•S grade-range performance indicators in a way that makes it clearer what skills need to be assessed at each grade range. Yet it's an important first step, for it gets us closer to defining how the NETS•S can serve as a powerful basis for student assessment by turning the high-level standards and performance indicators into a set of detailed objectives that can be used to develop appropriate assessment tools and resources.

NETS•S DEVELOPMENTAL RUBRIC

The detailed NETS•S Developmental Rubric for Grades PK–12 shown in Figure 2.2 specifies what constitutes technology proficiency at the end of Grades 2, 5, 8, and 12. Many of the items in this rubric are based on the NETS•S grade-range performance indicators shown in Figure 1.1 in chapter 1, but they've been expanded and organized in the familiar format of a rubric to help you better understand what the standards require of students at each benchmark.

While the NETS•S Developmental Rubric provides a useful conceptual guide for making decisions on curriculum development, teacher development, and assessment goal-setting, keep in mind that this rubric isn't intended to serve as the basis for a formal assessment. It will have to be further developed before it can be used to develop an effective and reliable assessment instrument—a process we will discuss in the next section.

FIGURE 2.2
NETS•S Developmental Rubric for Grades PK–12

NETS•S	PROFICIENCY			
	By End of Grade 2	By End of Grade 5	By End of Grade 8	By End of Grade 12
1. BASIC OPERATIONS AND CONCEPTS				
• Students demonstrate a sound understanding of the nature and operation of technology systems.	Students describe how to use basic input devices (e.g., keyboard fingering, mouse/track pad), output devices (e.g., monitor, printer), and software resources (e.g., MP3 player, DVD). Students name common technology found in homes (e.g., DVRs, tape or digital recorders, CD players, digital still and video cameras, telephones, radios). Students identify functions represented by symbols and icons commonly found in applications (e.g., font name, font size, bold, underline, alignment, color of type). Students know how to use correct sitting, hand, arm, and fingering positions to type complete sentences (including Shift for capital letters, the Space Bar for spacing, and punctuation keys). Students discuss how to properly care for and use software media (e.g., mini DV tapes, CDs, DVDs, memory cards, USB memory sticks).	Students know how to use basic input and output devices (including adaptive devices as needed); how to access network resources (e.g., printers, file servers); and how to use common peripherals (e.g., scanners, digital probes, digital cameras, video projectors). Students recognize, discuss, and visually represent ways technology has changed life and work at school and in the home, community, business, industry, and government during the past three decades. Students identify and know how to use Menu options in applications to develop text, graphics, spreadsheets, and Web documents; to save, print, format, add multimedia features; to store, access, and manage files; and to use dictionary, thesaurus, and spelling and grammar tools. Students know proper keyboarding position and technique to touch-type using the correct hands for alphabetic, numeric, and special-purpose keys (e.g., arrows, Escape, Backspace, Delete, Caps Lock, Control) and how to use these keys and the Edit Menu items to correct errors in a document.	Students recognize hardware and software components used to provide access to network resources and know how common peripherals (e.g., scanners, digital cameras, video projectors) are accessed, controlled, connected, and used effectively and efficiently. Students know how to evaluate, select, and use appropriate technology tools and information resources to plan, design, develop, and communicate content information, appropriately addressing the target audience and providing accurate citations for sources. Students know how to identify appropriate file formats for a variety of applications and apply utility programs to convert formats (as necessary) for effective use in Web, video, audio, graphic, presentation, word-processing, database, publication, and spreadsheet applications. Students continue touch-typing techniques, increasing keyboarding facility, and improving accuracy, speed, and general efficiency in computer operation.	Students evaluate new and/or advanced technology resources for information-dissemination options (e.g., video servers, webcasting, compressed video delivery, online file sharing, graphing calculators, multifunction communications devices, global positioning software) and technology-career opportunities. Students assess the capabilities and limitations of contemporary and emerging technology resources as well as the potential of these systems and services to address personal lifelong learning and workplace needs. In teams, students collaborate to illustrate content-related concepts integrating a variety of media (e.g., print, audio, video, graphic, probes, simulations, models) with presentation, word-processing, publishing, database, graphics design software, or spreadsheet applications. Students routinely exhibit touch-typing techniques with advanced facility, accuracy, speed, and efficiency as they complete their assignments.

continued

FIGURE 2.2 *continued*

NETS•S Developmental Rubric for Grades PK–12

NETS•S	PROFICIENCY			
	By End of Grade 2	**By End of Grade 5**	**By End of Grade 8**	**By End of Grade 12**
1. BASIC OPERATIONS AND CONCEPTS				
• Students demonstrate a sound understanding of the nature and operation of technology systems.		Students identify characteristics suggesting that the computer needs upgraded system or application software, virus-detection software, or spam-defense software to protect the information and functioning of the technology system.	Students examine changes in hardware and software systems over time and identify how changes affect businesses, industry, government, education, and individual users.	In teams, students collaborate to evaluate software, hardware, and networking systems to inform the development of a technology plan for a specific real-world business, educational entity, industry, organization, or other group.
• Students are proficient in the use of technology.	Students recognize functions of basic File Menu commands (e.g., New, Open, Close, Save, Save As, Print) and folders to manage and maintain computer files on a hard drive or other storage medium (e.g., CD, DVD). <hr> Students recognize accurate terminology to describe hardware, software, multimedia devices, storage media, and peripherals as well as to identify the basic functions of technology resources (hardware and software) commonly used in early elementary classrooms.	Students identify basic software commands used to manage and maintain computer files on a hard drive, CD, or DVD; manage and maintain their files on a network; and know how to exchange files with other students and the teacher through network file sharing and e-mail attachments. <hr> Students identify the used to describe basic hardware, software, and networking functions as well as to discuss the functions, processes, and/or procedures applied in common use of these technology resources.	Students identify strategies and procedures for efficient and effective management and maintenance of computer files in a variety of different media and formats on a hard drive and network. <hr> Students know how to solve basic hardware, software, and network problems occurring every day; protect computers, networks, and information from viruses, vandalism, and unauthorized use; and access online help and user documentation to solve common hardware, software, and network problems.	Students know how to use advanced utilities (e.g., compression, antivirus) with computer files in a variety of media and formats. <hr> Students know how to identify, assess, and solve advanced hardware, software, and network problems by using online help and other user documentation and support.
2. SOCIAL, ETHICAL, AND HUMAN ISSUES				
• Students understand the ethical, cultural, and societal issues related to technology.	Students identify common uses of information and communication technology in the community and in daily life.	Students identify issues related to how information and communication technology supports collaboration, personal productivity, lifelong learning, and assistance for students with disabilities.	Students identify legal and ethical issues related to using information and communication technology, recognize consequences of its misuse, and predict possible long-range effects of ethical and unethical uses of technology on culture and society.	Students analyze current trends in information and communication technology and assess the potential of emerging technologies for ethical and unethical uses in culture and society.

continued

FIGURE 2.2 *continued*

NETS•S Developmental Rubric for Grades PK–12

NETS•S	PROFICIENCY			
	By End of Grade 2	By End of Grade 5	By End of Grade 8	By End of Grade 12
2. SOCIAL, ETHICAL, AND HUMAN ISSUES				
• **Students practice responsible use of technology systems, information, and software.**	Students recognize that copyright affects how one can use technology systems, information, and software resources.	Students discuss basic issues related to the responsible use of technology and information, identify scenarios describing acceptable and unacceptable computer use, and describe personal consequences of inappropriate use.	Students discuss issues related to acceptable and responsible use of information and communication technology (e.g., privacy, security, copyright, file sharing, plagiarism), analyze the consequences and costs of unethical use of information and computer technology (e.g., hacking, spamming, consumer fraud, virus setting, intrusion), and identify methods for addressing these risks.	Students analyze the consequences and costs of unethical use of information and computer technology and identify how individuals can protect their technology systems from the unethical and unscrupulous user.
• **Students develop positive attitudes toward technology uses that support lifelong learning, collaboration, personal pursuits, and productivity.**	Students describe acceptable and unacceptable computer etiquette and how to work cooperatively with peers, family members, and others when using technology in the classroom or at home.	Students identify software or technology-delivered access valuable to them and describe how it improves their ability to communicate, be productive, or achieve personal goals.	Students examine issues related to computer etiquette and discuss means for encouraging more effective use of technology to support effective communication, collaboration, personal productivity, lifelong learning, and assistance for individuals with disabilities.	Students analyze current trends in information and communication technology and discuss how emerging technologies could affect collaboration, enhance personal productivity, meet the diverse needs of learners, and promote opportunities for lifelong learning among local and global communities.
3. TECHNOLOGY PRODUCTIVITY TOOLS				
• **Students use technology tools to enhance learning, increase productivity, and promote creativity.**	Students know how to use word processors, drawing tools, presentation software, concept-mapping software, graphing software, and other productivity software to illustrate concepts and convey ideas.	Students identify and apply common productivity software features such as menus and toolbars to plan, create, and edit word-processing documents, spreadsheets, and presentations.	Students describe and apply common software features (e.g., spelling and grammar checkers, editing options, dictionary, thesaurus) to maximize accuracy in development of word-processing documents; sorting, formulas, and chart generation in spreadsheets; and insertion of pictures, movies, sound, and charts into presentation software to enhance communication to an audience, promote productivity, and support creativity.	Students understand and apply advanced software features, such as templates and styles to improve the appearance of word-processing documents, spreadsheets, and presentations and to provide evidence of learning, productivity, and creativity.

continued

FIGURE 2.2 *continued*

NETS•S Developmental Rubric for Grades PK–12

NETS•S	PROFICIENCY			
	By End of Grade 2	By End of Grade 5	By End of Grade 8	By End of Grade 12
3. TECHNOLOGY PRODUCTIVITY TOOLS				
• **Students use productivity tools to collaborate in constructing technology-enhanced models, preparing publications, and producing other creative works.**	Students know how to work together to collect and create pictures, images, and charts for development of word-processed reports and electronic presentations.	Students know procedures for importing and manipulating pictures, images, and charts in word-processing documents, spreadsheets, presentations, and creative works.	Students describe how to use online environments or other collaborative tools to facilitate design and development of materials, models, publications, and presentations; and how to apply utilities for editing pictures, images, and charts.	Students analyze a plan and procedures for development of a multimedia product (e.g., model, presentation, webcast, publication, creative work) and identify authoring tools, other hardware and software resources, research, and team personnel needed to plan, create, and edit the product.
4. TECHNOLOGY COMMUNICATIONS TOOLS				
• **Students use tele-communications to collaborate, publish, and interact with peers, experts, and other audiences.**	Students—with assistance from teacher, parents, or student partners—identify procedures for safely and securely using telecommunications tools (e.g., e-mail, message boards, blogs) to read, send, or post electronic messages for peers, experts, and other audiences.	Students identify telecommunications tools (e.g., e-mail, message boards, blogs) and online resources for collaborative projects with other students inside and outside the classroom who are studying similar curriculum-related content.	Students know how to use telecommunications tools (e.g., e-mail, message boards, blogs, online collaborative environments) to exchange data collected and learn curricular concepts by communicating with peers, experts, and other audiences.	Students plan and implement collaborative projects (with peers, experts, or other audiences) using advanced telecommunications tools (e.g., groupware, interactive Web sites, simulations, joint data collection, videoconferencing) to support curriculum concepts or benefit the local, regional, or global community.
• **Students use a variety of media and formats to communicate information and ideas effectively to multiple audiences.**	Students know how to use a variety of developmentally appropriate media (e.g., presentation software; newsletter templates; Web sites as resources for clip art, music, and information resources) to communicate ideas relevant to the curriculum to their classmates, families, and others.	Students identify a variety of media and formats to create and edit products (e.g., presentations, newsletters, Web sites, PDFs) to synthesize and communicate information and ideas from the curriculum to multiple audiences.	Students know how to use a variety of media and formats to design, develop, publish, and present products (e.g., presentations, newsletters, Web sites) that effectively communicate information and ideas about the curriculum to multiple audiences.	Students know how to use a variety of media and formats to design, develop, publish, and present products (e.g., presentations, newsletters, Web sites) that incorporate information from the curriculum and communicate original ideas to multiple audiences.

continued

FIGURE 2.2 *continued*
NETS•S Developmental Rubric for Grades PK–12

NETS•S	PROFICIENCY			
	By End of Grade 2	By End of Grade 5	By End of Grade 8	By End of Grade 12
5. TECHNOLOGY RESEARCH TOOLS				
• Students use technology to locate, evaluate, and collect information from a variety of sources.	Students—with assistance from teachers, parents, or student partners—identify steps for using technology resources such as CDs (e.g., reference or educational software) and Web-based search engines to locate information on assigned topics in the curriculum.	Students describe steps for using common Web search engines and basic search functions of other technology resources to locate information, as well as guidelines for evaluating information from a variety of sources for its relevance to the curriculum.	Students know how to conduct an advanced search using Boolean logic and other sophisticated search functions; and know how to evaluate information from a variety of sources for accuracy, bias, appropriateness, and comprehensiveness.	Students know how to locate, select, and use advanced technology resources (e.g., expert systems, intelligent agents, real-world models and simulations) to enhance their learning of curriculum topics selected.
• Students use technology tools to process data and report results.	Students, with assistance from the teacher, know how to use existing common databases (e.g., library catalogs, online archives, electronic dictionaries, encyclopedias) to locate, sort, and interpret information on assigned topics in the curriculum.	Students describe how to perform basic queries designed to process data and report results on assigned topics in the curriculum.	Students know how to identify and implement procedures for designing, creating, and populating a database; and in performing queries they know how to process data and report results relevant to an assigned hypothesis or research question.	Students formulate a hypothesis or research question on a curriculum topic they choose, and design, create, and populate a database to process data and report results.
• Students evaluate and select new information resources and technological innovations based on the appropriateness to specific tasks.	Students identify technology resources (e.g., concept-mapping software, drawing software) to show steps in a sequence; to demonstrate likenesses and differences; and to recognize, record, and organize information related to assigned curricular topics.	Students identify, record, and organize information on assigned topics in the curriculum by selecting and using appropriate information and communication technology tools and resources (e.g., slideshow, timeline software, database, conceptual mapping).	Students know how to select and use information and communication technology tools and resources to collect and analyze information and report results on an assigned hypothesis or research question.	Students formulate a hypothesis or research question and select and use appropriate information and communication technology tools and resources for collecting and analyzing information and reporting results to multiple audiences.

continued

FIGURE 2.2 *continued*
NETS•S Developmental Rubric for Grades PK–12

NETS•S	PROFICIENCY			
	By End of Grade 2	**By End of Grade 5**	**By End of Grade 8**	**By End of Grade 12**
6. TECHNOLOGY PROBLEM-SOLVING AND DECISION-MAKING TOOLS				
• Students use technology resources for solving problems and making informed decisions.	Students know how to select information and communication technology tools and resources that can be used to solve particular problems (e.g., concept-mapping software to generate and organize ideas for a report, illustrate same/different, or illustrate the sequence of a story; drawing program to make a picture; presentation software to communicate and illustrate ideas; graph program to organize and display data; a Web browser and search engine to locate needed information).	Students know how to apply their knowledge of problem-solving tools to select appropriate technology tools and resources to solve a specific problem or make a decision.	Students identify two or more types of information and communication technology tools or resources that can be used for informing and solving a specific problem and presenting results or for identifying and presenting an informed rationale for a decision.	Students describe integration of two or more information and communication technology tools and resources to collaborate with peers, community members, experts, and others to solve a problem and present results or to present an informed rationale for a decision.
• Students employ technology in the development of strategies for solving problems in the real world.	Students identify ways technology has been used to address real-world problems.	Students know how to select and use information and communication technology tools and resources to collect, organize, and evaluate information relevant to a real-world problem.	Students describe the information and communication technology tools they might use to compare information from different sources, to analyze findings, to determine the need for additional information, and to draw conclusions for addressing real-world problems.	Students integrate information and communication technology to analyze a real-world problem, design and implement procedures to monitor information, to set timelines, and to evaluate progress toward the solution of a real-world problem.

DEVELOPING ASSESSMENT RUBRICS FOR THE NETS•S

The NETS•S Developmental Rubric for Grades PK–12 provides a snapshot of a student's progress through the four grade-range benchmarks. However, many on the NETS Project team believe this explanation was insufficient. What, they asked, would students need to know and be able to do at *each* grade level to meet these four benchmarks? As a result, the assessment model was extended to specify expectations at each grade level as students make their way to the four important benchmarks. Figure 2.3 shows examples of this organizational structure.

These extended assessment models, in addition to being tied to specific benchmarks, now provide an indication of what happens *before* students reach a benchmark. For instance, a student working toward the important NCLB eighth-grade technology literacy proficiency benchmark now passes through a novice level in Grade 6 and a basic level in Grade 7, finally reaching the proficient level in Grade 8. Reaching this level indicates the student is ready to meet the technology literacy proficiency benchmark.

The model also includes an advanced level that identifies those students who are demonstrating technology skills and abilities beyond their grade level. For example, a student at the advanced level in Grades 6 through 8 would be demonstrating knowledge and skills equivalent to the novice or basic levels in Grades 9 through 12. In this way, each of these grade-level benchmark

FIGURE 2.3
NETS•S Assessment Model Applied to Each Grade Level

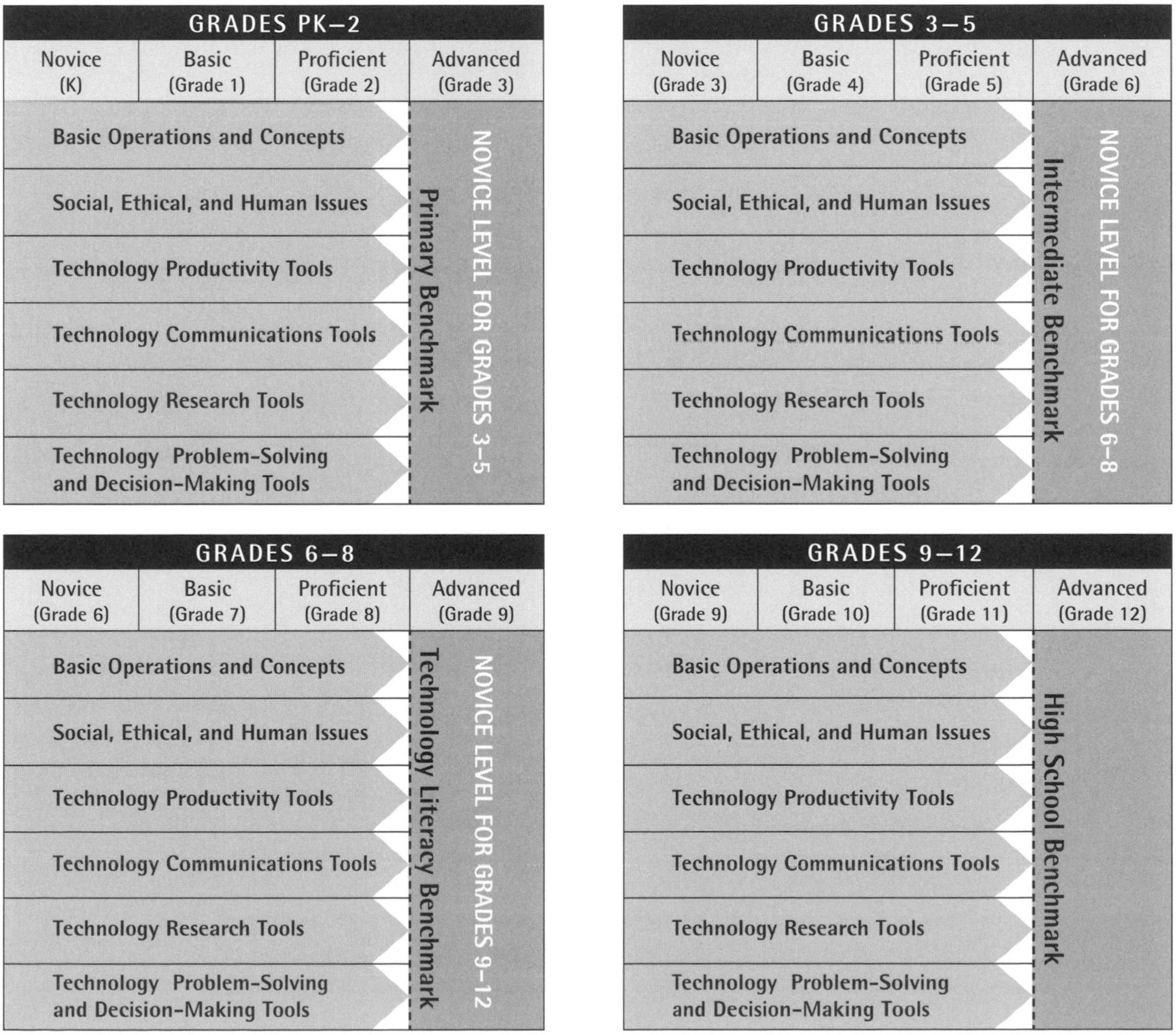

categories (novice, basic, proficient) builds on the next, defining a unified structure for specifying, and thus teaching and assessing, student technology literacy based on the NETS•S.

So the NETS•S Assessment Model has now reached the point where specific knowledge, skills, and abilities that students can demonstrate (and assessments can measure) can be mapped to specific grade levels. This mapping process leads to the creation of an *assessment rubric*, one that can be used as a basis for developing a reliable assessment instrument to measure student achievement of the NETS•S.

Examples of assessment rubrics, covering Grades PK through 12 and leading to the important technology literacy proficiency benchmarks, appear in appendix B. As you review the rubrics in appendix B, note the active verbs used to describe the knowledge, skills, and abilities that students are expected to demonstrate at the end of each grade level ("identify," "describe," "recognize," and so forth). These rubrics have been designed to facilitate the development of assessments that will gauge grade-by-grade progress toward technology literacy proficiency benchmarks. The specific descriptions in each of the six standards categories can serve as the basis for making decisions on how to measure these abilities, laying the foundation for a student technology assessment instrument imbued with the national consensus goals represented by the NETS•S.

ASSESSING TECHNOLOGY LITERACY

Having described very briefly the process of creating both a developmental rubric and an assessment rubric based on the NETS•S, the rest of this book will describe the different options you have for turning these rubrics into developmentally appropriate assessments of technology literacy. Chapters 3–6 provide examples of how individual teachers have used elements of the NETS•S Assessment Model to create integrated technology and content-area assessments.

Beyond the classroom, these or similar rubrics can also be used to create assessments at the school, district, state, or even national level to serve a variety of educational purposes. Chapters 7 and 12 describe the process that professional test developers go through to plan and deploy reliable assessments that can be delivered to large populations and scored consistently. Chapter 13 describes how one school district (Chicago Public Schools) used an assessment rubric very similar to the one in appendix B to develop a technology literacy assessment for all district eighth-graders. For any testing project, turning high-level goals and standards into measurable outcomes is the cornerstone of successful assessment.

The NETS•S Assessment Model outlined in this chapter represents one way to turn the NETS•S into the basis for an assessment. What happens next depends on the goals of your assessment program and the types of assessments you want to use to achieve those goals.

Reference

ISTE. (2003). *National educational technology standards for teachers: Resources for assessment*. Eugene, OR: Author.

Technology Assessment in the Classroom

Examinations are formidable even to the best prepared, for the greatest fool may ask more than the wisest man can answer.

—CHARLES CALEB COLTON

The NETS•S Developmental Rubric (Fig. 2.2 in chapter 2) defines important student technology benchmarks that can be measured for the four grade ranges that end at the 2nd-, 5th-, 8th-, and 12th-grade levels. Part 2 identifies creative ways teachers can use these benchmarks to measure how well their students are meeting the NETS•S within the classroom.

The chapters in part 2 present four projects that demonstrate how teachers and schools have used the NETS•S to create learning activities that combine technology assessment with academic content assessment. These projects highlight many of the strategies and techniques advocated in previous works published by ISTE, such as *Connecting Curriculum and Technology* and the *NETS•S Curriculum Series*. These include

- assessment that's integrated into the learning process,

- assessment over time using multiple measures, and

- assessment based on actual student classroom experience and student work.

In all cases, the technology skills needed to succeed on a particular assessment should be taught in the context of academic content learning long before they're formally assessed. Information gained from these integrated assessments can be used for both formative purposes (to help teachers understand what students need to learn to further their mastery of necessary skills) and summative purposes (to determine how well students are meeting goals specified by the NETS•S).

Each of the chapters in part 2 contains a benchmark assessment associated with one of the grade ranges illustrated in the NETS•S Assessment Model (Fig. 2.1 in chapter 2). As mentioned previously, this map of the grade ranges provides you with the big picture of students' progress in technology knowledge and skills as they move from the primary benchmark (Grades PK–2), to the intermediate benchmark (Grades 3–5), to the middle school benchmark (Grades 6–8), to the high school benchmark (Grades 9–12). The middle school benchmark represents the level at which students should reach "technology literacy proficiency" as defined by the No Child Left Behind legislation.

SCORING BENCHMARK ASSESSMENTS

In each chapter, rubrics for scoring the benchmark assessments are described and illustrated. In some cases, these tools are qualitative, assigning familiar rubric values such as "meets" or "exceeds" to describe a student's level of mastery of particular skills. These values can be assigned numeric scores if an assessment will be used for summative purposes, such as grading, or for aggregating and summarizing group scores.

Each of the projects described in part 2 offers you a number of ways to experiment with different teaching and assessment methodologies. You'll need to make decisions about how you want to score and report the results of the assessment. Will you use descriptive methods or quantitative scores? Will the results of the benchmark assessment be recorded in students' individual academic-record files or simply shared with the student and used to determine ongoing instructional needs? Will someone else check the scoring and complete a holistic analysis of classroom or school performance?

Once the results have been reported, you'll need to make decisions about what constitutes the "cut score," or the level at which those who score above have met the standards and those who score below have not. It may be the case that reporting individual assessment scores at the eighth-grade level becomes a state and district requirement. Consequently, it's important to have a mechanism in place for reliably scoring and reporting the data.

If a benchmark assessment reaches sufficient scale to warrant making comparisons of students taught by different teachers, testing issues such as validity and reliability will come into play. In this case, it's important to calibrate scoring procedures to ensure a high level of inter-rater reliability. Several methods for establishing anchor examples can be used to calibrate scoring (see part 3).

CHAPTER SNAPSHOTS

CHAPTER 3
"Everyone Is Important":
Grade 2 Benchmark Assessment

In the language arts project described in this chapter, second-graders explore biographies and autobiographies. Students use a graphic organizer as a way to organize their thoughts about a famous person. Students are encouraged to read more than one source of information about the chosen person (including electronic sources), and then they're asked to write a story and prepare a short PowerPoint presentation to share with their class and family.

CHAPTER 4
"You Were There!":
Grade 5 Benchmark Assessment

In the social studies project described in this chapter, students read Revolutionary War histories and biographies. Students write articles in journalistic style from a specific point of view, and use word processors, video cameras, and video editing software to create a series of interviews and news articles about the invidicuals involved in the Boston Massacre.

CHAPTER 5
"Physics Everywhere:"
Grade 8 Benchmark Assessment

In the science project described in this chapter, students demonstrate, through essay writing and video production, how principles they've learned in physics class are represented in their favorite sport or recreation. This project offers students a number of interdisciplinary links to the language arts curriculum as they work on their expository writing and presentation skills.

CHAPTER 6
The Senior Project:
Grade 12 Benchmark Assessment

The NETS•S benchmark assessment described in this chapter is incorporated into a formal senior project that's student-defined but must include several technology components, among other criteria. Elements of this project include a research paper, a work sample, a portfolio, a presentation, and a professional resumé.

CHAPTER 3

"Everyone Is Important": Grade 2 Benchmark Assessment

Using technology to teach and entertain young children has been commonplace since personal computers became a routine home purchase. Using technology with young children in a formal school setting, however, sparked disagreement among educators. Not all of them were convinced of its value.

The controversy reached its height with the publication of the book *Failure to Connect* (Healy, 1998). Healy accuses education technologists of sitting children in front of computers instead of encouraging brain development through social interaction. In the years since *Failure to Connect* was published, however, it's become clear that computers are important communication and research tools for students. They aren't just a means to increase their classroom productivity or interact with automated lessons or drill programs.

Most young children interact with many forms of technology before they enter school, and they see computers as tools for exploring, learning, and sharing with others. Computers have become tools for transforming the entire learning process. They're not just a supplement—much less a replacement—for the classroom teacher.

FIGURE 3.1

NETS•S Assessment Model

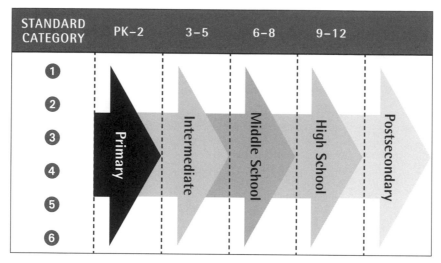

Because technology-rich learning has become more prevalent at all grade levels, students as young as Grade 2 should already be in the process of mastering the technology and critical-thinking skills they'll use throughout their education. By beginning with the NETS•S as the road map, young students will be in a better position to use technology to build higher-level problem-solving skills within the classroom.

Because primary-grade students are very young, NETS•S assessment should be mostly observational and include student work while learning academic content. The benchmark assessment described in this chapter is designed to measure only those portions of the standards that cannot be observed in the classroom. A checklist kept throughout the year can be used to record when students have met particular performance indicators.

The "Everyone Is Important" project is a summative assessment embedded in an English language arts writing project. In addition to providing students a unique way to learn academic content, the project provides multiple ways of measuring technology skills appropriate to the students' grade level. The project was developed using the backward design process described by McTighe and Wiggins (1999) in *Understanding by Design Handbook*. It assumes that many technology-rich experiences have preceded the assessment. To review what experiences should be taking place in your classroom before any assessment is performed, see *NETS•S Curriculum Series: Multidisciplinary Units for Prekindergarten Through Grade 2* (Carroll, Kelly, & Witherspoon, 2003).

This benchmark assessment is based on two elements:

- A set of rubrics that allows teachers to assess student work, such as a graphic organizer, written essay, and online slide presentation. In some cases, these rubrics are used to measure English language arts content standards, such as the ability to present arguments in a grade-appropriate essay project. In other cases, the rubrics are used to measure students' mastery of the NETS•S grade-range performance indicators.

- A checklist kept throughout the year that allows a teacher to track students' acquisition of key technology skills specified by the NETS•S.

As you look at the project, rubrics, and accompanying checklist, think about how this project might be used in your school or district within the context of an overall assessment plan. Make sure, too, that the assessment and checklist fit into your instructional process. Go back to the essential questions that should be answered by your assessment plan:

- How will the checklist information and assessment results provide the types of data that will assist you in determining what your students know and understand?

- How will the results help you with curriculum planning?

- Will the reported results provide parents and other stakeholders with the types of information they want reported for second-graders?

This project is designed as a benchmark assessment to determine proficiency in meeting the NETS•S at the primary grade level. Figure 3.2 shows the Grade 2 section of the NETS•S Developmental Rubric for Grades PK–12 which appears in Figure 2.2.

FIGURE 3.2

NETS•S Developmental Rubric—Focus on Grade 2

NETS•S	PROFICIENCY BY END OF GRADE 2
1. BASIC OPERATIONS AND CONCEPTS	
• Students demonstrate a sound understanding of the nature and operation of technology systems.	Students describe how to use basic input devices (e.g., keyboard fingering, mouse/track pad), output devices (e.g., monitor, printer), and software resources (e.g., MP3 player, DVD).
	Students name common technology found in homes (e.g., DVRs, tape or digital recorders, CD players, digital still and video cameras, telephones, radios).
	Students identify functions represented by symbols and icons commonly found in applications (e.g., font name, font size, bold, underline, alignment, color of type).
	Students know how to use correct sitting, hand, arm, and fingering positions to type complete sentences (including Shift for capital letters, the Space Bar for spacing, and punctuation keys).
	Students discuss how to properly care for and use software media (e.g., mini DV tapes, CDs, DVDs, memory cards, USB memory sticks).
• Students are proficient in the use of technology.	Students recognize functions of basic File Menu commands (e.g., New, Open, Close, Save, Save As, Print) and folders to manage and maintain computer files on a hard drive or other storage medium (e.g., CD, DVD).
	Students recognize accurate terminology to describe hardware, software, multimedia devices, storage media, and peripherals as well as to identify the basic functions of technology resources (hardware and software) commonly used in early elementary classrooms.
2. SOCIAL, ETHICAL, AND HUMAN ISSUES	
• Students understand the ethical, cultural, and societal issues related to technology.	Students identify common uses of information and communication technology in the community and in daily life.
• Students practice responsible use of technology systems, information, and software.	Students recognize that copyright affects how one can use technology systems, information, and software resources.
• Students develop positive attitudes toward technology uses that support lifelong learning, collaboration, personal pursuits, and productivity.	Students describe acceptable and unacceptable computer etiquette and how to work cooperatively with peers, family members, and others when using technology in the classroom or at home.
3. TECHNOLOGY PRODUCTIVITY TOOLS	
• Students use technology tools to enhance learning, increase productivity, and promote creativity.	Students know how to use word processors, drawing tools, presentation software, concept-mapping software, graphing software, and other productivity software to illustrate concepts and convey ideas.
• Students use productivity tools to collaborate in constructing technology-enhanced models, prepare publications, and produce other creative works.	Students know how to work together to collect and create pictures, images, and charts for development of word-processed reports and electronic presentations.

continued

FIGURE 3.2 *continued*

NETS•S Developmental Rubric—Focus on Grade 2

NETS•S	PROFICIENCY BY END OF GRADE 2
4. TECHNOLOGY COMMUNICATIONS TOOLS	
• Students use telecommunications to collaborate, publish, and interact with peers, experts, and other audiences.	Students—with assistance from teacher, parents, or student partners—identify procedures for safely and securely using telecommunications tools (e.g., e-mail, message boards, blogs) to read, send, or post electronic messages for peers, experts, and other audiences.
• Students use a variety of media and formats to communicate information and ideas effectively to multiple audiences.	Students know how to use a variety of developmentally appropriate media (e.g., presentation software; newsletter templates; Web sites as resources for clip art, music, and information resources) to communicate ideas relevant to the curriculum to their classmates, families, and others.
5. TECHNOLOGY RESEARCH TOOLS	
• Students use technology to locate, evaluate, and collect information from a variety of sources.	Students—with assistance from teachers, parents, or student partners—identify steps for using technology resources such as CDs (e.g., reference or educational software) and Web-based search engines to locate information on assigned topics in the curriculum.
• Students use technology tools to process data and report results.	Students, with assistance from the teacher, know how to use existing common databases (e.g., library catalogs, online archives, electronic dictionaries, encyclopedias) to locate, sort, and interpret information on assigned topics in the curriculum.
• Students evaluate and select new information resources and technological innovations based on the appropriateness for specific tasks.	Students identify technology resources (e.g., concept-mapping software, drawing software) to show steps in a sequence; to demonstrate likenesses and differences; and to recognize, record, and organize information related to assigned curricular topics.
6. TECHNOLOGY PROBLEM-SOLVING AND DECISION-MAKING TOOLS	
• Students use technology resources for solving problems and making informed decisions.	Students know how to select information and communication technology tools and resources that can be used to solve particular problems (e.g., concept-mapping software to generate and organize ideas for a report, illustrate same/different, or illustrate the sequence of a story; drawing program to make a picture; presentation software to communicate and illustrate ideas; graph program to organize and display data; a Web browser and search engine to locate needed information).
• Students employ technology in the development of strategies for solving problems in the real world.	Students identify ways technology has been used to address real-world problems.

"EVERYONE IS IMPORTANT"

In this project, students study the literary genre of biography/autobiography as an integral part of the second-grade English Language Arts Standards and in support of the Social Sciences Standard on the uniqueness of individuals. In addition to reading the genre, written and oral expression are included to create a holistic English language arts experience. After reading a biography or autobiography, students organize what they have learned about the famous person they have studied by using a graphic organizer. From the graphic organizer, students write a story about their important person. Each student creates at least one electronic presentation slide and orally shares the information with an audience.

BIG IDEA

Everyone is unique. Every person has a story to tell. Important people have stories written about them (biography) or they write a book about themselves (autobiography).

OBJECTIVES

Students will be able to

- identify the important aspects of the person's life after reading a biography or autobiography.

- create a graphic organizer that shows the important characteristics of the person's life.

- write a story that highlights at least three important points about the person based on the graphic organizer.

- create at least one multimedia presentation slide for an oral presentation about the subject of the biography/autobiography.

CONTENT STANDARDS ADDRESSED

NCTE English Language Arts Standards

This benchmark assessment activity can address any or all of the ELA Standards depending on what you choose to emphasize. You are encouraged to focus those state or local standards to meet the grade level benchmarks best assessed at the time of the year in which this assessment is administered.

TECHNOLOGY STANDARDS ADDRESSED

NETS•S 1, 3–5

OUTCOMES AND PRODUCTS

1. Graphic organizer depicting the chosen person's characteristics and contributions as well as events in the person's life.

2. Written story about the person based on information collected in the graphic organizer.

3. Oral presentation (using presentation software such as PowerPoint) of what the student has learned about the person.

ACTIVITY SEQUENCE

1. Preparation

Prepare for a visit to the library. Conduct a discussion of biographies and autobiographies. Guiding questions might

---

HANDWRITING VERSUS COMPUTER WRITING

Whether the story should be handwritten or drafted on a computer using a word processor is a local decision. We've found that it depends both on the prior experience of the students (whether they've composed on the computer before) and on the level of editing work expected by the teacher. In some cases, the requirement to write the story on a computer may hinder the assessment process. We've found that at this age level, no significant differences in the assessment outcomes occur between those groups who felt comfortable word processing the story and those who preferred to write the story by hand.

include: "What biographies have we read this year? What were the people known for? What impact did they have on our country? What makes a person important enough to write his or her life story?" Remind students that the biographies they choose to read could be of anyone, whether the person is well-known, important, or neither.

Go to the library and have students select at least one biography. Students can begin reading their choices immediately. There should be enough biographies so that everyone has a book. Students must consult at least one additional source, either in print or electronic format, to complete their research on the person whose biography they've chosen.

2. Graphic Organizer
Students use a graphic organizer to record information from the biography and organize it into a diagram, with the person's name in the center "bubble." Individual characteristics, contributions, and important events in the person's life should be placed in graphic organizer bubbles arranged around, and connected to, this central hub. Encourage students to use descriptive words to add detail to these linked bubbles. Have students share their diagrams with each other and discuss the important points learned.

3. Written Story
Students use the information they've gathered in the graphic organizer to write a narrative about the person they've studied. Be sure to review the writing process with them.

4. Slideshow
Students use presentation software to create at least one slide about the person they've read about. Remind students that the purpose of the slide is to provide a visual representation to help the audience learn more about the person being discussed. The slide, or slides, created must contain a title, important points, and at least one graphic. Students should be encouraged to obtain the graphic from any allowable source. Districts often have a library of purchased graphics, or students can create their own images.

5. Oral Presentation
Combine students' slides into a single file for ease of presentation. Students present their findings about the person they've studied by talking from the information on the slide they've created. Encourage the class to ask clarifying questions.

6. Lesson Extension
Have students create a similar graphic organizer about themselves, friends, or relatives. Repeat the sequence by having students either write stories or create a multimedia presentation, or both, based on themselves, a friend, or a relative. Discuss how each person is important.

ASSESSMENT
Assessment for the Grade 2 benchmark is completed in two phases:

1. **Assessing student work.** The rubrics that appear in Figure 3.3 can be used to assess the student work that results from the activities in this project. Each rubric is keyed to both the English Language Arts Standards and the NETS•S, allowing you to use this single project to assess multiple sets of skills and abilities in the context of content area learning. The writing portion of the rubric uses the Six Traits Writing structure (Culham, 2005), with modifications made for the grade range and the project.

2. **Checklist.** The checklist in Figure 3.4 is designed to keep track of student performance over time. Not all the performance indicators listed on the checklist are covered in this particular project; in fact, students should already have demonstrated many of the skills included on the checklist before they undertake this project. Whatever competencies have not been observed earlier in the year should become a focus of the observation during the performance of the activities in this project.

FIGURE 3.3

"Everyone Is Important" Grade 2 Rubric

GRAPHIC ORGANIZER				
CRITERIA	NOVICE Needs assistance	BASIC Approaching	PROFICIENT Meets	EXCEEDS
File Management (NETS•S 1)	Unable to title file and store in appropriate location	Either titles file appropriately or is able to store in proper location, but not both	Independently titles file with own last name and the important person's last name; stores in appropriate folder	Meets criteria and helps others; troubleshoots when others are having difficulty
Bubble Placement (NETS•S 3)	Cannot tell the difference between the important person and person's characteristics	The important person is in the center but characteristics are disjointed and not readable	The important person is in the center, with important characteristics connected around the main bubble	Meets criteria, with bubbles evenly placed around the important person's bubble
Bubble Labels (NETS•S 3, 4)	Labels do not reflect important characteristics	The important person's name is in the center, but some of the characteristics in surrounding bubbles are not most important	The important person's name is in the center, with appropriate, important characteristics in surrounding bubbles	Meets criteria and includes details for some of the characteristics in adjacent bubbles
Capitalization (NETS•S 1 and ELA Standard 6)	Does not use capital letters appropriately or at all, or all letters are capitalized	Uses capital letter for first or last name, but not both	Uses capital and lowercase letters for name	Capitalizes first word of phrases for each characteristic; can articulate that the phrase is not a sentence and has no period
Presentation (NETS•S 3, 4 and ELA Standards 1, 3, 5)	Uses default shape for organizer; linking lines are either not present or inappropriate	Uses same shape for both the important person and characteristics; linking lines are proper	Uses one shape for main person and another for characteristics; bubbles are linked properly	Uses several unique but appropriate shapes for bubbles; linking lines are appropriate

continued

FIGURE 3.3 *continued*

"Everyone Is Important" Grade 2 Rubric

WRITING				
6+1 TRAITS ASSESSMENT TERMS	**EMERGING** Need for revision outweighs strength	**DEVELOPING** Strengths and need for revision equal	**EFFECTIVE** Strengths outweigh weaknesses	**STRONG** Exceeds expectation for Grade 2
TRAIT 1 Content	No clear sense of purpose; missing details	Beginning to define topic but not completely clear; generally stays on topic	Supporting ideas are present; ideas are reasonably clear	Focused and clear; contains important details; insightful
TRAIT 2 Organization	Lacks a sense of direction; ideas strung together; illogical sequence to person's life	Organization sometimes supports main idea; uninspiring	Good introductory sentence; logical flow to details; uses transitions	Showcases the person; an inviting introduction; well-organized; excellent transitions; smooth to read; strong conclusion
TRAIT 3 Voice	Apparently does not care about subject; shows boredom; no awareness of audience	Safe writing; glimpse only touches of originality	Sounds like writer talking; clear the writer cares about the subject	Clearly connects with the subject, showing a desire to help the reader understand; voice is identifiable
TRAIT 4 Word Choice	Limited vocabulary; no unique words; some misused words	Repeats common words; mostly mundane vocabulary	Uses strong verbs and descriptive language	Uses strong descriptive language; good use of vocabulary
TRAIT 5 Sentence Fluency	Sentences are choppy, incomplete, and rambling; no connectedness; difficult to read aloud	Sentences are stilted and seem mechanical, but do flow; a few variatons in sentence structure	Generally easy to read; most sentences begin in unique ways; well-constructed; easy to read aloud	Easy to read; sentences begin in different ways; both long and short sentences; smooth
TRAIT 6 Conventions	Errors in spelling, punctuation, word usage, etc., make reading difficult; no evidence of proofreading	Reasonable control of writing conventions; only simpler words are spelled correctly; errors distract from understanding	Appropriate use of writing conventions, with minimal errors	Excellent punctuation and spelling; no errors
TRAIT 7 (6+1) Presentation (For handwritten papers)	Paper is difficult to read; handwriting is illegible; no use of margins and indentations	Readable handwriting, with some letter formation errors; margins are present but inconsistent	Paper is neat, no smudges; paper is written legibly with appropriate margins; no stray marks, cross-outs, or tears in paper	Excellent handwriting, margins, and indentations; illustration is planned, appropriate, and well-placed

continued

Adapted from rubrics produced by the Northwest Regional Education Laboratory, supplemented by http://www.nwrel.org/assessment/pdfRubrics/6plus1traits. PDF and http://www.edina.k12.mn.us/concord/teacherlinks/sixtraits/posterspage.htm. For student-friendly rubrics for each trait, see 6+1 Traits of Writing: The Complete Guide for the Primary Grades (Culham, 2005).

FIGURE 3.3 *continued*

"Everyone Is Important" Grade 2 Rubric

	POWERPOINT SLIDE(S)			
CRITERIA	**NOVICE** Needs assistance	**BASIC** Approaching	**PROFICIENT** Meets	**EXCEEDS**
File Management (NETS•S 1)	Unable to title file and store in appropriate location	Either titles file appropriately or is able to store in proper location, but not able to do both	Independently titles file with own last name and important person's last name; stores in appropriate folder	Meets criteria and helps others; troubleshoots when others are having difficulty
Slide Text (NETS•S 3)	Both title and bulleted points are inadequate size	Title or bulleted points are inadequate size	Title is at least 30 pt., with bulleted points at least 20 pt.	Font size meets criteria; font design uses advanced features
Slide Background (NETS•S 3)	Does not use a slide background color	Uses colors that do not have enough contrast to be viewed from a distance	Uses contrasting colors for background and text	Background color has appropriate contrast and has an advanced characteristic such as texture
Slide Graphics (NETS•S 3, 4)	No graphics included	Graphics included but do not support understanding of the person	Includes one graphic that was properly placed and adds to understanding of the person	Includes more than one graphic if only one slide or different graphics on multiple slides; all help with understanding
Content (NETS•S 4)	Shows no important facts about the person	Shows one or two important facts about the person	Shows three or four important facts about the person	Shows five or more important facts about the person
Oral Presentation— Content (ELA Standards 4, 5)	Reads slide(s) but cannot answer questions or provide additional information	Reads slide(s); only answers questions	Speaks from slide(s) by adding more information; responds to questions	Speaks from slide(s), sharing detailed stories about the person and responding to questions
Oral Presentation— Delivery (ELA Standards 10–12)	Does not look at audience; voice is too soft to hear	Either looks at audience or speaks with adequate volume and articulation	Looks at audience while speaking; voice has adequate volume and clear articulation	Meets criteria and is animated, enthusiastic, and engaging
Citation (NETS•S 2)	No citation	Cites one book as source	Cites book(s) read and other sources of information; provides at least two citations	Provides more than two print citations and at least one online citation

FIGURE 3.4
"Everyone Is Important" Observation Checklist

"EVERYONE IS IMPORTANT" OBSERVATION CHECKLIST															
PERFORMANCE INDICATOR	Angela	Anna	Billy	Borin	Chad	Clarissa	Coit	Danny	Daryl	Erin	Garrick	Glenn	Heather	Karen	Melissa
NETS•S 1															
IDs keyboard															
IDs mouse															
IDs monitor															
Sits properly at computer															
Uses keyboard															
Uses mouse properly															
Recognizes icons while on computer															
IDs technology in home and school															
Manages files without assistance															
NETS•S 2															
Participated in discussion on copyright															
Behaves appropriately while using technology															
Works cooperatively with others while using technology															
Shows positive attitude toward use of technology															
NETS•S 3															
Can word process															
Can create a graphic															
Can use...															
Can use...															
NETS•S 4															
Knows rules for safely using e-mail															
Uses electronic encyclopedia															
NETS•S 5															
Describes process for finding electronic information															
Uses various electronic resources to find information															
NETS•S 6															
Chooses appropriate electronic tool for task															
Identifies a situation in which technology was used to solve a real-world problem															

ONE TEACHER'S STORY

Carrie Geldard
San Marcos, California

By the third trimester of the school year, my students had already experienced several biographies including books about U.S. presidents, Martin Luther King, and Cesar Chavez. Since this project is an opportunity for students to go to the library and select a biography of a person they choose, I alerted the library media teacher in advance that we needed biographies in a variety of readability levels. I make no restrictions on who the biography should be about. Being able to make their own selections is quite a motivator for students. While still in the library, we talk about how important each person we know is, and how we each contribute to the class, our families, and others in unique ways. The students' job is to learn about contributions of the person they selected.

I have learned that, like adults, my children work well from examples that are tied to the rubric. I have samples of other students' work that I show as I introduce each part of the project. I have found that if I am very explicit about what I am looking for when sharing the rubric, my students rise to the occasion and self-assess as they go along. Even though they have examples, I keep the students focused on the essential question: How is each person important? You will be surprised how excited your students are to create their graphic organizers and presentation slides. It never ceases to amaze me how especially thrilled they are at the professional appearance of their presentations. When I put all the slides together into a single slideshow, they all want copies to show their families. This assessment task can also be used for open house. I place the slideshow on a classroom computer and set it for continuous replay. By the end of the project, the students are able to tell the stories of many of the famous people presented by their peers. Here's my advice for teachers planning to implement this project:

1. **Backing up student work.** Be sure to make backup copies of all student work. There's nothing worse than having a technical failure and losing their work. I've also found that having students print out their graphic organizer, story, and a notes page explaining their slides provides a written record of their work for their non-digital portfolio.

2. **Using a lab.** In my planning guide, I block out five time segments for doing this project. I use the computer lab for creating the graphic organizer and the multimedia slide. I use the presentation station in the classroom to show everyone's work. **If you don't have access to a lab,** classroom management is key. I've been able to complete the first two steps in two days. Then, it takes about a week of working with small groups, or in centers, to rotate the students through the classroom mini-stations. They're able to write and edit their stories in two additional days. You'll then have to rotate them through the classroom stations again to complete their presentations. In this setting, I often see students coaching each other on how to make the presentation more effective, which can affect your assessment validity.

3. **Sharing work.** Don't forget to share your students' work with others. My students love to show their work to their parents and friends.

4. **Using the checklist.** I keep the checklist on my clipboard all year long. When students are actively using technology, I glance at the checklist to remind myself what to look for, as well as to see if any performance indicators are being demonstrated. It's amazing how many you can check off early in the year if you give your students opportunities to learn with technology.

5. **Scoring and discussing.** After the project has been completed, my teaching team sits down to discuss the results. We proudly share the ones that are outstanding, of course, but we also take time to look at student work at each level. If we're unsure of any scoring issues, we discuss the work and help each other figure it out. We also discuss what we could have done better to prepare students for this project, and we make curriculum plans for the following year.

References

Carroll, J., Kelly, M.G., & Witherspoon, T. (2003). *NETS•S curriculum series: Multidisciplinary units for prekindergarten through Grade 2*. Eugene, OR: International Society for Technology in Education.

Culham, R. (2005). *6+1 traits of writing: The complete guide for the primary grades*. New York: Scholastic Inc.

Healy, J. (1998). *Failure to connect: How computers affect our children's mind—and what we can do about it*. New York: Touchstone.

McTighe, J., & Wiggins, G. (1999). *Understanding by design handbook*. Alexandria, VA: Association for Supervision and Curriculum Development.

Northwest Regional Educational Laboratory. (2001a). 6+1 trait writing assessment model. Retrieved January 5, 2005, from http://www.nwrel.org/assessment/department.php?d=1

Northwest Regional Educational Laboratory. (2001b). 6+1 Trait Writing Scoring Continuum. Retrieved April 20, 2005, from http://www.nwrel.org/assessment/pdfRubrics/6plus1traits.PDF and from http://www.edina.k12.mn.us/concord/teacherlinks/sixtraits/posterspage.htm

CHAPTER 4

"You Were There!": Grade 5 Benchmark Assessment

Fifth grade is the age at which abstract thinking and problem-solving skills begin to emerge in ways that can be effectively enhanced and showcased in a technology-rich environment. Students have developed academic content skills that enable them to do the complex tasks of researching, analyzing, and communicating information from primary resources.

The "You Were There!" project in this chapter combines English language arts, history, and technology, requiring students to research an important event (the 1770 Boston Massacre) that occurred during the Revolutionary War. From their research, students develop three technology-enhanced products. This project is a modification of an activity originally developed by Paula Conley, Coeur d'Alene, Idaho, and published in *Connecting Curriculum and Technology* (ISTE, 2000, pp. 48–51.)

This interdisciplinary project was developed using the backward design process developed by McTighe and Wiggins (1999) and discussed in *Understanding by Design Handbook*. Beginning with the end in mind, the project was created in the context of what is most commonly taught in the fifth grade and where the NETS•S could best be demonstrated through authentic learning experiences.

FIGURE 4.1
NETS•S Assessment Model

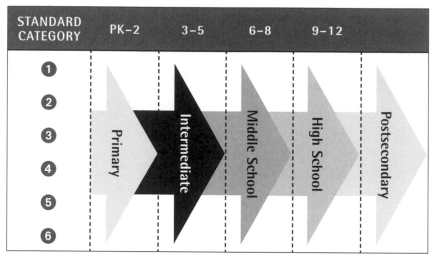

Because this is a summative assessment for Grades 3–5, it's assumed many technology-rich experiences will have preceded the assessment. To review what experiences should be taking place in your classroom before any assessment takes place, see *NETS•S Curriculum Series: Multidisciplinary Units for Grades 3 through 5* (Hannah, Ed., 2003).

As you'll read in chapter 7 and in the case studies found in part 4, multiple sources of data should be used to obtain a complete picture of how students' technology skills are developing. At the fifth-grade level, you may find it appropriate to supplement this performance assessment with either an observational tool such as those modeled in chapter 10 or an automated online assessment of technology knowledge and skills. An increasing number of options appropriate for this age level are available. Constructing a comprehensive assessment program to assess proficiency in all the NETS•S performance indicators requires examination of all appropriate assessment options.

As you review this summative assessment project and its associated rubrics, consider how it might fit into your overall assessment plan for all academic areas. Make sure the expectations built into the project activities fit your instructional process. Then, go back to the essential questions that should be answered by your education technology assessment plan:

• Will the results of this assessment project provide the types of data that will help you determine what your students know and are able to do with technology?

• Do you need additional assessment data? If so, how will that data be obtained?

This project is designed as a benchmark assessment to determine proficiency in meeting the NETS•S at the intermediate grade level. Figure 4.2 shows the Grade 5 section of the NETS•S Developmental Rubric for Grades PK–12 which appears in Figure 2.2.

FIGURE 4.2
NETS•S Developmental Rubric—Focus on Grade 5

NETS•S	PROFICIENCY BY END OF GRADE 5
1. BASIC OPERATIONS AND CONCEPTS	
• Students demonstrate a sound understanding of the nature and operation of technology systems.	Students know how to use basic input and output devices (including adaptive devices as needed); how to access network resources (e.g., printers, file servers); and how to use common peripherals (e.g., scanners, digital probes, digital cameras, video projectors).
	Students recognize, discuss, and visually represent ways technology has changed life and work at school and in the home, community, business, industry, and government during the past three decades.
	Students identify and know how to use Menu options in applications to develop text, graphics, spreadsheets, and Web documents; to save, print, format, add multimedia features; to store, access, and manage files; and to use dictionary, thesaurus, and spelling and grammar tools.
	Students know proper keyboarding position and technique to touch-type using the correct hands for alphabetic, numeric, and special-purpose keys (e.g., arrows, Escape, Backspace, Delete, Caps Lock, Control) and how to use these keys and the Edit Menu items to correct errors in a document.
	Students identify characteristics suggesting that the computer needs upgraded system or application software, virus-detection software, or spam-defense software to protect the information and functioning of the technology system.
• Students are proficient in the use of technology.	Students identify basic software commands used to manage and maintain computer files on a hard drive, CD, or DVD; manage and maintain their files on a network; and know how to exchange files with other students and the teacher through network file sharing and e-mail attachments.
	Students identify the used to describe basic hardware, software, and networking functions as well as to discuss the functions, processes, and/or procedures applied in common use of these technology resources.
2. SOCIAL, ETHICAL, AND HUMAN ISSUES	
• Students understand the ethical, cultural, and societal issues related to technology.	Students identify issues related to how information and communication technology supports collaboration, personal productivity, lifelong learning, and assistance for students with disabilities.
• Students practice responsible use of technology systems, information, and software.	Students discuss basic issues related to the responsible use of technology and information, identify scenarios describing acceptable and unacceptable computer use, and describe personal consequences of inappropriate use.
• Students develop positive attitudes toward technology uses that support lifelong learning, collaboration, personal pursuits, and productivity.	Students identify software or technology-delivered access valuable to them and describe how it improves their ability to communicate, be productive, or achieve personal goals.
3. TECHNOLOGY PRODUCTIVITY TOOLS	
• Students use technology tools to enhance learning, increase productivity, and promote creativity.	Students identify and apply common productivity software features such as menus and toolbars to plan, create, and edit word-processing documents, spreadsheets, and presentations.

continued

FIGURE 4.2 *continued*

NETS•S Developmental Rubric—Focus on Grade 5

NETS•S	PROFICIENCY BY END OF GRADE 5
• Students use productivity tools to collaborate in constructing technology-enhanced models, prepare publications, and produce other creative works.	Students know procedures for importing and manipulating pictures, images, and charts in word-processing documents, spreadsheets, presentations, and creative works.
4. TECHNOLOGY COMMUNICATIONS TOOLS	
• Students use telecommunications to collaborate, publish, and interact with peers, experts, and other audiences.	Students identify telecommunications tools (e.g., e-mail, message boards, blogs) and online resources for collaborative projects with other students inside and outside the classroom who are studying similar curriculum-related content.
• Students use a variety of media and formats to communicate information and ideas effectively to multiple audiences.	Students identify a variety of media and formats to create and edit products (e.g., presentations, newsletters, Web sites, PDFs) to synthesize and communicate information and ideas from the curriculum to multiple audiences.
5. TECHNOLOGY RESEARCH TOOLS	
• Students use technology to locate, evaluate, and collect information from a variety of sources.	Students describe steps for using common Web search engines and basic search functions of other technology resources to locate information, as well as guidelines for evaluating information from a variety of sources for its relevance to the curriculum.
• Students use technology tools to process data and report results.	Students describe how to perform basic queries designed to process data and report results on assigned topics in the curriculum.
• Students evaluate and select new information resources and technological innovations based on the appropriateness for specific tasks.	Students identify, record, and organize information on assigned topics in the curriculum by selecting and using appropriate information and communication technology tools and resources (e.g., slideshow, timeline software, database, conceptual mapping).
6. TECHNOLOGY PROBLEM-SOLVING AND DECISION-MAKING TOOLS	
• Students use technology resources for solving problems and making informed decisions.	Students know how to apply their knowledge of problem-solving tools to select appropriate technology tools and resources to solve a specific problem or make a decision.
• Students employ technology in the development of strategies for solving problems in the real world.	Students know how to select and use information and communication technology tools and resources to collect, organize, and evaluate information relevant to a real-world problem.

"YOU WERE THERE!"

One way to hook students into understanding the point of view of people of a particular time is by using literature to enhance social studies. In this project, students learn about the Boston Massacre through a novel titled *My Brother Sam Is Dead* (Collier & Collier, 1974), a personal story of the time, as well as using factual texts and other documents related to the event. Students use the Internet to view original source documents and related geographical sites. Using their research, they use journalistic writing style and multimedia to report about the events as if they were present and telecasting from the scene.

BIG IDEA

By researching what happened in the time period in which a historical figure lived, students can better understand why the person acted as he or she did and make a more informed judgment about the time period.

OBJECTIVES

Students will be able to

- express a point of view of a controversial historical event, even though it may not be their own view.

- demonstrate their understanding of the significance of the Boston Massacre and its effects on those who fought by exploring the death records and producing a eulogy.

CONTENT STANDARDS ADDRESSED

NCTE English Language Arts Standards
This benchmark assessment activity can address any or all of the ELA standards depending on what you choose to emphasize. You are encouraged to focus those state or local standards to meet the grade level benchmarks best assessed at the time of the year in which this assessment is administered.

NCSS Social Studies Standards
- Standard II – Time, Continuity and Change

- Standard III – People, Places, and Environments

- Standard VI – Power, Authority, and Governance

- Standard IX – Global Connections

- Standard X – Civic Ideals and Practices

TECHNOLOGY STANDARDS ADDRESSED

NETS•S 1, 3–6

OUTCOMES AND PRODUCTS

1. Video of an "on the scene" report of the Boston Massacre (group project).

2. Article about the Boston Massacre for publication in a classroom political newspaper (individual project).

3. Multimedia eulogy for one of the Boston Massacre victims (individual project).

ACTIVITY SEQUENCE

1. Preparation
Read chapter 1 of *My Brother Sam Is Dead* in class. (*My Brother Sam Is Dead* is typically used in the fifth-grade core literature or social studies curriculum.) Discuss the characters' points of view. Divide the class into teams of three to five students each. Assign teams a specific point of view regarding the incident or let them choose one. Make sure British and Patriot points of view are represented by an equal number of teams. Instruct the teams to use Web

sites provided to find and examine multiple accounts and documents related to the event. Tell them to review these materials using their assigned points of view. Suggested sites include:

The Boston Massacre: A Behind-the-Scenes Look at Paul Revere's Most Famous Engraving
www.earlyamerica.com/review/winter96/massacre.html

Anonymous Account of the Boston Massacre
http://odur.let.rug.nl/~usa/D/1751-1775/bostonmassacre/anon.htm
> Includes background information, inflammatory first paragraph, list of the killed and wounded.

Find a Grave: Boston Massacre Victims
www.findagrave.com/pictures/bostonmassacre.html
> Actual photos of grave sites. Select Crispus Attucks for a readable close-up image.

Boston National Historical Park Virtual Visitor Center
www.nps.gov/bost/home.htm

The Plumb Design Visual Thesaurus
www.plumbdesign.com/thesaurus/
> Students can use this online thesaurus to understand key concept words such as massacre, patriotic, and loyal.

The Revolutionary War and Children's Literature
www.carolhurst.com/subjects/ushistory/revolution.html
> Excellent activities and literature linked to the Revolutionary War.

2. Group Video Activity

Using information about the Boston Massacre obtained from Web sites and other sources, assign teams to produce on-the-scene video accounts of the event. Give each team a name that corresponds to their "sponsor"—either the RBC (Royal Broadcasting Company) or the LTBC (Liberty Tree Broadcasting Company)—and a number, for example, RBC-1, RBC-2, and so forth. Inform students that, as chair of the editorial review board, you'll be screening all videos. Your screening criteria are outlined in the rubric accompanying this project. Remind students that the reporter's account should represent the group's assigned point of view of the incident.

3. Individual Writing Activity

Following production of the videos, instruct students to use a word processing or publishing program to write and produce newspaper articles supporting the political point of view of their video group. Students may write on any aspect of the Boston Massacre they choose, but the point of view must be consistent with the video production. Gather and publish the articles in one of two class newspapers: *His Majesty's Daily Gazette* or *Liberty Tree Press*. Remind students that the editorial review board will screen all articles prior to publication in the paper.

4. Individual Multimedia Activity

1. Each student draws the name of a massacre victim. A list of the victims and actual photos of grave sites are available at www.findagrave.com/pictures/bostonmassacre.html.

2. Using multimedia software, students create a slide sequence that contains at least three testimonials for their victim from the perspective of survivors who knew the victim well. Although the factual information is incomplete, students can surmise information from the data provided.

WRITING FOR A NEWSPAPER

Before starting this activity, students should be familiar with the style of writing and the types of articles that typically appear in newspapers. As they write their articles, they should identify the section of the paper in which their articles should appear. The rubric for this project doesn't assess to what degree students follow standard journalistic writing practices. Assembling the newspaper can either be delegated to students or completed by an adult outside the assessment process.

3. Each presentation should include an introductory slide with the following: the victim's name, date of birth and death, image of the grave site (actual or student-visualized and -generated), drawing of the victim, and voice or text testimonials. Any other slides for testimonials may be organized as the student chooses.

4. At least one of the testimonials should be written from the point of view of a surviving female (e.g., wife, sister, aunt) to help clarify the role of women in this event.

For a celebration of student work, have team members present their final products to various audiences (entire class, cross-grade-level classes, parents, interested community members).

ASSESSMENT

Assessment of this project is based on three rubrics: one for the news video, one for the news article, and one for the multimedia eulogy. The rubrics in Figure 4.3 provide feedback on both the academic content standards and the NETS•S. As you examine the rubrics, keep in mind that they're designed to provide information about individual student achievement as well as about how well students work together as a group. As with any ISTE assessment rubrics, these can be customized to fit your needs.

THE VIOLENCE QUESTION

The violent nature of the Boston Massacre deaths may be of concern to some students. The project, however, should keep the focus on the humanity of the victims rather than on how they died. When students see the victims as human beings like themselves and not as statistics, they are more likely to see violence for what it really is and less likely to glorify it.

FIGURE 4.3
"You Were There!" Grade 5 Rubric

VIDEO NEWSCAST: ON-THE-SCENE REPORTER (GROUP PROJECT)				
CRITERIA	NOVICE Needs assistance	BASIC Approaching	PROFICIENT Meets	EXCEEDS
Teamwork	A few members do most of the work; no evidence of collaboration; teacher has to intervene frequently	Roles are followed by most in group; cooperation is evident, but not collaboration; teacher occasionally has to intervene	Cooperation and collaboration are evident; work is evenly divided; all members fulfill jobs; teacher rarely intervenes	Cooperation and collaboration are evident; group is synergistic in approach; all members are instrumental in the project; no teacher intervention is needed
TECHNICAL				
Opening	No opening title screen	Opening title screen is too long, too short, or unclear	Opening title screen is clear and relevant	Opening title screen is creative, unique; sets the stage while being clear and relevant
Camera	Image is unsteady; focus is irregular and distracting	Image is occasionally unsteady or out of focus	Image is usually steady and in focus	Image is clear, crisp, and in focus; camera angles enhance the point of view
Audio	Garbled and not clear; too low to understand; considerable distracting background noise	Occasionally unclear; some distracting background noise	Audio is clear; only occasional distracting background noise	Adds music background, transitions, or other audio enhancement

continued

FIGURE 4.3 *continued*
"You Were There!" Grade 5 Rubric

VIDEO NEWSCAST: ON-THE-SCENE REPORTER (GROUP PROJECT)				
CRITERIA	**NOVICE** Needs assistance	**BASIC** Approaching	**PROFICIENT** Meets	**EXCEEDS**
TECHNICAL				
Credits	No credits are included	Contains credits and citations, but some are missing	Credits and citations are complete, roll, and are readable	Credits are complete and well-organized; citations are in format used for report papers
Design	Background is inappropriate for subject; colors, props, and other elements of staging are distracting	Shows an attempt to make background and staging elements support point of view, but some elements are distracting and inconsistent	Background is relevant to point of view and not distracting; fonts are appropriate in color and size	Background and staging elements are unique and further convey point of view; fonts add continuity to video
CONTENT				
Introduction	No introduction	Introduction is unclear or jumbled	Introduction sets the stage for understanding point of view	Introduction is creative and grabs viewer attention while clearly conveying point of view
Vocabulary and Word Usage	Simplistic; grammatically incorrect	Generally appropriate vocabulary used; minor grammatical errors	Appropriate vocabulary used to convey point of view; no grammatical or usage error	Clearly conveys understanding of complex idea, appropriate vocabulary used to support point of view
Point of View	Unclear	Generally clear and explained	Clear to viewer and convincing	Clear, convincing, and supported with multiple examples
Logical Sequence	Sequence is jumbled and out of order	Sequence generally makes sense but needs additional work	Elements of the interview are in logical order and conveyed on storyboard	N/A
Conclusion	No conclusion; interview feels cut off	Conclusion present but may deviate from intent	Conclusion makes sense and follows point of view being conveyed	Conclusion sends strong message to viewer on point of view; logical conclusion to information is provided
Storyboard	Does not create storyboard	Deviates from storyboard	Adheres to storyboard	N/A
Time Frame	Does not adhere to time limit of three minutes	Video is significantly under time limit; insufficient material	Video is less than three minutes with no lag in interview	N/A

continued

FIGURE 4.3 *continued*
"You Were There!" Grade 5 Rubric

6 TRAITS ASSESSMENT TERMS	NEWSPAPER ARTICLE (INDIVIDUAL PROJECT)			
	EMERGING Need for revision outweighs strength	DEVELOPING Strengths and need for revision equal	EFFECTIVE Strengths outweigh weaknesses	STRONG Shows control and strength in ideas presented
TRAIT 1 Ideas and Content	No clear sense of purpose; missing details	Beginning to define topic but not completely clear; generally stays on topic	Supporting ideas are present; ideas are reasonably clear	Focused and clear; contains important details; insightful
TRAIT 2 Organization	Lacks sense of direction; ideas strung together; illogical sequence to convey point of view	Organization sometimes supports main idea; uninspiring	Good introductory sentence; logical flow to details; uses transitions; appropriate conclusion	Showcases the perspective; inviting introduction; well-organized; excellent transitions; smooth to read; strong conclusion
TRAIT 3 Voice	Writer indifferent to the point of view; development is limited	Sincere but not fully engaged in conveying point of view	Enthusiasm for point of view is apparent; aware of purpose of perspective	Speaks directly to the reader in a compelling way; convinces the reader that the point of view is the most compelling perspective
TRAIT 4 Sentence Fluency	Sentences are choppy, incomplete, and rambling; no connectedness	Sentences are stilted and seem mechanical, but flow	Generally easy to read; most sentences begin in unique ways; well-constructed	Easy to read; sentences begin in different ways; both long and short sentences are used; smooth flow
TRAIT 5 Word Choice	Limited vocabulary; no unique words; some misused words	Repeats common words; mostly mundane vocabulary	Uses strong verbs and descriptive language; uses appropriate vocabulary to convey point of view	Uses strong descriptive language; chooses complex but appropriate words to convey ideas
TRAIT 6 Conventions	Errors in spelling, punctuation, and grammar make reading difficult	Reasonable control of writing conventions; errors distract from understanding	Appropriate use of writing conventions; only minor errors	Excellent punctuation, spelling, and grammar; no errors

continued

FIGURE 4.3 *continued*
"You Were There!" Grade 5 Rubric

VICTIM TESTIMONIAL USING MULTIMEDIA (INDIVIDUAL PROJECT)				
CRITERIA	**NOVICE** Needs assistance	**BASIC** Approaching	**PROFICIENT** Meets	**EXCEEDS**
File Management (NETS•S 1)	Unable to title file and store in appropriate location	Either titles file appropriately or stores in proper location, but unable to do both	Independently titles file appropriately (e.g., student last name_ assignment); stores in appropriate folder	Meets criteria and helps others; troubleshoots when others have difficulty
Slide Text (NETS•S 3)	Both title and bulleted points are too small	Either title or bulleted points are too small	Slide title is at least 30 pt.; bulleted points are at least 20 pt.	Font size meets criteria, font design uses advanced features
Slide Background (NETS•S 3)	Background is default white	Uses contrasting color and text	Uses template found in software	Uses template found in software; changes template to suit needs
Use of Images (NETS•S 3, 4)	No images are included, or irrelevant graphics are used	Appropriate images are included, but by placement or size inconsistently enhance understanding	Includes at least one image on each slide of proper placement and size; images add to understanding of the person	Meets standard; shows creative use of images in size or placement; images may be artistically cropped or altered from the original
Content (ELA Standards 2, 7, 8; NETS•S 4)	Uses few relevant important facts about the person; inconsistent point of view	Uses adequate important facts about the person; inconsistent point of view	Uses adequate important facts about the person; consistent point of view	Meets standard; uses additional facts that come from resources other than provided Web sites; information enhances point of view
Number of Slides (ELA Standards 9; NETS•S 4)	Creates basic slide only	Creates introductory slide and one or two testimonial slides	Creates introductory slide and one slide for each of three testimonials	Creates introductory slide and more than three testimonial slides, each of which are appropriate to the person
Oral Presentation Content (ELA Standards 4, 5, 7)	Reads slide(s) but cannot answer questions or provide additional information	Reads slide(s) to class; only answers questions with limited information	Speaks from slide(s) by adding more information and responds to questions with additional information	Meets standard; while presenting, provides linking information to other presentations that preceded or will come, adding coherence to class presentation
Oral Presentation Delivery (ELA Standards 10–12)	Does not look at audience; voice is too soft to hear	Either looks at audience or speaks with adequate volume and clear articulation	Looks at audience while speaking; speaks with adequate volume and clear articulation	Meets criteria and is animated, enthusiastic, and engaging
Citation (NETS•S 2)	No citation	Cites one Web site provided on list but misses others used	Cites all Web information used	Uses more sources than provided; cites all sources

ONE TEACHER'S STORY

Paula Conley
Coeur D'Alene, Idaho

I've used this lesson sequence in my classroom for several years. Infusing required lessons with technology never fails to produce highly motivated students. By the conclusion of this project, students understand the concepts of propaganda and point of view in historical events.

The excitement generated by the activities even carries beyond the classroom walls: I've heard students planning and discussing their newspaper articles and videos out on the playground! History comes alive and the students are involved—a guarantee for success. They don't think of this project as an assessment project, but one that moves from working together to working independently while trying to retain a specific point of view.

References

Collier, J., & Collier, C. (1974). *My Brother Sam Is Dead*. New York: Macmillan.

Hannah, L. (Ed.). (2003). *NETS•S curriculum series: Multidisciplinary units for grades 3 through 5*. Eugene, OR: International Society for Technology in Education.

ISTE. (2000). *National educational technology standards for students: Connecting curriculum and technology*. Eugene, OR: Author.

McTighe, J., & Wiggins, G. (1999). *Understanding by design handbook*. Alexandria, VA: Association for Supervision and Curriculum Development.

CHAPTER 5

"Physics Everywhere": Grade 8 Benchmark Assessment

According to the National Middle Schools Association (NMSA), middle school students are at a crossroads in their educational journey. Students in this age group "must be engaged in learning that is relevant, challenging, integrative, and exploratory" (National Middle Schools Association, n.d.).

During the important middle school years, from sixth through eighth grade, students move from familiarity to mastery of important technologies they'll be using throughout the rest of their education and into their adult lives. They also develop critical-thinking and analytical skills that can help them understand technology in a broader context.

For embedded assessment in the middle school setting, learning tasks must reflect the "relevant, challenging, integrative, and exploratory" nature of the learning environment. Following the philosophy of the NMSA statement, middle school teachers often work together to create interdisciplinary learning experiences for students. These learning experiences help students understand the interconnectedness of the academic discipline areas, often in an experiential mode.

While we know that embedded assessment can provide a clear picture of a student's performance, for data to be reliable when using performance tasks issues such as scalability, deployment, scoring, and calibrating become important (see part 3). Using multiple measures to assess students—such as an online, electronically scored assessment—can balance the picture of achievement by including individual achievement of basic skills and

FIGURE 5.1
NETS•S Assessment Model

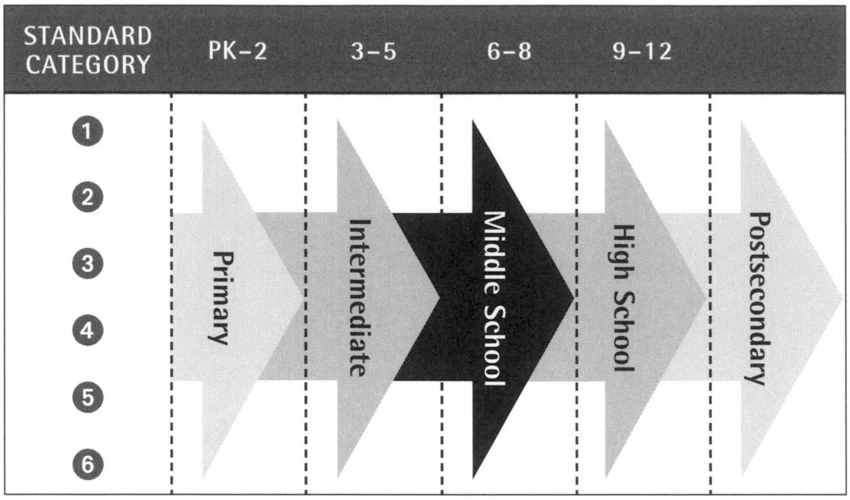

operations and other related standards and performance indicators. As you examine the benchmark assessment task "Physics Everywhere," think about the fundamental assessment questions raised in part 1. Consider the types of data being collected, how the data will be reported, and whether the data answers the necessary questions for your school or district.

Because of the eighth-grade computer literacy requirements contained in the No Child Left Behind legislation, eighth grade may be the point where some form of standardized NETS•S performance assessment is provided—or required—on a school, district, or state level. These types of large-scale assessments, discussed in more detail in parts 3 and 4, generally focus on specific technology skills. While professionally developed assessments of this type can be of great value to the education process, creative and interdisciplinary classroom assessments, such as the one described in this chapter, offer you an excellent way to assess many of the higher-order thinking and collaborative skills referenced in the NETS•S. The NETS•S can be difficult to measure with tests that focus primarily on objective skills and knowledge. The "Physics Everywhere" assessment project demonstrates not only how technology can be infused into the curriculum in ways that combine learning and assessment, but also how technology can enable "relevant, challenging, integrative, and exploratory" experiences that link disciplines as diverse as science and language arts.

For this project, assessment is based on a set of rubrics that allows the teacher to assess each student's individual work (an expository essay) as well as a group product (a video production). Using the rubrics provided, you'll be able to measure achievement of the content standards for both science and English language arts, as well as achievement of the NETS•S eighth-grade performance indicators.

As you examine this assessment project, think about the fundamental assessment questions raised in part 1:

- What types of data is this project designed to generate?

- How will these data be reported?

- To what degree will they answer your school's or district's technology assessment needs?

This project is designed as a benchmark assessment to determine proficiency in meeting the NETS•S at the middle school level. Figure 5.2 shows the Grade 8 section of the NETS•S Developmental Rubric for Grades PK–12 which appears in Figure 2.2.

FIGURE 5.2
NETS•S Developmental Rubric—Focus on Grade 8

NETS•S	PROFICIENCY BY END OF GRADE 8
1. BASIC OPERATIONS AND CONCEPTS	
• Students demonstrate a sound understanding of the nature and operation of technology systems.	Students recognize hardware and software components used to provide access to network resources and know how common peripherals (e.g., scanners, digital cameras, video projectors) are accessed, controlled, connected, and used effectively and efficiently.
	Students know how to evaluate, select, and use appropriate technology tools and information resources to plan, design, develop, and communicate content information, appropriately addressing the target audience and providing accurate citations for sources.
	Students know how to identify appropriate file formats for a variety of applications and apply utility programs to convert formats (as necessary) for effective use in Web, video, audio, graphic, presentation, word-processing, database, publication, and spreadsheet applications.
	Students continue touch-typing techniques, increasing keyboarding facility, and improving accuracy, speed, and general efficiency in computer operation.
	Students examine changes in hardware and software systems over time and identify how changes affect businesses, industry, government, education, and individual users.
• Students are proficient in the use of technology.	Students identify strategies and procedures for efficient and effective management and maintenance of computer files in a variety of different media and formats on a hard drive and network.
	Students know how to solve basic hardware, software, and network problems occurring every day; protect computers, networks, and information from viruses, vandalism,and unauthorized use; and access online help and user documentation to solve common hardware, software, and network problems.
2. SOCIAL, ETHICAL, AND HUMAN ISSUES	
• Students understand the ethical, cultural, and societal issues related to technology.	Students identify legal and ethical issues related to using information and communication technology, recognize consequences of its misuse, and predict possible long-range effects of ethical and unethical uses of technology on culture and society.
• Students practice responsible use of technology systems, information, and software.	Students discuss issues related to acceptable and responsible use of information and communication technology (e.g., privacy, security, copyright, file sharing, plagiarism), analyze the consequences and costs of unethical use of information and computer technology (e.g., hacking, spamming, consumer fraud, virus setting, intrusion), and identify methods for addressing these risks.

continued

FIGURE 5.2 *continued*

NETS•S Developmental Rubric—Focus on Grade 8

NETS•S	PROFICIENCY BY END OF GRADE 8
• Students develop positive attitudes toward technology uses that support lifelong learning, collaboration, personal pursuits, and productivity.	Students examine issues related to computer etiquette and discuss means for encouraging more effective use of technology to support effective communication, collaboration, personal productivity, lifelong learning, and assistance for individuals with disabilities.
3. TECHNOLOGY PRODUCTIVITY TOOLS	
• Students use technology tools to enhance learning, increase productivity, and promote creativity.	Students describe and apply common software features (e.g., spelling and grammar checkers, editing options, dictionary, thesaurus) to maximize accuracy in development of word-processing documents; sorting, formulas, and chart generation in spreadsheets; and insertion of pictures, movies, sound, and charts into presentation software to enhance communication to an audience, promote productivity, and support creativity.
• Students use productivity tools to collaborate in constructing technology-enhanced models, preparing publications, and producing other creative works.	Students describe how to use online environments or other collaborative tools to facilitate design and development of materials, models, publications, and presentations; and how to apply utilities for editing pictures, images, and charts.
4. TECHNOLOGY COMMUNICATIONS TOOLS	
• Students use telecommunications to collaborate, publish, and interact with peers, experts, and other audiences.	Students know how to use telecommunications tools (e.g., e-mail, message boards, blogs, online collaborative environments) to exchange data collected and learn curricular concepts by communicating with peers, experts, and other audiences.
• Students use a variety of media and formats to communicate information and ideas effectively to multiple audiences.	Students know how to use a variety of media and formats to design, develop, publish, and present products (e.g., presentations, newsletters, Web sites) that effectively communicate information and ideas about the curriculum to multiple audiences.
5. TECHNOLOGY RESEARCH TOOLS	
• Students use technology to locate, evaluate, and collect information from a variety of sources.	Students know how to conduct an advanced search using Boolean logic and other sophisticated search functions; and know how to evaluate information from a variety of sources for accuracy, bias, appropriateness, and comprehensiveness.
• Students use technology tools to process data and report results.	Students know how to identify and implement procedures for designing, creating, and populating a database; and in performing queries they know how to process data and report results relevant to an assigned hypothesis or research question.
• Students evaluate and select new information resources and technological innovations based on the appropriateness for specific tasks.	Students know how to select and use information and communication technology tools and resources to collect and analyze information and report results on an assigned hypothesis or research question.
6. TECHNOLOGY PROBLEM-SOLVING AND DECISION-MAKING TOOLS	
• Students use technology resources for solving problems and making informed decisions.	Students identify two or more types of information and communication technology tools or resources that can be used for informing and solving a specific problem and presenting results or for identifying and presenting an informed rationale for a decision.
• Students employ technology in the development of strategies for solving problems in the real world.	Students describe the information and communication technology tools they might use to compare information from different sources, to analyze findings, to determine the need for additional information, and to draw conclusions for addressing real-world problems.

"PHYSICS EVERYWHERE"

Eighth-grade students use Web-based resources to research how basic physics concepts are demonstrated by a favorite sport, hobby, or other type of recreation. Students then write an expository essay using a word processor to explain the connection between the physics concepts and the favorite recreation.

Humanities and science teachers collaborate to complete this interdisciplinary benchmark assessment. Both teachers evaluate the essay to assess the students' understanding of physics and their expository writing skills. Because of this, the sequence of the two activities is important: the essay is assigned in science class after basic physics concepts are explored, then the writing of the essay is coached in Humanities class. After the essay, students collaboratively produce a short, narrated video in the science class that demonstrates and explains how three physics concepts are used in their favorite recreation.

BIG IDEA
Concepts learned in physics relate to what we do every day.

OBJECTIVES
Students will be able to

- identify three physics concepts that are illustrated by their favorite recreation.

- explain through written expository narrative how physics concepts are demonstrated in their chosen recreation.

- show how physics concepts work within the chosen recreation by creating a video of the concepts in action.

CONTENT STANDARDS ADDRESSED

NCTE English Language Arts Standards
his benchmark assessment activity can address any or all of the ELA standards depending on what you choose to emphasize. You are encouraged to focus those state or local standards to meet the grade level benchmarks best assessed at the time of the year in which this assessment is administered.

NAS National Science Education Standards
Grades 5–8 Science Content Standard B: Physical Science

- B-1 Properties and changes of properties in matter

- B-2 Motion and forces

- B-3 Transfer of Energy

TECHNOLOGY STANDARDS ADDRESSED
NETS•S 1, 3–6

OUTCOMES AND PRODUCTS

1. An expository essay explaining physics concepts demonstrated in a chosen recreation (individual product).

2. A narrated video explaining and illustrating physics concepts demonstrated in the recreation (group product).

ACTIVITY SEQUENCE

1. Preparation
Each student selects a sport, hobby, or other form of recreation. A wide variety of activities are suitable for this purpose, from hitting a baseball, to playing a musical instrument, to riding a roller coaster. The only requirement is

that the activity in some way demonstrate principles of physics in action. Concepts covered in a typical eighth-grade science course include:

- potential energy: kinetic energy transfer
- friction: sliding, rolling, fluid, and static
- air resistance
- drag
- projectile motion: arced flight of objects
- Newton's First Law: inertia
- Newton's Second Law: force = mass x acceleration
- Newton's Third Law: action force = reaction force
- Bernoulli's Principle: forces within fluids
- Law of Conservation of Momentum

2. Expository Essay

With guidance from their science teacher, students research how three physics concepts relate to their chosen recreation. Then, with guidance from their humanities teacher, students write an expository essay explaining how these three physics concepts are demonstrated in their chosen recreation. The essay must include at least three sources, one of which must be printed and one electronic. All sources must be cited appropriately, and the essay must be written using a word processor. The technical, structural, and stylistic requirements for the essay (detailed in the scoring rubrics in Figure 5.3) should be provided to the students by the humanities teacher.

Many good Web sites can help students work through steps in the writing process, such as www.members.tripod.com/~lklivingston/essay/index.html. The Citation Machine Web site (www.citationmachine.net) can help students learn the proper formatting for citations. The following list of research sites can give you and your students a head start on finding relevant material for this project; however, if research skills are to be demonstrated, don't provide students with a list of Web sites. Alternatively, you can minimally provide students with the Exploratorium Web site address (www.exploratorium.edu), which they can then use to find additional sites.

Baseball
www.exploratorium.edu/baseball/index.html
www.pbs.org/saf/1206/video/watchonline.htm (scroll down to Baseball Tech video)

Tennis
www.physics.usyd.edu.au/~cross/tennis.html

Hockey
www.exploratorium.edu/hockey/index.html

Surfing
www.exploratorium.edu/theworld/surfing/physics/index.html

Skateboarding
www.exploratorium.edu/skateboarding/index.html

Cycling
www.exploratorium.edu/cycling/index.html

Basketball
http://mrfizzix.com/basketball/

Swimming
http://ffden-2.phys.uaf.edu/211_fall2002.web.dir/Craig_McMullen/CoverPage.htm

CONCEPT MAPS

This assessment project does not include the development of a concept map of the writing process. However, use of concept-mapping software can be included as another element of the assessment of writing and technology skills.

3. Group Video Project

Completion of the expository essay is necessary before starting the video portion of the project. It's important to build on the essay experience as students would have completed their research and discussed the physics involved before considering how to illustrate the concept. Because this is an assessment activity, students should have had some previous experience in making short videos before they're asked to complete this activity.

For each group of students, you'll need basic video-editing software (often preinstalled on newer computers) and a video camera. Because there are many stages to the project, it isn't necessary to have one camera per group as groups can easily share cameras. If access to an adequate number of video cameras isn't possible, consider using free video clips available on the Internet. AltaVista has such clips at www.altavista.com/video/default.

1. Break the class into groups of four or five to complete the video portion of this project. (If resources are limited, the entire class can work as a group on a single video). Depending on the size of the groups, students should assign each other one or more roles in the video production process, such as director, producer, writer, copy editor, actor(s), film editor(s), stagehand, and so forth. It will be necessary for the group members to have multiple roles. Rely on the group process normally used in the class. As with the essay portion of this project, the rubrics that will be used to score the final product should be shared with students in advance so that they'll have clear guidelines to follow.

2. Have students share their expository essays and decide which essay represents the sport, hobby, or other recreational pursuit they want to use as the basis for their video. The video should illustrate the main points in the essay.

3. Students work together to write the group's script, showing how physics is evident in a common recreation. They can demonstrate and explain the concepts in a straightforward manner or use other formats by creating a commercial, a poem, music video, impersonation, or dramatic scene—the ideas are almost unlimited. Because the focus is on video production, the script can be in rough form as it will be transferred to a storyboard (see sample on next page).

4. Students plan the production by creating a storyboard. A storyboard is an outline of the video showing the script and the effects to be used for each scene of the video.

5. Students will need to practice scenes before filming begins. They should be encouraged to complete the activity in segments so that video editing can begin as soon as possible.

6. Have students collaboratively edit the video and add music and other enhancements as they choose. Many sites offer royalty-free music for easy downloading. Try Partners in Rhyme at www.partnersinrhyme.com/pir/PIRsfx. html or Apple's Sound Effects site at www.apple.com/ilife/imovie/soundeffects.html

7. Hold a Student Physics Film Festival to share the students' work. Students in lower grades can learn physics concepts and get a glimpse of an experience they'll have in eighth grade.

ASSESSMENT

The products resulting from this benchmark assessment project provide a wealth of diverse assessment information. You can use the products to evaluate students' research, writing, and technology skills, as well as their understanding of fundamental physics concepts. The collaborative nature of the video production project also allows you to evaluate students' ability to work together and use technology tools collaboratively. The rubrics shown in Figure 5.3 provide a model for capturing and evaluating all aspects of this integrated assessment. Rubrics are typically based on standards, such as content area standards and the NETS•S, or on a specific conceptual framework, such as the 6+1 Trait Writing Assessment Model (Northwest Regional Educational Laboratory, 2001a) that's used as the basis for the essay rubric in Figure 5.3.

SCIENCE VIDEO STORYBOARD

TITLE:	AUTHORS:	
Video	Sketch (to scale)	Audio

FIGURE 5.3

"Physics Everywhere" Grade 8 Rubric

EXPOSITORY ESSAY				
6+1 TRAITS ASSESSMENT TERMS	**EMERGING** Need for revision outweighs strength	**DEVELOPING** Strengths and need for revision equal	**EFFECTIVE** Strengths outweigh weaknesses	**STRONG** Professional or collegiate level
TRAIT 1 Ideas and Content	Accurately explains only one physics concept; ideas are unclear, rambling, or off-topic; lacking details	Beginning to define the topic but not completely clear; accurately explains only two of the required three concepts; details somewhat support topic; generally stays on topic	Accurately explains three concepts; supporting ideas are present; ideas are focused, clear, and informative	Focused and clear; contains important details; insightful; accurately explains more than three physics concepts related to the recreation
TRAIT 2 Organization	Lacks a sense of direction; ideas strung together; needs more structure; confusing	Writing is fairly organized; introduction is obvious but weak; closing is attempted; transitions are limited; uninspiring	Good introduction that includes thesis; logical flow to concrete details; uses transitions; conclusion relates to thesis/topic, and then goes beyond to "so what" information	Clearly showcases the concept; inviting introduction; well-organized; sequence is effective in moving the reader through the topic; excellent transitions; smooth to read; strong conclusion
TRAIT 3 Voice	Writer seems indifferent to the topic; connection to the audience is unclear; tone is flat; little emotion	Sincere but not fully engaged; inconsistent; tone is generally appropriate	Personality, confidence, and feelings are evident; commitment is obvious; tone is sincere; writing engages reader in material	Speaks directly to the reader in a natural, compelling way; personality of writer is obvious; overall effect is expressive, creative, and engaging
TRAIT 4 Sentence Fluency	Sentences are choppy, incomplete, and rambling; no connectedness; lacks fluency when read aloud	Sometimes concise and sometimes too wordy; sounds mechanical	Generally easy to read, with strong and varied sentence structure; well-constructed	Strong and varied sentence structure; appropriately concise; natural flow and rhythm when read aloud
TRAIT 5 Word Choice	Limited vocabulary; makes no attempt to use words from curriculum; no unique words; misuses some words	Repeats common words; attempts to use vocabulary from curriculum; expression is limited	Uses appropriate descriptive language; uses appropriate vocabulary from the curriculum to clarify explanation	Uses strong descriptive language; chooses complex but appropriate words from curriculum and other sources to convey ideas
TRAIT 6 Conventions	Minimal grasp of basic conventions makes reading very difficult	Basic grasp of standard writing conventions is apparent; errors distract from understanding	Appropriate use of writing conventions; a few minor errors in the more difficult words but not distracting	Excellent command of writing conventions; no errors; uses enhancements such as subheadings, in-text notes, footnotes, etc.
TRAIT 7 (6+1) Presentation	Disregards format requirements for expository writing; presentation distracts from understanding of topic; formats with spaces; does not use style sheet	Limited attempt to follow format requirements of expository essay; presentation is flat or slightly distracting; relies on basic word processing formatting to produce paper	Follows format requirements for expository essay; presentation is neat and appropriate; uses style sheet to create consistency in paper layout and design	Follows format requirements for expository essay; presentation is neat and creative and enhances understanding of the topic; uses style sheet as basis for formatting

continued

FIGURE 5.3 *continued*

"Physics Everywhere" Grade 8 Rubric

VIDEO PRODUCTION				
CRITERIA	NOVICE	BASIC	MEETS	EXCEEDS
Script	Did not complete a script	Partially completed script	Completed rough script; connection from script to storyboard is clear	Completed a detailed script; connection between script and storyboard is clear
Storyboard	Not complete; did not use	Partially completed; departed from storyboard when producing video	Completed storyboard; adhered to original storyboard	Thoroughly thought through process, as shown on completed storyboard; adhered to storyboard in production
Completion (Group Score)	Not much is done on the project	The project is almost finished but did not make the deadline	The project is completed and met the deadline	The project was completed early; finished team members helped others during time left
Science Content (Group Score)	Concepts are not addressed, are unclear, or are confused; one science concept is covered	Concepts are included, but not explained well; two concepts are covered	Concepts explained well; examples are connected to three science concepts	Concepts are explained well and clearly linked to the recreation; more than three concepts are included
Group Cooperation (Individual Score)	Not an active member of the group; other group members did all of the work	Works well with the group most of the time; some teacher intervention needed to keep on task	Active member of the group; was working well at all times during production; teacher intervention not needed	Active member of the group; willingly helped others in the group but not domineering; demonstrated leadership among peers
TECHNICAL				
Opening NETS•S 1, 4, 6	No opening title screen	Opening title is screen too long, too short, or unclear	Opening title screen is clear and relevant	Opening title screen is creative and unique; sets the stage while being clear and relevant
Camera NETS•S 1, 3	Image is very unsteady; focus is irregular and distracting	Image is occasionally unsteady or out of focus	Image is steady and in focus	Image is clear, crisp and in focus; camera angles enhance the point of view
Audio NETS•S 1, 3,	Garbled and unclear; volume too low to understand; considerable distracting background noise	Occasionally unclear; some distracting background noise	Audio is clear, with no distracting background noise	Has a music background, transitions, or other audio enhancement
Credits NETS•S 2	Missing citations or credits	Contains credit and citations, but some are incomplete	Credits and citations are complete, roll, and are readable	Credits are complete and well-organized; citations are in the format used for report papers
Design NETS•S 4	Background is inappropriate for subject; colors, props, and other elements of staging are distracting	Shows an attempt to make background and staging support understanding of the concept, but elements are distracting and inconsistent	Background is relevant to subject and not distracting; fonts are appropriate in color and size	Background and staging elements are unique and further support understanding of the concepts; design elements add continuity to video

ONE TEACHER'S STORY

Russ Bird

Mesa Verde Middle School, Poway, California

I've found this project to be the most rewarding thing I've done with students in my 18 years of teaching. The students are engaged and learning without a lot of teacher intervention.

The group interaction is positive, and each student finds a contributing role within the group. The students are amazingly proud of their final product, and all want a copy. The knowledge that we're going to have a film festival at the end of the project, and that their production will be seen by others, is a strong motivator for students to produce quality work.

My role during this project is very dynamic. I go from technical director, to expert resource, to software problem solver in a matter of minutes. There's a lot going on in the classroom, but the students are producing the material and I'm definitely the "guide on the side." From the videos, I'm truly able to see whether the students understand the concepts. For the first time, I can really tell if the students get it!

References

Culham, R. (2005). *6+1 traits of writing: The complete guide for the primary grades.* New York: Scholastic Inc.

National Middle Schools Association. (n.d.). *This I believe….* Retrieved February 12, 2005, from www.nmsa.org

Northwest Regional Educational Laboratory. (2001a). 6+1 trait writing assessment model. Retrieved January 5, 2005, from http://www.nwrel.org/assessment/department.php?d=1

Northwest Regional Educational Laboratory. (2001b). 6+1 trait writing scoring continuum. Retrieved April 20, 2005, from http://www.nwrel.org/assessment/pdfRubrics/6plus1traits.PDF

CHAPTER 6

The Senior Project: Grade 12 Benchmark Assessment

By the end of 12th grade, students should be able to demonstrate under-standing of the NETS•S. Mastery of the Grade 12 performance indicators represents the culmination of a development process begun in the primary grades. By the end of high school, students should be adept at finding prac-tical applications for their skills as they prepare to enter the workforce or begin a program of higher education.

Technology standards such as those found in NETS•S 6, which address prob-lem-solving and decision-making tools, should provide not just a theoretical framework for teaching, but a focus for assessing student achievement of practical, real-world technology skills.

FIGURE 6.1
NETS•S Assessment Model

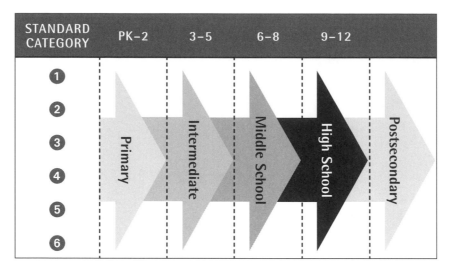

Many districts require a portfolio of work to demonstrate that a student has met district and state graduation requirements. Demonstrating understanding of the NETS•S should be an integral part of this portfolio. For some, the portfolio is one large multidisciplinary task. For others, the portfolio is a directed set of work samples that meet a set of criteria. Still others include testing data as well as work samples in such a portfolio.

Increasingly, high schools are requiring a senior project or exhibition, a rigorous piece of work that demonstrates application of knowledge and skills necessary to be productive members of society. The philosophy behind such a "capstone" senior project is the belief that what really shows who students are and what they have learned is their ability to demonstrate their academic education and life experiences through a project that makes a contribution to the community.

In his work establishing the principles of the Coalition of Essential Schools, Theodore Sizer states that capable individuals who graduate from high school should be able to apply their skills to analyze problems, propose solutions, communicate effectively, work successfully in groups, and coordinate the work of others when necessary (Sizer, 1992). In the context of NETS•S assessment, this means a student's capstone achievement project should demonstrate the ability to successfully interact with a world of continuously emerging technologies.

The 12th-grade benchmark assessment described in this chapter is based on the senior project or exhibition model that has grown out of the Coalition of Essential Schools project and other efforts to improve secondary education:

> One of the most pressing issues facing educators today is the necessity to adequately prepare students to meet the growing demands of both higher education and the work force. These two arenas require not only mastery of such fundamentals as history,

mathematics, reading, science, and writing, but also the ability to analyze, integrate, and synthesize materials and present the results to diverse audiences.

The senior project is a culminating performance assessment for 12th-graders. The project incorporates the skills of writing, researching, public speaking, planning, and time management by requiring students to complete four components: a research paper, a related project or product, a portfolio, and a presentation to a panel of school staff and community members (Coalition of Essential Schools).

Because of the scale and scope of most senior projects, they require considerable coordination and support by parents, teachers, administrators, and other members of the community. Research has shown that a school's or district's capacity to implement a senior project is based on criteria similar to the NETS Essential Conditions discussed in chapter 1. A shared vision; professional development; adequate infrastructure; and supportive policies, standards, and curriculum are all part of what the Senior Project Center calls the "Senior Project Certification Yes Test" (SERVE Center, 2004).

If your school or district doesn't have a senior project program, consider implementing the benchmark assessment that follows as part of a required interdisciplinary course for all seniors. As with the eighth-grade benchmark assessment, teachers from different subject areas should work together to decide who will be responsible for each portion of the assessment.

It's likely you'll find the individual activities that make up this project already being completed at your school, but perhaps each in a different course. Therefore, completing this benchmark assessment will involve active collaboration in mapping the assessment across the curriculum and collecting data for analysis and evaluation.

For this project, assessment is based on a set of rubrics that allows teachers to assess a wide range of senior project products, including a research paper, a project-related work sample, a portfolio, a presentation, and a resumé. Not every student project will require all of these products, and not every product will have a technology component for assessment. However, each product associated with a senior project should be evaluated with carefully constructed rubrics, such as those modeled in this chapter. These rubrics provide fair and consistent scoring of student work. Products that include a technology component should be assessed based on the high school NETS•S performance indicators. Figure 6.2 shows the Grade 12 section of the NETS•S Developmental Rubric for Grades PK–12 which appears in Figure 2.2.

FIGURE 6.2
NETS•S Developmental Rubric—Focus on Grade 12

NETS•S	PROFICIENT BY END OF GRADE 12
1. BASIC OPERATIONS AND CONCEPTS	
• Students demonstrate a sound understanding of the nature and operation of technology systems.	Students evaluate new and/or advanced technology resources for information-dissemination options (e.g., video servers, webcasting, compressed video delivery, online file sharing, graphing calculators, multifunction communications devices, global positioning software) and technology-career opportunities.
	Students assess the capabilities and limitations of contemporary and emerging technology resources as well as the potential of these systems and services to address personal lifelong learning and workplace needs.
	In teams, students collaborate to illustrate content-related concepts integrating a variety of media (e.g., print, audio, video, graphic, probes, simulations, models) with presentation, word-processing, publishing, database, graphics design software, or spreadsheet applications.
	Students routinely exhibit touch-typing techniques with advanced facility, accuracy, speed, and efficiency as they complete their assignments.
	In teams, students collaborate to evaluate software, hardware, and networking systems to inform the development of a technology plan for a specific real-world business, educational entity, industry, organization, or other group.
• Students are proficient in the use of technology.	Students know how to use advanced utilities (e.g., compression, antivirus) with computer files in a variety of media and formats.
	Students know how to identify, assess, and solve advanced hardware, software, and network problems by using online help and other user documentation and support.
2. SOCIAL, ETHICAL, AND HUMAN ISSUES	
• Students understand the ethical, cultural, and societal issues related to technology.	Students analyze current trends in information and communication technology and assess the potential of emerging technologies for ethical and unethical uses in culture and society.
• Students practice responsible use of technology systems, information, and software.	Students analyze the consequences and costs of unethical use of information and computer technology and identify how individuals can protect their technology systems from the unethical and unscrupulous user.
• Students develop positive attitudes toward technology uses that support lifelong learning, collaboration, personal pursuits, and productivity.	Students analyze current trends in information and communication technology and discuss how emerging technologies could affect collaboration, enhance personal productivity, meet the diverse needs of learners, and promote opportunities for lifelong learning among local and global communities.
3. TECHNOLOGY PRODUCTIVITY TOOLS	
• Students use technology tools to enhance learning, increase productivity, and promote creativity.	Students understand and apply advanced software features, such as templates and styles to improve the appearance of word-processing documents, spreadsheets, and presentations and to provide evidence of learning, productivity, and creativity.
• Students use productivity tools to collaborate in constructing technology-enhanced models, prepare publications, and produce other creative works.	Students analyze a plan and procedures for development of a multimedia product (e.g., model, presentation, webcast, publication, creative work) and identify authoring tools, other hardware and software resources, research, and team personnel needed to plan, create, and edit the product.

continued

FIGURE 6.2 *continued*
NETS•S Developmental Rubric—Focus on Grade 12

NETS•S	PROFICIENT BY END OF GRADE 12
4. TECHNOLOGY COMMUNICATIONS TOOLS	
• Students use telecommunications to collaborate, publish, and interact with peers, experts, and other audiences.	Students plan and implement collaborative projects (with peers, experts, or other audiences) using advanced telecommunications tools (e.g., groupware, interactive Web sites, simulations, joint data collection, videoconferencing) to support curriculum concepts or benefit the local, regional, or global community.
• Students use a variety of media and formats to communicate information and ideas effectively to multiple audiences.	Students know how to use a variety of media and formats to design, develop, publish, and present products (e.g., presentations, newsletters, Web sites) that incorporate information from the curriculum and communicate original ideas to multiple audiences.
5. TECHNOLOGY RESEARCH TOOLS	
• Students use technology to locate, evaluate, and collect information from a variety of sources.	Students know how to locate, select, and use advanced technology resources (e.g., expert systems, intelligent agents, real-world models and simulations) to enhance their learning of curriculum topics selected.
• Students use technology tools to process data and report results.	Students formulate a hypothesis or research question on a curriculum topic they choose, and design, create, and populate a database to process data and report results.
• Students evaluate and select new information resources and technological innovations based on the appropriateness for specific tasks.	Students formulate a hypothesis or research question and select and use appropriate information and communication technology tools and resources for collecting and analyzing information and reporting results to multiple audiences.
6. TECHNOLOGY PROBLEM-SOLVING AND DECISION-MAKING TOOLS	
• Students use technology resources for solving problems and making informed decisions	Students describe integration of two or more information and communication technology tools and resources to collaborate with peers, community members, experts, and others to solve a problem and present results or to present an informed rationale for a decision.
• Students employ technology in the development of strategies for solving problems in the real world.	Students integrate information and communication technology to analyze a real-world problem, design and implement procedures to monitor information, to set timelines, and to evaluate progress toward the solution of a real-world problem.

THE SENIOR PROJECT

OVERVIEW

Unlike the other assessment tasks, the Grade 12 Benchmark Assessment Task is defined by the student and reflects the student's interests and talents. They must demonstrate achievement of the NETS•S as part of the requirements for completing the five components of the senior project: paper, project, product, presentation, and resumé (Senior Project, n.d.).

BIG IDEA

Each student graduating from high school has the ability to apply his or her knowledge and skills to make a contribution to the community.

OBJECTIVES

Students will be able to

- identify and research an area of personal interest in which they believe they can make a contribution to the community.

- independently conduct background research on the topic and convey the results in a formally written research paper.

- plan and execute a project that solves a problem and makes a contribution to the community.

- show how the project was planned and executed by assembling a portfolio of artifacts documenting the process and outcomes.

- create a presentation showing the project's process and outcomes.

- write a resumé for employment.

CONTENT STANDARDS ADDRESSED

In addition to the meeting the NETS•S, the academic content standards covered in the Senior Project are defined by the school with the graduation outcomes of the district and state in mind.

Because writing ability is so important for all students—whether they're entering the workforce or continuing in higher education—English Language Arts Standards are likely to be an essential component of any senior project. Other content area standards will be addressed depending on the subject matter of the student's project. Having students select the standards they want to exemplify is another way for students to take control of the project and make it meaningful for them. However, teachers and administrators should work with students to make sure the projects they choose and the work they create will adequately demonstrate the student's mastery of the core academic content areas required for graduation.

TECHNOLOGY STANDARDS ADDRESSED

NETS•S 1–6

OUTCOMES AND PRODUCTS

Paper. A research paper focusing on background information that will support the project.

Product/Project. A work sample composed of something made or invented, or a procedure created for the project. Alternatively, the work sample can be a problem solved or an issue clarified through research.

Portfolio. A portfolio of artifacts documenting the process students go through while completing the other elements of the senior project.

Presentation. A formal presentation to a public audience, including those assessing the senior project, that describes both the project process and the project outcomes.

Resumé. A professional resumé for employment.

ACTIVITY SEQUENCE

1. Preparation

Unlike other assessment projects described in earlier chapters, the implementation of a senior project requires input and support from the entire school, not just individual teachers or a few departments. The elements needed to support senior projects vary from school to school or district to district, depending on the nature of the program being implemented. However, the following preparation steps generally apply to all such programs.

- Introduce the project to students before they enter 12th grade. If current seniors are exhibiting their work, 11th-graders and their parents should have the chance to view the exhibits or otherwise review senior work, with an understanding that they will be performing comparable senior project activities when they enter 12th grade. Students should be encouraged to think ahead and even begin researching their projects the summer before their senior year.

- Hold an orientation session for students and parents early in the process, preferably before the start of senior year. At this session, provide parents and students with handouts about each component of the senior project, instructions on the timeline(s) that students will need to follow, and information on the rubrics to be used for scoring. Hold additional sessions the week before the school starts, and again several weeks into the school year, for new students and those wishing a refresher. Make provisions for students who enter later in the school year.

- Make sure faculty members are well-versed in the senior project process so they can answer questions as they arise.

- Make available information on the program. If your school maintains a Web site, include information on the expectations of the senior project process, as well as an FAQ section.

2. Identifying Project Parameters and Components

Individual schools determine what components will be required for the senior project based on district and state graduation requirements. Figure 6.3 presents several examples of senior projects developed by students at Nogales High School, Nogales, Arizona (2005).

While the topics selected for senior projects can be wide-ranging, it's important that teachers, administrators, and students agree on an underlying set of principles common to the design of all projects. The "Six Tenets of the Senior Project" from Parker School, Devens, Massachusetts (n.d.), provide a model for designing projects that will encourage and support high expectations from students, parents, and community members.

3. Research Paper

The research paper demonstrates students' ability to use primary and secondary sources to search for, gather, and organize information about a specific topic. The paper can vary in length and format. Provide students with guidelines for formatting and citations, such as those used by the American Psychological Association (APA), or provide school-defined guidelines for research papers. While teachers may want to give students room for creativity in their organization of the paper, typical elements include

- an introduction
- a statement of the problem or thesis statement

- information that supports a solution to the problem

- information that's contrary to the proposed solution

- a conclusion that includes the proposed solution as well as the academic content standards which completion of the project will address

- footnotes and bibliography

Because of the importance of this research to all other senior project activities, the paper should cite a minimum of 10 sources. Of these sources, at least five must be from electronic sources and three from print sources. Electronic sources can include online interviews, videoconferencing with individuals, documents and samples from the Internet, and e-mail exchanges in consultation with experts. Be sure to reinforce the importance of exercising information literacy standards for judging the credibility of information.

Require students to write their research papers on a word processor. This allows you to assess student technology skills related to creating, editing, and formatting documents, including documents containing professionally formatted footnotes and bibliographic entries.

FIGURE 6.3
Sample Senior Projects and Exhibitions

ESSENTIAL QUESTION	RESEARCH	PROJECT
I want to eventually open a Mexican health food restaurant. How can I help people understand the health benefits of Mexican food?	Nutritional value of common ingredients; Mexican food industry	Write a healthy foods cookbook focusing on traditional Mexican recipes. Put together a series of menus low in cholesterol and carbohydrates.
Can a bridge that doesn't destroy the environment be built over the river?	Civil engineering; environmentally friendly designs	Design a suspension bridge.
Children are coming to school without being ready to learn. What can be done?	Early childhood education; poverty	Teach preschool and kindergarten in a low-income area.
How can we lower the number of people in our area dying of preventable diseases?	Deadly diseases in our area; mortality information and related health issues	Produce a video.
Should the Internet be censored?	Censorship on the Internet; legality of censorship; concerns of the library community; impact of open access to the Internet; filtering	Build a Web site exploring both sides of the issue. Include links for parents to appropriate filtering software and links for community members on rights.
Children are learning to follow, not lead. How can we foster leadership skills?	Leadership in children	Coach a basketball team with a focus on developing leadership skills and full-participation experience
My community has no jobs. How can I start a successful business that will last?	Small business ownership Key elements of success and failure in the community	Start a small business that provides a service.
How can we help adults learn English?	Literacy Program of America; adult literacy	Volunteer to teach English in a school for adults
How can we protect the rights of teenagers?	Teen court; legal rights of minors; judicial services for minors	Volunteer for teen court

This list was modified from a sample provided by Nogales High School, Nogales, Arizona (2005).

4. Product/Project

The product/project represents the experiential part of the learning process. While the nature of this product can range considerably—from a business plan, to a diary or blog of student experiences, to a new invention—the project is meant to demonstrate how students are applying their knowledge, skills, and experiences to solve the problem outlined in their research papers. Teachers should work with students to establish one or more specific objectives whose outcomes can be measured through a review of the work.

Each student should create a plan for completing this activity and have it approved by a school adviser or senior project mentor. Elements of the activity may include

- a clear statement of objective

- a timeline (supported by the use of project management software)

- digital documentation of the steps involved in the project (digital pictures, video, and so forth)

- an electronic journal documenting the steps in the project

- student reflection on how the project has addressed the identified academic content standards

- an archive of all communication with the senior project mentor

---

SIX TENETS OF THE SENIOR PROJECT

1. **The Essential Question.** Because a successful and meaningful senior project necessarily involves genuine inquiry around a topic of the student's choosing, seniors will focus their work around a complex, interesting, and sustainable essential question.

2. **Benefit to the Larger Community.** Because we are all members of a broader community, each senior project must incorporate some aspect of giving back to others. In this regard, each senior's work, time, and energy will result in a lasting contribution that is bigger than the project itself.

3. **Multifaceted Approach.** Because of the complex nature of each senior project, seniors must incorporate a variety of modes of thinking in the planning, implementation, and exhibiting of their projects.

4. **Research Component.** No senior project will be successful without a substantial element of new learning. This learning can take place in many ways, one of which must be research. Research must be both experiential (e.g., internships, surveys) and text-based (e.g., library, Internet), although the degree to which each form is emphasized will vary from student to student.

5. **Collaboration.** One of the most important skills in life is the ability to work with and learn from other people. Each senior project must incorporate some element of collaboration with individuals outside the immediate community. In many cases, these outsiders will serve as secondary mentors for the senior project.

6. **Academic Rigor.** Each senior project must be conceived in a way that challenges the student to think deeply and critically beyond what the student already knows and is able to do. The topic must be big enough for the student to consider multiple perspectives but not so big that it will lead only to superficial understanding.

This list is provided by Parker School, Devens, Massachusetts (n.d.).

In addition to demonstrating the student's achievement of the chosen outcome(s), the project can also be used to evaluate the student's

- level of independence in completing the project

- resource and time-management skills

- interpersonal skills and collaboration with others involved in the project, either directly or indirectly

5. Portfolio

The portfolio is a compilation of all the artifacts generated, from development of the original idea through completion of the project. Required elements include the project artifacts listed above as well as the other elements of the senior project—research paper, presentation, and resumé. The portfolio should be kept in electronic format, either as a Web page with links to the artifacts or managed with the district's portfolio software, such as TaskStream or LiveText. The portfolio rubric in Figure 6.6 is designed to assess a Web-page portfolio.

The organization of the portfolio should be left to the student. The portfolio should communicate how the project was created, what problems were solved, and what objectives were met. If the senior project is one component of a district-prescribed, standards-based portfolio, such as the assessment portfolios described in chapter 11, you may need to customize the required elements of the portfolio to fit district guidelines.

6. Presentation

This culminating step in the senior project should take place near the end of the school year. Public review of senior projects can take the form of an exhibition, with students using multimedia presentation software to explain and illustrate

- the development of the central research idea, including references to the research conducted

- the process used to complete the project, including all steps and missteps to completion

- the outcome of the project, with reflections on what was learned

The presentation should be supported by multimedia, Internet-based resources as well as other visual aids, such as posters and exhibits.

To stress the importance of senior projects, many schools ask students to dress professionally as they make their presentation in a public forum to school faculty, family, peers, and community members. Students are also often asked to generate a professional resumé to distribute to people attending the event. A trained panel of faculty and community members should evaluate the presentation using a rubric-based scoring procedure.

7. Resumé

As part of their senior English class, students are expected to create a professional resumé that can be used to apply for employment. The resumé should include the following standard elements:

- objective (vocational goals)

- education (current GPA, favorite classes, college plans)

- community activities (volunteer and service-learning activities)

- work experience (all jobs and responsibilities as well as length of time in each job)

- extracurricular school activities (clubs, music, athletics, and so forth)

- interests and hobbies (off-campus activities)

- awards and honors

The resumé should also include information about a student's senior project, including links to Web pages documenting the project, if appropriate. By using one of the resumé templates provided in many word processors, students can demonstrate their word processing and document-formatting skills.

Make sure students abide by district privacy policies and adjust the personal contact information on their resumés. If the resumé is to be evaluated as part of the senior project presentation (see above), students should bring a minimum of six copies to the event. Many students bring more copies for community members who are interested in hiring students. The resumé stresses to seniors the importance of their student work in providing avenues to future employment. In many cases, senior project resumés lead to immediate opportunities for summer or long-term employment.

ASSESSMENT

Because senior projects vary so widely in terms of topics covered and products created, no single set of assessment rubrics is likely to cover all components of the project. The rubrics in Figures 6.4 through 6.8 offer a solid start—you can customize these or use them as a basis for creating your own rubrics. Most rubrics are based on standards: in this case, the NETS•S and the 6+1 Trait Writing Assessment Model (Northwest Regional Educational Laboratory, 2001a). Rubrics for complex products such as portfolios and presentations often must be customized to cover all the necessary evaluation criteria, including measures of student technology use.

SEVERAL SCHOOLS' REFLECTIONS ON SENIOR PROJECTS

- To develop a successful senior project, schools must make a commitment to integrate the elements of the project into the senior year curriculum. Providing time for students to meet with their faculty adviser, devising a plan for obtaining community advisers, and setting a clear timeline for the completion of each element of the project are all consistently cited as essential to success by schools that have implemented senior projects.

- From a student perspective, the senior project might seem to be just another burden before graduation. Yet feedback from students involved in senior projects confirms that the experience has connected them to the community and provided a new perspective on ways of learning. Teachers often talk about lifelong learning, but rarely do students understand how that might play out when they leave school for jobs or higher education. Students also attest to enjoying the freedom that senior projects give them to choose a topic of interest and explore it in depth, with the focus on making a difference in the community.

- Moving from a poster session-style exhibition to an electronic, multimedia exhibition has changed the nature of many senior projects from one that was exclusively for a few faculty and community members to one that has become a formal community event and celebration. The professional appearance of the presentation, the large display on an auditorium screen, and the ability to respond to questions in an open forum give the exhibition a higher level of importance.

Some schools and communities view the exhibition as an opportunity to unveil for local businesses and industry the high quality of potential new employees. Some schools structure the public exhibition in such a way that projects similar to one another are scheduled in blocks, with a public announcement of when these grouped projects will be shown and who will be presenting. Community members interested in specific topics can attend the blocks most pertinent to them.

- Senior projects and exhibitions often have unanticipated outcomes. For example, most students feel uneasy in front of an audience, but by presenting their projects alongside their peers and being there to support and observe one another's work, they gain both newfound confidence and respect for members of their class. This public display of student work also wins over many community members when they see how capable their local graduates are.

References

Coalition of Essential Schools. (n.d.). Retrieved June 5, 2005, from www.essentialschools.org

Nogales High School, Nogales, Arizona. (2005). *Sample senior projects.* Retrieved January 20, 2005, from http://www.nusd.k12.az.us/nhs/seniorproject/why.SP.html

Northwest Regional Educational Laboratory. (2001a). 6+1 Trait writing assessment model. Retrieved January 5, 2005, from http://www.nwrel.org/assessment/department.php?d=1

Northwest Regional Educational Laboratory. (2001b). *6+1 Trait Writing Scoring Continuum.* Retrieved April 20, 2005, from http://www.nwrel.org/assessment/pdfRubrics/6plus1traits.PDF

Parker School, Devens, Massachusetts. (n.d.). *Six tenets of the senior project.* Retrieved from http://www.parker.org/DivisionIII/Senior%20Project%20Handbook/senior_project_handbook.htm

Senior project. (n.d.). Retrieved June 10, 2005, from http://www.seniorproject.net.

Sizer, T. (1992). *Horace's school: Redesigning the American high school.* Boston: Houghton Mifflin.

SERVE Center, University of North Carolina Greensboro. (2004). *Senior Project.* Retrieved June 10, 2005, from http://www.serve.org/SDImprov/#senior

FIGURE 6.4
Research Paper Rubric

The rubric is based on the 6+1 Trait Writing Scoring Continuum, modified to fit the research task.

RESEARCH PAPER				
6+1 TRAITS ASSESSMENT TERMS	EMERGING Need for revision outweighs strength	DEVELOPING Strengths and need for revision equal	EFFECTIVE Strengths outweigh weaknesses	STRONG Professional or collegiate level
TRAIT 1 Ideas and Content	No clear sense of purpose; missing details; no balance of view points	Beginning to define topic but not completely clear; generally stays on topic	Supporting ideas are present; ideas are focused and clear; provides a balance of primary and secondary ideas	Focused and clear; contains important details; insightful; a balanced presentation
TRAIT 2 Organization	Lacks a sense of direction; ideas strung together; needs more structure; confusing; transitions need improvement	Writing is fairly organized, introduction is obvious; closing is attempted; transitions are limited; uninspiring	Good introductory sentence; logical flow to details; uses transitions; appropriate conclusion	Showcases the perspective on the issue; inviting introduction; well-organized; sequence is effective in moving the reader through the topic; excellent transitions; smooth to read; strong conclusion
TRAIT 3 Voice	Writer seems indifferent to the topic; connection to the audience is unclear; tone is flat; little emotion	Sincere but not fully engaged; inconsistent; tone is generally appropriate	Personality, confidence, and feelings are evident; commitment is obvious; tone is sincere; writing evokes emotion in reader	Speaks directly to the reader in a natural, compelling way; personality of writer is obvious; overall effect is individualistic, expressive, and engaging
TRAIT 4 Sentence Fluency	Sentences are choppy, incomplete and rambling; no connectedness; lacks fluency when read aloud	Sentences are stilted, seem mechanical, but flow; sometimes concise and sometimes too wordy	Generally easy to read due to strong and varied sentence structure; well constructed	Strong and varied sentence structure; appropriately concise; natural flow and rhythm when read aloud
TRAIT 5 Word Choice	Limited vocabulary, restricted or too technical for understanding; no unique words; some misused words	Repeats common words; mostly mundane vocabulary; expression is limited	Uses strong verbs and descriptive language; uses appropriate vocabulary to convey point of view	Uses strong descriptive language; chooses complex but appropriate words to convey ideas
TRAIT 6 Conventions	Minimal grasp of basic conventions is apparent; errors in spelling, punctuation, word usage, and grammar make reading difficult; no special conventions used	Basic grasp of standard writing conventions is apparent; errors distract from understanding; special conventions may be distracting	Appropriate use of writing conventions, with a few minor errors of more difficult words; special conventions (titles, subtitles, etc.) enhance text	Excellent punctuation, spelling, and grammar; no errors; punctuation enhances meaning; special conventions (titles, subtitles, in-text notes etc.) enhance the text
TRAIT 7 (6+1) Presentation	Disregards format requirements for research paper outlined by district; presentation creates distractions to understanding topic; formats through spaces and tabs, not using style sheet or formatting conventions	Limited attempt to follow format requirements outlined by district; presentation is flat or slightly distracting; relies on basic word processing formatting to produce paper	Follows format requirements for research paper outlined by district; presentation is neat and appropriate; uses style sheet to create consistency in paper layout and design	Follows format requirements for research paper outlined by district; presentation is neat and creative and enhances understanding of the topic; customizes electronic style sheet to produce paper

FIGURE 6.5
Project/Product Rubric

This rubric is an excerpt from a sample project evaluation form. Teachers and other evaluators should modify this form to assess skills specific to a particular project or work sample. For example, a project involving the use of a computer-aided design (CAD) program should include rubric-based measurements developed specifically to assess the student's ability to use such a technology tool.

PROJECT/PRODUCT					
STUDENT:			YOUR NAME:		
PROJECT TITLE:			YOUR POSITION:		DATE:
CRITERIA	NOVICE	BASIC	MEETS	EXCEEDS	COMMENTS
Level of independence in completing the project	Dependent on others	Some independence, not consistent	Independent	Independent and helps others	
How the student manages the project, including time management	Misses deadlines; doesn't adhere to timeline	Occasionally misses deadlines; tries to stay on timeline.	Adheres to timeline; meets all deadlines	Adheres to or is in advance of timeline; meets all deadlines.	
Completion of the project in meeting the objective	Makes progress but doesn't complete project or meet objective	Almost completes project; objective is likely to be met	Completes project; meets objective	Exceeds expectations for project; meets objective on time or earlier than anticipated	
Interpersonal skills and collaboration with others involved, either directly or indirectly	Has difficulty collaborating with others	Generally works well with others; experiences some difficulty in collaborating	Works well with others; has no difficulty collaborating	Becomes a part of the team; works well other others; makes a significant contribution to the work environment	
Impact of project	Project doesn't make impact; needs more work or revision to have impact	Project has temporary impact but will not endure after student discontinues doing project	Project makes the desired impact in meeting objective; project results will remain	Project makes a significant contribution beyond all expectations; project results will endure over time	

FIGURE 6.6
Portfolio Rubric

Assessment of portfolio content should reflect all the essential elements—comprising both content and structure—defined in the original instructions to students. The rubric presented here evaluates several aspects of a student's use of Internet-based tools to create the portfolio. While Web-based portfolios aren't required for all student projects, the inclusion of Internet tools allows teachers to evaluate many NETS•S objectives as they review the artifacts and reflections that make up the portfolio. If one objective is to assess the student's ability to produce an effective Web page, the items beneath the heading Web-Page Portfolio should be included. If the portfolio is contained in a vendor-based product such as TaskStream or LiveText, the portfolio assessment can be managed with the software.

PORTFOLIO				
CRITERIA	**NOVICE** Needs ssistance	**BASIC** Approaching	**PROFICIENT** Meets	**EXCEEDS**
Timeline	Incomplete and difficult to understand	Complete with major events, but lacks some detail	Complete with major events and includes details of time, place, people, and activity	Complete with major and minor events and includes details of time, place, people, and activity
Digital Documentation	Includes only one media; extent of involvement in project is unclear	Includes multiple media; extent of involvement in project is unclear	Includes video, digital pictures, and other relevant artifacts; extent of involvement in project is clear	Includes video, digital pictures, and a variety of other relevant artifacts that thoroughly and clearly document involvement in project
Electronic Journal	Journal entries are skimpy or nonexistent; does not document development of project	Journal tracks development of project; entries may not be clear and logical	Journal clearly and logically tracks development of project; reflections included on key project events	Journal entries are frequent, clear, descriptive, and reflective
Reflection on Meeting Standard	Is unclear how standard links to project; project may not be implemented as planned, making identified standard inappropriate	Links a few standards to project; reflection and explanation are not clear	Clearly links project development and results to identified academic content standard	Clearly links project development and results to identified academic content standard; identifies additional standards and provides reflection
Organization	Disorganized, making it difficult for the reader to comprehend project	Generally organized but needs additional work	Clear; designed so viewer can clearly see portfolio elements and follow project	Clearly organized, providing an additional level of detail (e.g., subheadings) about the contents of each item
Also Includes • Research Paper • Presentation Slides • Resumé	Missing two of the three items	Missing one of the items	Includes all items	Includes all items as well as others that support project but were not required

continued

FIGURE 6.6 *continued*
Portfolio Rubric

PORTFOLIO				
CRITERIA	**NOVICE** Needs assistance	**BASIC** Approaching	**PROFICIENT** Meets	**EXCEEDS**
WEB-PAGE PORTFOLIO				
Identification	Missing name	Name is present; relevant information focusing on project is unclear or missing	Name and relevant information are clear	Name and relevant information are clear and creatively displayed
Layout	Disorganized and cluttered; does not use design principles	Organized but some portions detract from content; design principles are not consistently followed	Organized, clean, and attractive; clearly uses design principles	Well-organized, clean, creative use of design principles
Multimedia	Does not include video or other media	Includes video, digital pictures, etc.; links do not work consistently	Includes clear links to video, digital pictures, and other multimedia	Clearly links to video, digital pictures, and other multimedia; includes enhancements of sound and animation that support objective
Navigation	Links function inconsistently; does not provide link to school's senior project page or home page	Most links to artifact function; includes links to school's senior project page and home page	Links are logical and function well; includes links to school's senior project page and home page	Links are logical and function well; includes links to school's senior project page and home page as well as to important portions of artifacts for easier navigation
Copyright and Privacy	Inconsistently follows fair use guidelines; fails to eliminate personal information from resumé before attempting to post	Generally follows fair use guidelines but has omitted some citations; eliminates personal information from resumé before posting	Follows fair use guidelines by citing appropriately; eliminates personal information from resumé before posting	N/A
Writing Conventions	Does not consistently follow writing conventions; makes many errors; vocabulary is simple or inappropriate	Mostly follows writing conventions; contains a few errors; uses appropriate vocabulary	Follows all writing conventions; uses appropriate vocabulary	N/A
HTML/Authoring	HTML code does not include basic formatting, image, hyperlink, or table tags	HTML includes basic tags, with most code displays working appropriately	HTML includes basic tags, with all codes and displays functioning correctly	HTML includes descriptive or advanced tags, with all codes and displays functioning correctly
File Management	Does not name files appropriately or follow the school's naming convention; does not save files to the correct location	Saves files to the correct location but does not name consistently or follow the school's naming convention	Names files according to the school's naming convention; saves in the appropriate location; does not organize into folders	Names files according to the school's naming convention; saves in the appropriate location; organizes into folders

FIGURE 6.7
Presentation Rubric

Like the portfolio rubric, the presentation rubric shown here assumes the use of technology tools (in this case, a multimedia presentation program) to create this portion of the senior project. When such tools are used, students can be evaluated on their NETS•S skills as well as their presentation and communication skills. Since a team of assessors—including faculty, administrators, and community members—will evaluate student presentations, care should be taken to ensure they have a common understanding of the rubric elements before beginning the scoring process. Keep in mind that assessors may become fatigued when scoring for long periods of time, so schedule regular breaks in the presentations to ensure the reliability of the scoring process.

PRESENTATION				
CRITERIA	**NOVICE** Needs assistance	**BASIC** Approaching	**PROFICIENT** Meets	**EXCEEDS**
File Management (NETS•S 1)	Unable to title file and store in appropriate location	Either titles file appropriately or is able to store in proper location, but not both	Independently titles file appropriately (e.g., own last name_assignment); stores in appropriate folder	Meets criteria and helps others; troubleshoots when others are having difficulty
Slide Text (NETS•S 3)	Title and bulleted points are inadequate size	Either title or bulleted points are inadequate size	Slide title is at least 30 pt., with bulleted points at least 20 pt.	Font size meets criteria; font design uses advanced feature
Slide Background (NETS•S 3)	Background is default white	Uses contrasting color and text	Uses template found in software	Uses template found in software; changes template to suit needs
Use of Images (NETS•S 3, 4)	No video, images, or links are included, or irrelevant graphics are used	Appropriate video, images, or links are included, but placed or sized inconsistently	Includes video, images, and links properly placed and sized; images add to the understanding of the topic	Creatively uses video, images, and links; images have been cropped or altered to enhance understanding
Content (ELA Standards 2, 7, 8, NETS•S 4)	Not logical; few relevant facts provided; missing considerable material needed to make presentation understandable	Uses adequate important facts about project; inconsistent, unbalanced material, requires organization; logical in presentation	Uses adequate important facts about process used in project; provides balanced information; logical in presentation	Uses many important facts about process used in project; provides balanced information; logical in presentation
Number of Slides (ELA Standard 9, NETS•S 4)	Creates basic slides only; lacks introduction and conclusion	Creates one introductory slide, three factual slides, and one concluding slide	Creates one introductory slide, three or more factual slides that adequately explain the project, and one concluding slide; includes credits slide	Creates more than 10 factual slides that fully explain the project, including an introduction, a conclusion, and credits
Oral Presentation Content (ELA Standards 4, 5, 7)	Reads slides to audience but can't answer questions or provide additional informatioon	Reads slides to audience; answers questions with limited information	Speaks from slides and adds some additional information; content is logical; responds to questions with some additional information	Easily speaks from slides, adding additional information from memory; content is logical and natural; is able to answer questions easily and refers back to information in slides

continued

FIGURE 6.7 *continued*
Presentation Rubric

PRESENTATION				
CRITERIA	NOVICE Needs assistance	BASIC Approaching	PROFICIENT Meets	EXCEEDS
Oral Presentation Delivery (ELA Standards 10, 11, 12)	Does not look at audience; voice is too soft to hear	Occasionally looks at audience; speaks with inconsistent volume and articulation	Looks at audience while speaking; speaks with adequate volume and clear articulation	Makes eye contact with audience while speaking; is enthusiastic and engaging; speaks with appropriate volume and clear articulation
Oral Presentation Appearance	Not appropriately dressed for professional presentation (e.g., wears inappropriate footwear or accessories)	Neat but not satisfactorily dressed for professional presentation (e.g., wears inappropriate footwear or accessories)	Satisfactorily but not professionally dressed; appearance is neat and clean; wears appropriate footwear and accessories	Professionally dressed (e.g., pressed shirt, tie, and suitcoat; career dress or suit); appearance is neat and clean; wears appropriate footwear and accessories
Citation (NETS•S 2)	No citation	Inconsistent citations for video, images, links, and other items	Cites all information used from list provided	N/A

FIGURE 6.8
Resumé Rubric

This simple rubric allows teachers to assess a student's resumé for content and formatting. Additional criteria can be used to evaluate the student's use of a word processor to create the resumé, using either an existing template or their own format. The resumé should be critiqued and revised prior to the presentation, when the final version will be distributed to evaluators.

RESUMÉ				
CRITERIA	NOVICE Needs assistance	BASIC Approaching	PROFICIENT Meets	EXCEEDS
Format	Unprofessional in appearance; doesn't use template at all; format detracts from content	Format detracts from content; poor or impropriate use of template; length too short or too long	Professional in appearance; uses template; keeps to one or two pages	Creative and professional appearance; creates or modifies template; keeps to one or two pages
Content	Does not provide enough information; misspellings; disorganized; incorrect use of conventions	Provides most of the needed information; some misspellings; some confusing organization; some errors in writing	Provides adequate information; no misspellings; well-organized; correct use of writing conventions	Provides all required information, with appropriate descriptive phrases; no misspellings; well-organized; solid understanding of writing conventions

PART 3

Assessment Concepts and Options

Experience is a hard
teacher because she gives
the test first, the lesson
afterwards.

VERNON SANDERS LAW

P art 3 looks at the design, construction, benefits, and limitations of a variety of types of assessment, including assessment projects that are scalable beyond the classroom. This section provides an introduction to basic concepts applicable to any assessment program:

- test planning
- item-writing
- test assembly and deployment
- test development methods used by professional test developers to ensure the reliability and validity of an assessment

The following chapters explore the types of test items to consider when creating an assessment of student technology skills, with a focus on assessing achievement of the NETS•S and their performance indicators.

Depending on the overall goals of a technology assessment plan, the most appropriate method and style of assessment can vary widely. Classroom teachers interested in gauging technology literacy for a technology class, or evaluating technology skills before introducing a technology-enhanced math or English unit, have access to a variety of automated tools for creating and delivering different types of test items. Many of these tools can be easily implemented within a single classroom or computer lab.

At the other end of the spectrum, states or districts attempting to implement technology assessments for large numbers of students face the same development, validation, deployment, and grading challenges that accompany the implementation of any large-scale standardized exam. The following chapters discuss large-scale assessment projects and the methodologies used to assess student technology literacy, with numerous examples of schools, districts, and states that have successfully implemented a variety of assessment programs.

CHAPTER SNAPSHOTS

CHAPTER 7
Assessment Basics

What should educators know first? Chapter 7 provides basic information about test planning and development. It also contains basic information about the fundamental elements and concepts to consider when either creating your own assessment or evaluating commercial assessment options. It sets the stage for a more detailed consideration of the particular assessment options presented in the remaining chapters of part 3.

CHAPTER 8
Linear Assessments

This chapter concentrates on using multiple-choice, fill-in-the-blank, and essay formats, the most common methods of testing used in classrooms, in large-scale testing situations, and commercially.

CHAPTER 9
Survey Assessments

Chapter 9 looks at the various ways self-reported data can be used to collect information about students' and teachers' perceptions of technology competence.

CHAPTER 10
Observational Assessments

The number of ways teachers and external observers can monitor and evaluate actual student technology use in the classroom are examined in this chapter.

CHAPTER 11
Portfolio Assessments

Chapter 11 looks at how student work and other measures of performance can be collected in a standards-based portfolio to validate students' technology skills and knowledge in the context of academic performance.

CHAPTER 12
Automated Assessments

The final chapter of part 3 examines an emerging type of technology performance assessment that's designed to be delivered by a stand-alone computer, over a network, or over the Internet. These automated assessments allow technology skills to be measured using performance-based items that ask students to perform tasks in context, thus enabling automated scoring for large-scale testing projects.

CHAPTER 7

Assessment Basics

Everyone involved in K–12 education is working in an environment of mounting accountability pressures. Fortunately, the increased availability of assessment software allows teachers to try new and innovative assessment methods. These include computerized performance-based tests, portfolio assessments tied to rigorous scoring rubrics, and integrated technology and content area assessments. These methods can serve as models for assessment across the curriculum.

When it comes to technology assessment, you are looking for options that support your educational priorities. You want to be able to measure

- how well students use the technology available to them to learn academic content and
- how well students can transfer that knowledge to the real world.

Accountability pressures also affect students. Increasingly, students are reporting fatigue associated with the amount of time they spend preparing for and taking standardized tests. In a recent survey conducted by graduate students for a teaching methods course, and reported in the *Indianapolis Star*, only 52% of student respondents indicated they tried their best on state tests, while 23% said they didn't try at all and 25% tried only sporadically (Gammil, 2005).

While no conclusions should be drawn from this single informal survey, there's increasing concern nationwide over the backlash among secondary students regarding the current testing environment. Students at Torrey Pines High School in San Diego, for example, recently boycotted state exams due to their frustration with the overemphasis on testing (Parmet, 2005). Consequently, when considering assessment options, it's important to keep in mind the impact that increased testing demands will have on you and your students.

To meet the needs of all stakeholders—teachers, students, parents, state and federal agencies—educators at every level must carefully consider what kinds of assessments to use and how to report the results. To make an informed decision about whether to purchase an existing commercial assessment or create your own customized tool, you'll need to understand not only what you're trying to assess but also how the assessment tool has been or will be developed to ensure the validity and reliability of results. Whether you're a teacher creating a paper-based final exam for your class or a member of an education committee responsible for evaluating commercial options for a statewide technology assessment project, an understanding of the fundamentals of test development can help make you a more informed consumer or developer of assessments, or both.

This chapter is a primer on the processes and procedures used by testing professionals to create high-quality, valid assessments. If you're creating a classroom test, you probably don't need to go through the same extensive process that a district or company creating a standardized educational exam or professional certification must go through. However, understanding the techniques used in professional test development can help make any type of testing more effective.

TEST? ASSESSMENT?

Even among those who specialize in test development, such as professional psychometricians and industrial psychologists, terminology standards can be inconsistent. The terms "test," "assessment," and "exam" are often used interchangeably, even though "exam" (as in "final exam" or "college-entrance exam") implies a test with higher stakes than does "assessment." For the purposes of this chapter, the terms "assessment" and "test" will be used interchangeably to mean any instrument that measures the knowledge, skills, and abilities of an individual or group.

TEST PLANNING

Before an assessment is created or any items written, a test developer normally creates an overall plan for the assessment. This plan usually consists of the following documents:

Test blueprint. This specifies and organizes the content to be covered in the assessment. Creating boundaries for the content that will be covered (and, just as important, *not* covered) in an assessment is a critical step in test development, just as it is in the development of an education curriculum.

Test construction plan. This delineates all factors in the development of the assessment that are unrelated to content, such as length of testing time, how the assessment will be administered, test setting, method of grading, and so forth.

As a teacher, when you create a final exam, your course syllabus can serve as the blueprint for the exam, since it should outline all the information that's been taught and might be covered on the final. The test construction plan for the final exam may be largely determined by class schedule and the immediate resources available to you. For example, if the final exam will be administered to the entire class during one class period, this may dictate test time (one hour), test delivery method (paper testing delivered simultaneously to all students), and other elements of the assessment's design.

Developers of standardized commercial tests go through a process that's analogous to the process teachers go through when creating a classroom exam. Normally, however, developers follow more formalized procedures for creating test-planning documents; these procedures allow multiple individuals to provide input during the planning, creation, and validation of the assessment. In addition to informing the test-development process, the documents can provide test consumers, such as schools and districts, with important information about the design, scope, and deployment of an assessment.

Test Blueprint

An assessment blueprint details and organizes the test content so that it can be reviewed by subject-matter experts and statistically analyzed during the content validation process. Figure 7.1 shows part of an assessment blueprint for a hypothetical eighth-grade technology assessment.

While a test blueprint can be put together in any number of ways, an outline format is often the most useful way to organize information and ensure that topic coverage is complete. In Figure 7.1, the content is organized by domain, sub-domain, and objective, in alignment with the NETS•S. This taxonomy can be summarized as follows:

Domains. The domains of a test are the highest conceptual levels covered by the assessment. In this example, the assessment domains are based on the NETS•S, the first of which—Basic Operations and Concepts—is shown in Figure 7.1. Other organizing frameworks, such as a state's education technology standards, may be equally appropriate ways to organize these high-level domains.

Sub-Domains. Sub-domains are logical categories that further define the content covered in a particular domain. For example, in Figure 7.1, the domain Basic Operations and Concepts can be broken down into sub-domains that include hardware (sub-domain 1.1, shown), software, and networks (sub-domains 1.2 and 1.3, not shown).

Objectives. Individual objectives capture one or more measurable elements that are key to understanding and assessing each domain and sub-domain. Each item in the third level of the outline in Figure 7.1 (e.g., "1.1.1 Identify terminology related to computer hardware…") represents an objective.

FIGURE 7.1

Example from Blueprint for Eighth-Grade Technology Assessment

DOMAIN 1.0 • BASIC OPERATIONS AND CONCEPTS

This domain includes the knowledge and skills required to demonstrate a sound understanding of the nature and operation of technology systems in order to be proficient users of information technology. Concepts covered in this domain include fundamentals of computer hardware, computer software and networks. Terminology and concepts are grade appropriate for an eighth-grade assessment.

Content Limits

1.1 Identify the purpose and function of computer hardware

Content may include the following:

1.1.1 Identify terminology related to computer hardware, including:
- Microprocessor/Central processing unit (CPU)
- Monitor
- Keyboard
- Mouse
- Printer
- Scanner
- Disk drive
- Hard drive
- CD-ROM
- Memory (including RAM, ROM, and disk storage)

1.1.2 Identify different types of computers and the purposes/best uses of each computer type, including:
- Mainframe computer
- Minicomputer
- Microcomputer/Personal computer
- Laptop/notebook computer
- Handheld computer/Personal Digital Assistant (PDA)

1.1.3 Identify parts of a computer by how they appear in a diagram of computer components, including:
- CPU box/case
- Mouse
- Keyboard
- Microphone
- Monitor
- Printer
- Speakers
- Floppy diskette drive
- CD-ROM drive

1.1.4 Identify the important role of the central processing unit as the "brain" of the computer

From the classroom or curriculum point of view, a course syllabus, curriculum outline, or set of education standards resembles a test blueprint document in many ways, as do the NETS•S rubrics described in chapter 2. However, while education curricula can include goals to be strived for but never assessed, an assessment blueprint must consist only of those objectives that can be adequately measured in some way.

While the goals of a test blueprint may be different from those of a course, curriculum, or education standard, the assessment plan (test blueprint) and the teaching plan (course syllabi, and so forth) are inextricably linked. As discussed in Wiggins' and McTighe's *Understanding by Design* (1998), before planning any kind of instruction, it's important to begin by understanding the desired results. The parallel processes of creating a course curriculum, which focuses on what is teachable, and creating a test blueprint, which focuses on what is measurable, are improved when done together.

Test Construction Plan

Whether the test is for a grade level, specific course, integrated curriculum, or set of standards, many factors unrelated to content go into designing an assessment. These include

- the length of time intended for the assessment
- the method of delivery (e.g., paper, computer, Internet)
- scoring/grading system (e.g., raw percentage, scaled)
- scoring mechanics (human-scored or machine-scored)
- scalability (number of students taking the test)
- number of test forms (number of versions of the test)
- commercial issues (e.g., price, delivery channel).

While some of these factors—such as time, format, and scoring—are relevant for all types of tests, other factors—such as commercial issues and scalability—are important for only certain types of assessments, such as standardized tests and professional licensure exams.

Taken together, the test blueprint and test construction plan provide developers with a map of how many items are needed to create the assessment. For example, a blueprint may list 100 objectives that could be included in the assessment. If the construction plan identifies a 60-minute time limit for the test, it will probably limit the number of items. Test developers would have to reduce the test's scope or consider whether they need to create an item to match every objective.

In addition, the planning process helps define the types of items that are practical for an assessment. The need to deliver paper exams to large numbers of students simultaneously may mean that the assessment will have to consist of linear test items, such as multiple-choice questions, rather than other item types. Consideration of the strengths and limitations of the various types of test items described in the next section will play a large role in the overall planning process.

CONSIDERATIONS FOR AN "ANY PLACE" EXAM

A standardized college entrance exam, such as the SAT or ACT, must adhere to established time limits and be deliverable on a large scale in a wide variety of environments (classrooms, hotel conference rooms, and so forth).

Because of these constraints, a test construction plan for this type of exam might indicate that a paper administration of the test is critical to ensure access from any location. Such a plan would also specify the number of questions to be included in the test (to fit time requirements).

Since these exams are often given simultaneously across the country, the use of a single exam form (as opposed to multiple, equivalent exam forms) may be sufficient to minimize cheating.

CONSIDERATIONS FOR AN "ANYTIME" EXAM

A+ is a popular certification for hardware and software maintenance professionals. It's developed by the Computer Technology Industry Association. The exam consists of two 90-minute tests that can be taken separately or together. Like many information technology certifications or professional licensure exams, the A+ exam is administered through a select set of commercial testing facilities.

Because the test is intended to be delivered on demand throughout the country, developers were required from the beginning to create multiple, equivalent test forms that could be delivered online in accordance with technical standards acceptable to, and achievable by, each testing center. This online requirement defines how the test is scored and reported as well as the parameters for the type of questions to be used.

TEST ITEM TYPES

If you've ever developed and graded a test, you're probably familiar with the test item types listed in this section. You already have some experience in determining whether a test item succeeds or fails in measuring specific knowledge or skills. Guidelines for creating these various test item types appear later in part 3.

Linear Items

Multiple-choice questions, true-false statements, and matching tasks are all examples of linear test items (discussed in more detail in chapter 8). Most assessments used in schools, as well as most professionally developed standardized tests, make extensive use of linear items. The benefits of linear test items include

- their usefulness in measuring a wide variety of knowledge, skills, and abilities
- the ease of scoring linear items accurately and objectively using either human graders or a computerized scoring process
- the low cost of deployment, whether reproduced on paper or delivered over computers or the Internet
- the availability of numerous statistical models for analyzing the performance of linear test items.

Open Response Items

Open response items require test takers to supply their own answers and provide open-ended information, rather than select from a number of predetermined options. The most popular forms of open response items are fill-in-the-blank, short-answer, and essay.

Fill-in-the-Blank

A fill-in-the-blank item provides a test taker with a sentence or paragraph containing missing information, such as a word, phrase, or number. The test taker needs to provide the missing information. This type of item requires test takers to recall the correct answer, not just recognize it from a list. It's useful when testing areas such as vocabulary or math skills in which answers are specific (Figure 7.2).

FIGURE 7.2
Sample Fill-in-the-Blank Questions from an Exam

1. _____ was the U.S. government agency that created the Internet.

2. 189.43 x 2.55 = _____

Fill-in-the-blank items can usually be converted into equivalent linear items. For example, the questions in Figure 7.2 can be turned into multiple-choice questions quite easily (Figure 7.3).

FIGURE 7.3
Fill-in-the-Blank Exam Questions Converted to Linear Multiple Choice

1. _____ was the U.S. government agency that created the Internet.
   A. EPA   C. OSHA
   B. DOE   D. DARPA

2. 189.43 x 2.55 = _____
   A. 438.05   C. 483.05
   B. 438.50   D. 483.50

A fill-in-the-blank, open-ended item is a more challenging and thorough measurement of a test objective than is a comparable multiple-choice item. Because the number of possible incorrect answers to an open-ended item is infinite, the answers can also provide you with interesting information about the misconceptions of your students.

While fill-in-the-blank questions have been used for machine-scored assessments, which require an exact match between the student's input and the correct answer, this format is most often used in assessments scored by a human grader.

Short-Answer

A short-answer test item normally requires students to provide information either in the form of a phrase or in one or more sentences. Since short-answer items are usually human-scored, this format provides a method to assess a candidate's understanding of concepts that might be difficult to pinpoint using linear test items (Figure 7.4).

FIGURE 7.4
Sample Short-Answer Questions from an Exam

1. List two ways in which computers have changed the workplace.

2. What would you type into an Internet search engine to find a list of tragedies written by William Shakespeare?

In the first question, the test taker is asked to provide information that could be wide-ranging but would most likely take the form of two short phrases or sentences. In the second question, the test taker is asked to provide a set of words that would be used as a search string.

While short-answer items allow test makers to ask for and collect potentially subjective information, as illustrated above, this format is also useful for testing objective information that would be difficult to assess using item types that limit the number of potential answers.

Essays

Essay exams are easy to administer in the classroom, but they can be labor-intensive to grade. Despite this, the extent to which essay responses demonstrate critical thinking and conceptual understanding often makes essay items the best method for assessing higher-order thinking skills. Essay exams can open a window onto the thinking processes of your students and provide diagnostic information that may help inform the next teaching unit.

Beyond the classroom, however, essay exams have not been widely deployed until fairly recently. Scaling an assessment that includes essay-style items is a challenge, for it requires developers to ensure that scoring is done consistently, particularly when multiple human graders are used to score student essays.

Some familiar academic exams, such as the AP English and AP history exams, have used essays for years. Recently, essays have also been introduced in standardized college entrance exams, such as the ACT and SAT. The increased use of essays in high-volume standardized exams is the result of technology tools and procedures that help automate the scoring process. Software tools have been created that provide a computerized "first-pass" review of an essay, allowing human graders to use this automated grading information for guidance as they perform their own review and scoring.

Whether or not computerized tools are used to help score student essays, systematic procedures must be in place to ensure that human evaluation and scoring of essays is based on objective standards. This is often accomplished through the creation of rubrics and "anchor" essays, called *exemplars*, that exemplify each scoring level and against which all graders must base their assessment of each student's work. While it's impossible to fully eliminate subjectivity in an essay-grading process that involves multiple graders, methodologies which have been in place for decades have created a good deal of confidence that this type of item can be implemented fairly on a large-scale basis.

One other concern to keep in mind when you're considering an essay exam is the extent to which it may disadvantage second language learners. Because syntax and rhetoric aren't easily transferable from one language to another, second language learners often don't have command of the grammatical structures and rhetorical cues that graders look for when evaluating essays. The dependence of essay exams on culture-specific writing conventions requires second language students to have detailed command of those conventions, a proficiency that may be lacking even when conceptual understanding of the content may be present. Therefore, unless assessment of writing ability is integral to the exam, scoring rubrics for essay exams should be explicitly focused on the content being assessed rather than on conventions or language usage.

Despite the challenges of scoring essay exams, technology knowledge and skills can be assessed using an essay exam format (Figure 7.5). Essay items provide the means to assess not just the student's ability to respond to a question with a well-written and well-reasoned essay, but also the ability to use a technology tool such as a word processor to create and display work. As in the example below, essay-based tests make it possible for you to assess student achievement of both academic content standards and some aspects of the NETS•S.

The activity illustrated in Figure 7.5 has three key areas of assessment:

1. Can the student effectively create a persuasive argument? Are the elements of the argument present and in logical order?

2. Does the student have knowledge of the issues and facts that prompted the Boston Tea Party? Does the student understand the British point of view well enough to create a convincing argument for action?

3. Can the student create a document that's in two-column format and has a full-width title? Can the student access the Internet to find a historically accurate image that supports the argument? Is the image inserted into the mock editorial page in a manner that enhances the document?

FIGURE 7.5
Multiple Assessments: U.S. History and Technology Skills

Write a persuasive argument for the editorial page of a Revolutionary War-era newspaper in which you try to convince British sympathizers that something is going to happen soon and mitigative action needs to be taken right now. Your essay will be published in the paper just two days before the Boston Tea Party occurs. Format your essay as it would appear in the paper: two-column text and a full-page title. Include a historically accurate image from a library archive.

Don't Ignore Rumblings of Revolution

Citizens in taverns around Boston are hearing rumors that colonists are fed up with British rule and just might take action. One of the rumors involves tea imported from Britain.

Ships are due to dock day after tom~

can do something now. If we don't, not only will tea importers lose their profits, things might get really out of hand. There is even talk of a revolution, so keep your musket close at hand.

God save the king!

Performance-Based Items

A performance-based test item asks a test taker to perform a specified task and measures how successfully and accurately that task is performed. Some examples of performance-based testing in technology include:

- An *observational* assessment. A test taker is observed and scored while using a tool, such as a computer running a specific operating system, to complete a list of assigned tasks. Observational assessments are covered in detail in chapter 10.

- A *mechanical* assessment. A test taker is asked to create a product, such as a slideshow using presentation software. The end product (the presentation file) is reviewed by a trained grader to determine if the task assigned has been accomplished as specified. The creation of technology-enhanced products that can be used to evaluate achievement of the NETS•S and grade-range performance indicators is often part of a portfolio assessment program, which is discussed in chapter 11.

- An *interactive simulation*. The simulation asks a test taker to perform a specific task (setting margins in a word processor, for example) and automatically determines whether the task has been performed successfully. Interactive simulations are discussed in detail in chapter 12.

- A *concurrent* testing product. This places a test taker in an actual application and asks the candidate to perform a specific task, such as changing column widths in a spreadsheet program. The testing product "hooks" into the live application to determine if the test taker has accomplished the task successfully. Concurrent tests are covered in chapter 12.

Generally speaking, performance-based test items are best used to measure skills, while other types of test items can be more useful when testing *concepts*, *knowledge*, or *attitudes*. Figure 7.6 illustrates the comparative effectiveness of a linear test item versus a performance-based test item when measuring a skill-based objective, in this case how to set margins using a word processor.

Performance-based test items can give students confidence that they're being tested fairly and accurately. They are also efficient, as one performance-based item can replace several linear items on the same subject. Many tests, especially technology assessments that cover both knowledge and skills, may make use of multiple item types within the same test.

FIGURE 7.6
Linear Versus Performance-Based Tests

LINEAR TEST ITEM	PERFORMANCE-BASED TEST ITEM
Which of the following commands will allow you to change margins? A. From the File Menu, select Margins. B. From the File Menu, select Page Setup C. From the Format Menu, select Margins. D. From the Format Menu, select Paragraph.	
This linear test item is testing just one component of the objective: which menu choice contains an option to change margins. The question is not put into the context of the software program and does not ask the student to perform a complete software task. In this case, the student could memorize the answer and still not be able to perform the task. These items are easily constructed by teachers.	In contrast, this performance-based test item places the student in a simulation of the software environment and requires that the task be performed from start to finish in any correct way the software allows. Only a fully interactive performance-based item allows assessment of all components of the objective. Constructing this type of item requires extensive support. Exams including simulation items are commercially available.

ESTABLISHING TEST VALIDITY

Test developers need to make certain the assessment they're building actually tests and measures the targeted skills and abilities. To be certain, developers must establish a test's validity using a variety of well-known procedures. Evidence should demonstrate that the test accurately measures a target group's knowledge and skills. When evaluating commercial assessments, make sure validity has been established through one of these important methods:

Content Validity. Content validity is demonstrated by assembling evidence that items in an assessment address the most essential knowledge and skills needed to achieve objectives measured by the test. Subject-matter experts normally provide the evidence. For example, a test covering word processor use is said to be *content valid* if it can be shown that test items, such as printing or setting margins, represent functions all users of the software should be able to perform.

Test developers will often conduct a content study to determine the appropriate balance of content within the assessment. A content study for a technology assessment covering both computer hardware and software may indicate that the assessment should include twice as many items on hardware as on software.

Construct validity. This is demonstrated by assembling evidence that the individual items in a test are accurate measurements of the subject being tested. For example, an item in a word processing assessment that asks a test taker to set margins, either in a performance-based simulation or in a concurrent test that uses a real word processor, is based on a perfect or near-perfect construct.

A test can also be based on an overall construct. For example, a college entrance exam that tests vocabulary and mathematical knowledge is built on the construct that measurement of these two skills provides an accurate predictor of success in higher education.

Criterion validity. This test validity is demonstrated by assembling evidence that the overall results of a test accurately correlate with an independent measure. For example, to determine if test scores accurately predict job performance, an employer can assess employee performance while using a spreadsheet program on an actual job one month after the person took a test on that subject. This type of criterion validation is known as *predictive* validation.

Alternatively, a test can be administered to people whose job skills are already known, and the test scores can be correlated with an independent measure of those skills. This type of criterion validation is known as *concurrent* validation.

An independent assessment often takes the form of a carefully worded survey given to teachers, employers, or supervisors, allowing them to quantify someone's skills or job performance. In both types of criterion validation (predictive and concurrent), it's

---

DIFFERENT TESTS FOR DIFFERENT FOLKS

Tests are usually validated for a specific type of person or job. For example, an electronic spreadsheet test that covers the use of basic features to create and modify simple tables might be equally valid for students and teachers, but it may not be valid for testing accountants who use advanced spreadsheet features to perform financial analysis. Likewise, when creating assessments of education technology, using developmentally appropriate items that align with the NETS•S performance profiles is important. What may be a valid measure for a second-grader may not be valid for an eighth-grader.

important that the independent assessment be administered consistently and without reference to the test scores. (See chapter 9 for more information on surveys.)

Reliability. This is another important component of test validation. It's demonstrated by assembling evidence that a test provides consistent measurement of scores. For example, a scientific instrument that gives different readings each time it's used, perhaps due to a mechanical defect, would likely have low reliability. Similarly, a hands-on driving test may be unreliable if the human evaluators aren't trained to measure the candidates' driving performance according to the same objective standard.

Tests can be evaluated for reliability by giving the same test to the same people at different times to determine if measurement is consistent. This is called *test-retest reliability*. A variety of statistical techniques, including *split-half reliability* and *internal consistency*, measure test reliability by comparing performance on specific test items with one another.

ASSEMBLING AN ASSESSMENT

As you can see, considerable assessment planning and research often takes place before a single test item is written or an assessment assembled. Before item-writing and test assembly begins, professional test developers normally have in place

- a blueprint created after careful research that ideally includes the input of many subject-matter experts.

- a test construction plan that provides further information on the length and nature of the assessment.

- a content validation exercise to determine the balance of items needed for the different subjects covered in the assessment.

With this information in hand, item-writers can use the guidelines outlined in this and subsequent chapters to create high-quality questions that match the requirements identified during the assessment planning stage.

Field-Testing

After an assessment has been planned and created, its performance needs to be measured in real-world testing situations. Only by putting a test "to the test" can its ability to measure what it claims to measure be evaluated.

In a classroom setting, when you give an exam to students and results are collected, a number of different outcomes may occur. You may calculate scores using simple arithmetic to generate a percentage score and then assign grades based on fixed percentages—90% to 100% for an A, 80% to 89% for a B, and so forth.

However, you may notice that some items are missed more frequently than others, or they may be missed more frequently than expected. These items may be evidence of either a common conceptual misunderstanding or a lack of adequate classroom coverage of the objective, thereby providing a rationale for reteaching. Or you may discover that the item itself is problematic—that it's poorly worded or scored incorrectly. The instructions for a short-answer question may be confusing, or a multiple-choice item may contain more than one answer that can reasonably be construed as correct.

When a professional test developer reviews the performance of a field test, he uses statistical models to analyze these same issues. This process—formally known as *item analysis*—can reveal important details about test items and the test as a whole. The table in Figure 7.7 shows performance data for five items in an assessment.

This type of statistical analysis can be quite similar to a teacher reviewing test items for unexpected results. For example, the statistics for the five items in this example can lead reviewers to some important conclusions:

> **Item 1.** Item 1 has a very high p-value (.93), indicating that most test takers answered this item correctly. However, the low r-value for this item (.22) indicates that of those who answered this item incorrectly, several did well overall on the test and several

FIGURE 7.7
Performance Data for Five Items in an Assessment

ITEM	p-VALUE (Difficulty)	r-VALUE (Performance consistency)
1	.93	.22
2	.94	.55
3	.50	.56
4	.20	.48
5	.25	.14

The *r-value* measures *internal consistency*, an extremely important measure for test items. This value is calculated by statistically comparing the difficulty of a particular test item with test takers' overall performance on the test. Put simply, if people who did well overall on the test generally got a moderately difficult question right, while people who did poorly overall generally got the same question wrong, that question will have a high r-value. If high performers and low performers score about the same on a given question, that question will have a low r-value.

The *p-value* corresponds to the *difficulty* of the test item and reflects the proportion of students who answered the question correctly. A test item with a p-value of .25 can be said to be twice as difficult as one with a p-value of .50.

Note: While p-value does not always relate directly to the number of people who answered a question correctly, for purposes of this example, one can think of item #5, which close to three-quarters of test takers answered incorrectly, as being twice as difficult as item #3, which half of test takers answered incorrectly.

others did poorly. Consequently, while this item is easy—and easy items can certainly be included in a test—the item fails to discriminate between high performers and low performers, making it less useful and desirable.

Item 2. This item is also quite easy, even easier than item 1. However, the item has a high r-value, indicating that those who answered this item incorrectly are also likely to be the ones who did poorly overall on the test.

Item 3. Statistically speaking, this is an almost perfect test item, in which half the test takers answered correctly and half incorrectly. Coupled with a high r-value, this item does an excellent job of discriminating between high and low performers.

Item 4. This is a difficult item, with a p-value of only .20. However, the high r-value indicates that students who answered this question correctly also did the best overall on the test. While you should take care to limit the number of highly difficult or highly easy items, this item discriminates well between high and low performers.

Item 5. This item is also quite difficult, though not as difficult as item 4. However, the low r-value means both high performers and low performers on the test answered this item incorrectly. This indicates that there may be a reason students aren't answering the item correctly, aside from difficulty alone. The item may be poorly worded or, if automated, programmed incorrectly. Given this item's poor performance, it can either be rejected and not included in the final exam form, or analyzed further to determine the reasons behind the poor performance.

Test Analysis

It's not uncommon for schools and districts to be asked to participate in the field-testing of an assessment that's intended to be used statewide. Multiple types of analysis are done on tests to ensure they meet the rigorous validity and reliability requirements needed for large-scale, high-stakes use. These can include

Item/Test Trialing. While you would ideally like to have a test consisting only of items with perfect statistics, this often isn't possible in the real world. For instance, content validation may require the inclusion of objectives that are measured by items with less than perfect statistics. Professional test developers will often field-test hundreds of items just to create a single 50-question exam. Once a statistical analysis of all items is run, the developer can select items with the best statistics to create a test that meets all content-balance requirements.

Norming Analysis. A norming analysis organizes test score data into percentiles in much the same way a teacher scales an exam. For example, if a student had a raw score of 75% on an assessment, this might translate to a 90th percentile score, indicating a candidate performance better than 89% of all others who took the exam. Norming provides a meaningful way to compare test scores between test takers.

Cut Score Determination. If an exam must have a pass/fail mark, various methods can be used to determine where this "cut score" may lie. Some use the judgment of test developers to assign a cut score while others rely on either a test taker's self-rating or a third-party rating to determine a passing grade.

Criterion Validation. If a test is to be used to make high-stakes decisions, particularly related to hiring or educational advancement, a criterion validation in which test scores are correlated with an independent measure, such as job performance or grades, gives further evidence of a test's ability to determine or predict success. As a basis of validation, criterion studies involve generating an independent measure, such as the results of a third-party evaluation survey that has not been informed by test scores.

Adverse Impact. The higher the stakes, the more critical the need to prove that an assessment does not discriminate against legally protected groups, such as women, the elderly, or minorities. Many tests collect race, age, and gender information from test takers. Test developers use this information to determine if the test shows *adverse impact*, that is, statistically significant lower scores for protected groups that might imply the test is somehow unfair.

Test Reliability. Just as individual items can be determined to be reliable measures of particular objectives, a complete test can also be the subject of study to determine overall test reliability.

Whether you're developing a custom assessment or selecting from among several commercial assessment options, you should look at all the information available for the tests being considered. The reliability and validity of the testing instrument and test results add credence to decisions made based on the assessment data. The process used to construct the test, the data obtained during field-testing, and the item and test analysis performed after field-testing are all valuable pieces of evidence. This evidence will help you determine if the assessment was constructed with the rigor needed to ensure the results will meet your needs.

References

Gammil, A. (2005, August 17). Survey of teens raises questions about education: Where students say they feel afraid and unchallenged—and think teachers don't care. *The Indianapolis Star*. Retrieved August 15, 2005, from http://www.indystar.com

Parmet, S. (2005, May 11). *Test drive in motion at Torrey Pines High*, San Deigo Union-Tribune. Retrieved July 10, 2005, from http://www.signonsandiego.com/news/education/20050511-9999-7m11torrey.html

Wiggins, T., & McTighe, J. (1998). *Understanding by design*. Alexandria, VA: Association for Supervision and Curriculum Development.

CHAPTER 8

Linear Assessments

Linear test questions are the most common type of assessment item, whether used in the classroom or as part of a standardized test. We've all answered thousands of linear test items, in all kinds of settings and for many different purposes. Most assessment programs around the country—indeed, the world—make regular use of linear test items. So they're likely to be among the first options you consider when planning or evaluating a technology assessment.

Exactly what makes a good linear test item, and how hard is it to develop these items? As noted in the previous chapter, linear test items are extremely useful—and, in fact, are the best item format—for assessing certain types of objectives, especially the demonstration of knowledge. Linear test items can be deployed on paper, on computers, or over the Internet at relatively low cost. This makes them a popular choice for large and small testing projects. Figure 8.1 shows the range of linear test items.

In theory, linear items are also easy to write. As a teacher, you've probably created hundreds of tests with multiple-choice questions and other types of linear test items. However, looking at how professional test developers create linear test items can teach us a lot about a process most of us approach on instinct, as in, "I know a good test question when I see it!" Linear items you create for a classroom quiz may never need to go through the rigorous statistical analysis applied to standardized exam items. But the practices test developers use to create items that will withstand analysis and scrutiny can improve any test-development process.

FIGURE 8.1

Types of Linear Test Items

ITEM TYPE	DESCRIPTION	EXAMPLES
MULTIPLE CHOICE	A question or statement (the *stem*), followed by several *responses*, one of which is correct (the *answer*), and the rest of which are incorrect (*distracters*). A multiple-choice item can also be accompanied by one or more *exhibits* (such as graphics or text passages) that provide information needed to answer the question.	Information in a database related to the same person (such as name, address, and phone number) is stored in a database _____. A. field B. query C. report D. record
MULTIPLE RESPONSE	A question or statement followed by several responses, *more than one* of which is correct.	From the list below, select two terms that refer to types of computer memory. A. RAM B. REM C. RIM D. ROM E. RUM
TRUE/FALSE	A statement followed by options to indicate that the statement is correct (TRUE, YES, etc.) or incorrect (FALSE, NO, etc.)	Only a computer with an Internet browser can send and receive electronic mail. TRUE FALSE
MATCHING	Two lists or sets of items in which there are unique associations between the individual items in one list and the individual items in the other list.	If cell A1 contains the number 10 and cell B1 contains the number 15, match the spreadsheet formula with the result of that formula. A. +A1+B1 1. 150 B. +A1*B1 2. 25 C. +A1-B1 3. -5
SURVEY	A statement followed by options that allow the test taker to evaluate the statement based on criteria other than whether the statement is correct or incorrect. A survey is usually used to collect demographic, self-report, or opinion data. (See chapter 9 for more on survey items.)	How many years of experience do you have using an electronic mail program? A. None B. Less than 1 year C. 1–2 years D. 3–4 years E. More than 4 years

The examples in this chapter demonstrate how linear test items can be used to measure objectives drawn from the NETS•S and grade-range performance indicators. Yet the principles apply to the assessment of any subject. Figure 8.2 illustrates problems commonly found in linear test items and offers suggestions for improving these items.

USING LINEAR TEST ITEMS TO ASSESS ACHIEVEMENT OF THE NETS•S

While linear test items are best used to assess knowledge, they can also be used to measure certain skills. When the purpose of a test is to define what students know about technology applications or concepts, linear test items can meet that purpose very well. On the other hand, linear items are less likely to be successful in examining higher-order thinking skills or confirming that a student can actually perform a task using a technology tool. For assessing these types of abilities, the testing methodologies discussed in chapters 9 through 12—including observation, portfolios, and automated assessments—are more suitable.

GUIDELINES FOR WRITING AND EVALUATING LINEAR TEST ITEMS

Whether you're looking at a commercially developed linear assessment or developing one yourself, you should know the generally accepted characteristics of high-quality linear test items.

- Each item should measure a single, clearly defined objective.

- Items should be written in language that's at or below the average reading level of the students targeted by the assessment.

- Items should be clearly written and unambiguous.

- Items should be free of cultural or other forms of bias.

- When writing multiple-choice items, all responses should be of equivalent length. Avoid items where one or more answers are much longer or much shorter than the others.

- When writing multiple-choice items, arrange responses in a logical order—by length or, in the case of numeric answers, by numeric value.

- Avoid the use of responses such as "all of the above" or "none of the above."

- Avoid repetitive language. If an article or preposition appears in all responses, reword the question stem to include the article or preposition rather than repeating it in all the responses.

- Distracters, while incorrect, should still be plausible. Try to select distracters of equal plausibility.

- All responses (correct and incorrect) should be constructed similarly. Avoid anything that makes a correct answer stand out from the distracters.

- When writing multiple-response items, the number of correct answers should be indicated in the question stem.

- Be consistent in item-writing style. Items that require a test taker to select a word or phrase to fill in a blank should represent these blanks consistently throughout the test. Lines that are always the same length would be one method.

- Exhibits such as text passages or graphics should relate directly to the test questions and not provide distracting, extraneous information. Similarly, an exhibit should not disclose the correct answer or help a test taker easily eliminate one or more distracters.

- Avoid trick questions—that is, questions in which a careful reading of the question and responses for hidden meanings is required to answer the question correctly.

- Avoid items that may disclose the answer to other items that appear on the same test.

FIGURE 8.2

Common Problems Found on Linear Test Items

ITEM	PROBLEM	BETTER
A binary number consists of what digits? A. 3 B. 1 C. 2 D. 0 E. 4	This item has two problems. To begin with, a multiple-response item should indicate the number of correct answers. Also, answers should be arranged in a logical order (in this case, numerically).	From the list below, select the two digits that make up a binary number. A. 0 B. 1 C. 2 D. 3 E. 4
APPLE::RED as LEMON:: A. Yellow B. Green C. Blue D. Orange	This item actually contains cultural bias: in some countries, lemons are just as likely to be green as yellow. Also, the fact that not all apples are red makes this a poor analogy-style item. Finally, the choices should be arranged in a logical order (in this case, by word length).	STOP::RED as GO:: A. Blue B. Green C. Orange D. Yellow
A sonnet is an example of _____. A. a poem B. a painting C. a form of music D. an airplane	The distracters are not equivalent (three represent art forms, the fourth a vehicle). Distracters should be of equal plausibility and parallel in structure. Also, the article ("a" or "an") should appear in the question stem rather than in the responses.	A sonnet is an example of a _____. A. story B. poem C. painting D. symphony

The North Central Regional Education Laboratory (NCREL), as the designated technology lab in the national education laboratory network, has been working for some time to develop a bank of test items to assess achievement of the NETS•S. Adhering to strict standards of reliability and validity, NCREL has developed questions like those shown in Figure 8.3, which are all good examples of linear test items for technology assessment. These sample items are measuring objectives from the NETS•S fifth-grade performance indicators. As you examine them, look at the types and range of questions included—from basic-knowledge questions with simple question stems and lower-level readability, to more complex questions with contextualized stems and on-grade-level readability.

This sample shows how diverse linear test questions can be and how other variables, particularly reading level, can influence student response and complicate the results of an assessment. Carefully selecting test items that meet the needs of the assessment and are appropriate to the student population(s) being assessed are crucial to success.

Figure 8.4 presents a number of test items covering the NETS•S eighth-grade performance indicators. As you review these samples, keep in mind that a test can consist of more than one item type. For example, an automated assessment (described in chapter 12) might include

FIGURE 8.3

Sample Fifth-Grade Test Items

1. A computer mouse

   o stores programs and data

   o keeps track of which computer programs are used

   o controls the curser or pointer on the computer screen

2. An Internet service that finds resources based on key words or phrases is a

   o Web site

   o newsgroup

   o search engine

3. Which spreadsheet formula would you use to find the total profit for all products?

◇	A	B	C
1	Product	Price	Profit
2	Notebook	$2.00	$0.50
3	Markers	$3.25	$0.75
4	Crayons	$2.50	$0.75
5	Eraser Set	$1.25	$0.40
6	Calculator	$7.00	$2.00

   o =SUM(C2:C6)

   o =ADD C2 TO C6

   o =PLUS(C2, C3, C4, C5, C6)

4. What technology tool would your class use to post reflections about a book and ask other classes to respond to the reflections?

   o blog

   o Webcam

   o search engine

5. Which search would give you the best results for information about New York City?

   o NYC

   o "New York City"

   o New +York +City

6. An example of acceptable use of technology would be

   o letting my friend borrow my password to the network

   o copying for a friend a new CD by your favorite musical artist

   o taking a picture with a digital camera and e-mailing it to a friend

continued

FIGURE 8.3 *continued*

Sample Fifth-Grade Test Items

7. To change the name of the main character in your story from Joe to Matt, which editing feature would you use?

   o Go To

   o Replace All

   o Paste Special

8. What would you do to get Query Results B from the data in Student Table A?

Student Table A		
Name	Grade Level	Lunch
Josh Engles	5	A
Amy Smith	6	A
Matt Battles	5	A
Sue Sumi	6	B

Query Results B		
Name	Grade Level	Lunch
Josh Engles	5	A
Matt Battles	5	A

   o a query to search for students with lunch B

   o a query to search for students in the fifth grade

   o a query to search for students with the highest grades

9. You are searching for Web sites to use as resources for a science report. What is a good indicator that the Web site is a trustworthy source?

   o The site has mostly words and very few pictures.

   o The site lists the authors, and sources are referenced.

   o The site has a counter and shows it has many visitors.

10. Which tool would you choose to record the local weather for 3 weeks and create a chart for each week to compare the data?

    o database

    o spreadsheet

    o weather CD-ROM

11. Your teacher asks you to edit a story written by another student in your class. You open the story in a word processor from your classmate's floppy disk. The best way to suggest changes in the plot of the story would be to use the _____ feature of the word processor.

    o spelling check

    o autocorrect

    o insert comments

linear test items covering both knowledge-based and performance-based items that assess specific skills.

While all the assessment items in Figures 8.3 and 8.4 are multiple choice, they cover a broad range of objectives, some requiring simple memory recall, others providing situational questions that require judgment. These samples show how you can address a variety of grade-range NETS•S performance indicators using the linear question format.

FIGURE 8.4
Sample Eighth-Grade Test Items

1. A _____ is similar to a copy machine, except that it creates a digital copy of the document instead of a paper copy.

    o scanner

    o digitizer

    o graphics board

2. A Boolean search for a topic on the Web uses

    o AND, OR, and NOT in the search.

    o IF, THEN, and WHEN in the search.

    o HOW, WHEN, and WHY in the search.

3. As part of an English assignment, you are to act as a peer editor and respond to a classmate's story. The story was composed in a word processing program. The most effective feature to use to suggest changes would be

    o the autocorrect feature, which will allow you to insert smart tags to mark errors in writing

    o the comment feature, which will allow you to recommend changes that are easy to read and document

    o the spelling and grammar features, which would allow you to correct mistakes on your classmate's document

4. A word processing feature that can automatically insert a title on each page is called

    o pagination

    o search-and-replace

    o headers and footers

5. You are using a handheld device to collect information about the temperature of the stream that runs alongside your school. What should you do to facilitate easy calculation of your findings?

    o attach your handheld to a printer and print the results

    o attach your handheld to a PC and download data into a spreadsheet

    o attach your handheld to a projector and share the results with your class

6. A student locates a story online, copies it by hand, and submits it to the teacher as the student's own work.

    o This is called copying and is OK because the information was online.

    o This is an appropriate use of information and is OK because everyone does it.

    o This is called plagiarism and is unethical because it is calling someone else's work your own.

7. Which of the following information is it safe to share in a public chat room or blog?

    o name and school

    o screen name only

    o age and screen name

continued

FIGURE 8.4 *continued*

Sample Eighth-Grade Test Items

---

8. Which of the following activities would be best accomplished using a spreadsheet?

   o writing a paper for math class

   o creating a catalog of your math books

   o using formulas to solve math word problems

9. Which search strings would be most efficient for searching the Web for information on growing orange trees in the Western United States?

   o trees

   o "trees" and southwest*

   o "orange trees" + western + grow

10. Which of the following is an appropriate use of database software?

    o organizing facts about several cities in your state

    o generating graphs showing rainfall over a set period of time

    o writing and illustrating a report about a class field trip to a farm

11. _____ is the process of converting readable data into unreadable characters.

    o phishing

    o call back

    o encryption

12. Internet _____ software allows parents, teachers, and others to block access to certain materials on the Internet.

    o cookie

    o filtering

    o authoring

13. Which of the following statements is true?

    o Computers remove chances for human error.

    o Computers can help summarize data to make inferences.

    o Computers guarantee that conclusions reached from data are correct.

14. To send a form letter using many different names and addresses, use the _____ feature of your word processing program.

    o mail merge

    o sort and send

    o format paragraph

CHAPTER 9

Survey Assessments

Surveys are sometimes viewed as an easy and simplistic method for collecting opinions or feedback from large numbers of people. However, surveys can be excellent tools for efficiently and effectively assessing elements of your students' technology progress using the NETS•S performance indicators. Surveys have been frequently used to gauge perceived levels of technology skill for both students and teachers, as well as to assess student, teacher, and administrator attitudes toward technology. Well-constructed surveys can be reliable and valid methods of assessment, especially when survey results are analyzed in conjunction with other sources of evidence.

Technology surveys are essentially assessments in which answers to the questions posed are neither right nor wrong. Their purpose is to gauge respondents' education technology knowledge, skills, and aptitudes, as well as their attitudes toward technology. These surveys are similar to those used in other fields to gather data on attitudes toward customer service or—before elections—political preferences.

SURVEY CONSTRUCTION

When considering the use of surveys, keep in mind that surveys normally rely on self-reported data and assume that respondents will provide candid and honest answers. As such, surveys are subjective instruments that work best when those being surveyed fully understand the purposes for which the survey data will be used.

For example, if someone is under the impression, accurate or not, that the information asked for in a survey will be used to make individual hiring, promotion, or grading decisions, the survey taker is more likely to skew responses toward whatever is thought to be the right or best answers. If it's clearly communicated beforehand that survey information will be anonymous and used only to analyze aggregated data, survey participants are more likely to provide honest input that will lead to more accurate and useful results.

Surveys can be created and distributed on paper. However, most large-scale surveys used today in business and education take advantage of low-cost, Internet-based tools. These tools allow students and teachers to respond to survey questions posted on a Web site or distributed by means of e-mail. Organizations with Web-development experience can implement online surveys using a variety of development tools. Educators can also take advantage of subscription surveying products, such as Zoomerang (www.zoomerang.com; Figure 9.1) and Survey Monkey (www.surveymonkey.com). These products allow individuals or groups without programming experience to create and deploy standard survey forms.

These online tools make it easy to create forms with standard survey elements, such as Likert Scale items that ask respondents to react to statements based on a five-point scale. The resulting surveys can be accessed from a third-party Web site by hyperlinks or embedded in an e-mail message that can be sent to a specific list of respondents. As the survey is deployed, most online survey packages include the ability to monitor and analyze results. A final report can be downloaded into a spreadsheet or a statistical package for further analysis.

While full access to tools such as Zoomerang or Survey Monkey requires a subscription or fee, many products also offer free limited access to services that may provide enough capability to support a particular educational survey project.

Because of their low cost and ease of deployment and analysis, surveys have been used by many education entities to gather timely data from students, teachers, parents, and community members concerning attitudes toward technology. The results have often been used to set school- or district-wide priorities. District coordinators and classroom teachers have created online surveys to collect attitudinal data, as well as perceptions of competency in grade-specific technology skills.

It's relatively easy to create and automate a set of survey questions. The creation of an effective, high-quality survey, however, requires careful planning, writing, editing, and analysis following the same procedures described in chapter 7 for creating any type of assessment. As with all assessment instruments, a survey-based assessment project should begin with a blueprint and a test-construction document, described in chapter 7. These documents determine the survey's content and structure. When writing survey questions, it's particularly important to make sure

FIGURE 9.1.

Sample Online Survey Question Using Zoomerang

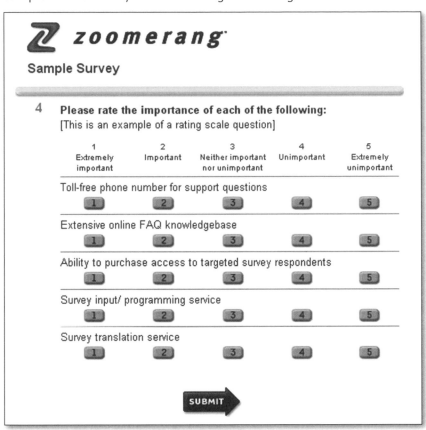

the items are clear, focused, and well-written. This minimizes the chance that respondents will interpret them in ways that weren't intended. Wherever possible, concrete examples should be used to illustrate options available to the survey taker.

Surveys can also be validated using some of the same statistical techniques described in chapter 7, including content validation, criterion validation, and reliability analysis. Content validation ensures that the coverage of the survey matches the content-balance requirements of the assessment blueprint. Criterion validation compares the survey results against some other performance measure, such as grades or scores on an objective or performance assessment. Reliability analysis compares the data for each survey item with other items in the same survey and with the results of the survey overall.

Survey results can be used in a number of ways. Two very different uses are illustrated in the following case studies. The TAGLIT survey focuses on self-assessment of technology competence. The Bellingham School District survey, on the other hand, is an annual survey specifically designed to gather data on technology use in the district. Data are then used to create professional development opportunities for teachers.

As you review these two case studies, notice the types of items included in each survey. Both TAGLIT and Bellingham have created four-point scales for survey takers to use to respond to specific statements regarding their technology aptitudes and attitudes. These scales are well defined, ensuring that respondents will clearly understand how to rate their own level of skill or knowledge. Behind the scenes, each response is assigned a specific point value (1–4), and this information is used to generate reports based on aggregate data from thousands of respondents.

CASE STUDY: TAGLIT SURVEY
www.taglit.org

Taking a Good Look at Instructional Technology, or TAGLIT, was originally designed for education leaders to collect data regarding how technology is used in teaching and learning. The TAGLIT survey has since grown to include versions for upper elementary, middle, and high school students, as well as for teachers and administrators.

TAGLIT was created by the Center for School Leadership Development at the University of North Carolina, in conjunction with the Principals' Executive Program. With the support of Bell South, SAS in Schools, and the Bill and Melinda Gates Foundation, TAGLIT has been used extensively around the country in administrator training sessions funded by Gates Foundation grants. Research questions included in TAGLIT surveys include:

- What is the impact of technology in the classroom?
- How often is technology used in the classroom?
- What are the technology skill levels of teachers and students?

FIGURE 9.2.
TAGLIT Survey of Computing Skills for Upper Elementary Students

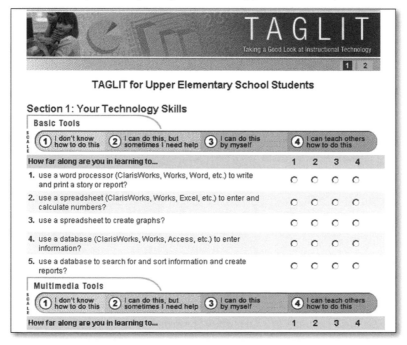

The information collected by the student version of the TAGLIT survey is aligned with the NETS•S. Items are written using modified language from the NETS•S performance profiles. The student surveys ask students to evaluate their ability to accomplish specific technology tasks using simple, personal language. The example shown in Figure 9.2 is from the Basic Tools section of the survey.

Notice how the TAGLIT survey elicits responses that correspond with different degrees of understanding. Rather than simply asking students to rate their skills with raw numbers, the TAGLIT scale asks students to rate themselves in terms of classroom performance or interaction with others, or both. It uses ratings that correspond to particular levels of performance, such as, "I can do this but sometimes need help" or "I can teach others how to do this." This forces students to examine their own comfort level with a particular computer skill in the context of a real-world classroom. The competency-rating method is based on research that has shown that the best way to determine how well students understand a subject is to ask them to teach it to others.

Figure 9.3 shows an excerpt of the kind of report that the TAGLIT survey generates. The survey results in Figure 9.3 are based on aggregate data from 210 survey respondents and provide information about general levels of understanding across the population of student respondents.

By using the same survey to assess students at different grade levels, or the same grade level in different years, this type of assessment can also be used to determine and analyze trends over time (Abbott, 2003). In addition to determining aggregate skill levels and trends, TAGLIT has also been used to assess individual students' self-reported growth in knowledge and skills over a specified period of time.

CASE STUDY: BELLINGHAM SCHOOL DISTRICT
http://www.bham.wednet.edu/technology/EISIfAsmt.htm

Bellingham Public Schools in Bellingham, Washington, requires that all teachers and students participate in a self-assessment process at regular intervals to inform professional development plans. Figure 9.4 illustrates the style of questions used in the BPS survey.

Like the TAGLIT survey, the Bellingham instrument uses a four-point scale. Unlike TAGLIT, the Bellingham instrument uses a rating system based on skill-level definitions specific to the skill being measured. For instance, a question related to basic computer use defines each of four skill levels based on concrete examples of what the student can and cannot do with the computer, such as open, use, and close programs; use more than one program at the same time; and so forth. This is another example of how a creative use of standard survey item formats can be used to gauge students' perceptions of their own performances and skills.

Self-assessment instruments based on the NETS•S have been used in the district for many years, and cumulative data have been collected and analyzed. Seven years of accumulated data on how well students are meeting the basic operations and concepts area of the NETS•S are presented in Figure 9.5.

FIGURE 9.3
TAGLIT Survey Results

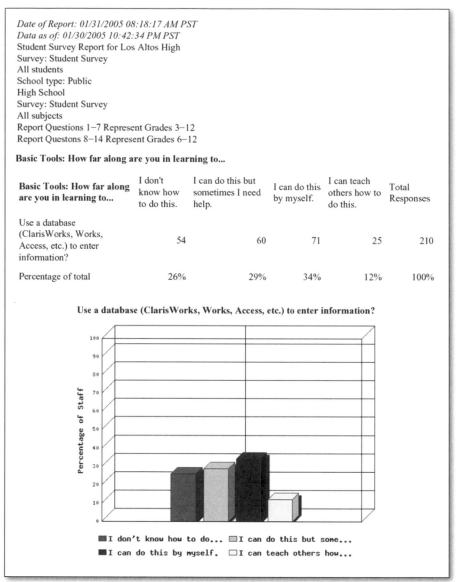

Date of Report: 01/31/2005 08:18:17 AM PST
Data as of: 01/30/2005 10:42:34 PM PST
Student Survey Report for Los Altos High
Survey: Student Survey
All students
School type: Public
High School
Survey: Student Survey
All subjects
Report Questions 1–7 Represent Grades 3–12
Report Questons 8–14 Represent Grades 6–12

Basic Tools: How far along are you in learning to...

Basic Tools: How far along are you in learning to...	I don't know how to do this.	I can do this but sometimes I need help.	I can do this by myself.	I can teach others how to do this.	Total Responses
Use a database (ClarisWorks, Works, Access, etc.) to enter information?	54	60	71	25	210
Percentage of total	26%	29%	34%	12%	100%

Use a database (ClarisWorks, Works, Access, etc.) to enter information?

The table at the top of Figure 9.5 presents percentage data derived from survey respondents. For example, the 100% value listed under Word Processing for the Spring of 2001–2002 indicates that all (or close to all) respondents selected either Level 3 or Level 4 (representing the highest level of skill) when asked to rate their ability to use a word processor. The high ratings for Responsible Use in 1998–2002 (89%–98%) indicate that most respondents rated themselves at the highest two levels (Level 3 and Level 4) when asked to assess their understanding of responsible use.

By looking at aggregate data over time, important trends emerge. For example, dynamic growth in the understanding of responsible use, which grew to 98% from 57% between

FIGURE 9.4.
Questions Posed to Elementary Students in the BPS District

Bellingham
Public Schools

Elementary Student Use of Technology
2004-2005 Self-Evaluation

Students: Please check the highest level that describes what you can do at the present time. Marking Level 4 shows you can also do Levels 2 and 3.

1. Responsible Use
__ Level 1 - I do not understand what responsible use means.
__ Level 2 - I take care of the equipment I use and leave it in ready condition for the next user.
__ Level 3 - I understand and follow school rules concerning harassment, language, passwords, privacy, copyright,
          appropriate use and citation of resources, etc.
__ Level 4 - I model responsible use and teach others how to be responsible users.

2. Basic Computer Use
__ Level 1 - I do not use a computer.
__ Level 2 - I log on, log off, open, use and close programs on my own.
__ Level 3 - I open programs from icons and the Start bar and use more than one program at the same time.
__ Level 4 - I learn new programs and discover additional program features on my own.

3. File Management
__ Level 1 - I do not save any documents I create using the computer.
__ Level 2 - I select, open and save documents in my folder on the H: drive.
__ Level 3 – I create folders to organize the files I save in my H: drive.
__ Level 4 – I use Windows Explorer or My Computer to locate files on different drives, and I move files between drives.

FIGURE 9.5
Cumulative Data on BPS Students' Technology Self-Assessment

Sample Elementary School--Cumulative Student Data 1995-2002

Spring 2001-02	Respon-sible Use	Comput-er Basic Use	File Manage-ment	E-Mail	Word Process-ing	Graphics	Desktop Publish-ing	Spread-sheet	Library Data-base	Research Info-Search	Internet	Technol-ogy Pre-sentation
% at 3 &	98%	98%	86%	77%	100%	91%	58%	58%	98%	95%	95%	77%
Spring 99-2000												
% at 3 &	90%	81%	49%	81%	97%	54%	59%	39%	32%	63%	83%	76%
Spring 1998-99												
% at 3 &	89%	83%	72%	76%	91%	57%	72%	72%	39%	57%	67%	72%
Spring 1												
% at 3 &	86%	84%	80%	86%	96%	82%	50%	46%	38%	60%	68%	46%
Spring 1996-97												
% at 3 &	91%	83%	65%	83%	95%	84%	38%	69%	33%	64%	52%	31%
Spring 1995-96												
% at 3 &	85%	91%	55%	72%	91%	77%	40%	57%	38%	72%	30%	28%
Spring 1994-95												
% at 3 &	57%	61%	44%	13%	93%	65%	22%	39%	17%	46%	7%	15%

2001-2002--Technology Self-Evaluation survey revised. Database changed to Library Database: emphasizes using Library Catalog database; database creation removed. Internet: emphasizes information location and evaluation skills; web page creation removed.

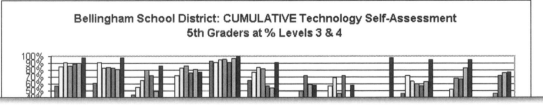

Bellingham School District: CUMULATIVE Technology Self-Assessment
5th Graders at % Levels 3 & 4

1994 and 2002, demonstrates that this important area has become better understood by students over time. This may be the result of improved teaching of the subject, or it may be because of more students being exposed to responsible use issues as the Internet was gradually integrated into the classroom.

USING SURVEYS FOR TECHNOLOGY ASSESSMENT

The previous case studies illustrate how surveys can collect valuable information on subjects related to education technology, particularly aggregate information that can illustrate trends. To accomplish this, the surveys must be

- well-planned, well-designed, and tied to specific objectives, such as the NETS•S grade-range performance indicators, and
- constructed with well-written items based on concrete language.

While surveys are less useful than other assessment techniques in assessing individual student ability, they can form an important element of a comprehensive technology assessment plan.

Reference

Abbott, M.L. (2003, November). *State challenge grants TAGLIT data analysis.* Fouts and Associates. Retrieved July 15, 2005, from http://www.gatesfoundation.org/nr/downloads/ed/researchevaluation/TAGLITDataAnalysis.pdf

CHAPTER 10

Observational Assessments

Observing your students' use of technology in class is a powerful way to obtain performance information, especially when it's in the context of learning. Observational assessment can be particularly useful when measuring the higher-order thinking skills that are components of several of the NETS•S, such as, "Students use productivity tools to collaborate on constructing technology-enhanced models, preparing publications, and producing other creative works" and "Students employ technology in the development of strategies for solving problems in the real world."

Observational assessments that are reliable and scalable can also be resource-intensive. They require the involvement of skilled observers who must be trained to analyze and report on classroom behavior in a consistent manner. A trained observer can effectively determine a student's skill level with software, such as a spreadsheet program, by observing and evaluating the student's ability to create a worksheet based on specified instructions. However, such "hard" skills may be more efficiently measured with an automated, performance-based assessment that's scored by computer.

Within the context of an individual classroom, teacher observation of student performance can be an extremely valuable assessment tool. A teacher's knowledge of both the subject matter and students' performances over time can produce observations of abilities that would be difficult to measure using any other assessment method. When a teacher performs all the observations and uses the data within the classroom for diagnostic or assessment purposes, issues of reliability and consistency are no more significant than with any other type of assessment used by a classroom teacher. In this case, classroom data are not being compared with *other* classrooms or calibrated with data generated by *other* teacher observers.

This chapter looks at the use of observational assessments in contexts beyond the individual classroom. Given the human resources and time required for observational assessment of large groups of students, it's important that this assessment option be used wisely and focus primarily on those objectives that are difficult to measure using other assessment techniques.

CONSISTENCY IN OBSERVATIONAL ASSESSMENT

Like self-report surveys, observational assessments are subjective instruments. In this case, however, it's the observer who can be the source of subjectivity, rather than the person being assessed. *Inter-rater reliability* is the formal term used to describe how well those who score, or rate, an assessment can be counted on to assign comparable scores to comparable observations. Inter-rater reliability can be greatly enhanced by following these guidelines:

- Carefully construct observational tools, such as the NETS-based rubrics and checklists described in this chapter, so that they provide clear, concrete categories for assigning specific scores to particular observations.

- Create processes that allow raters to compare the results of their observations with one another.

- Train raters on the use of these tools and processes so that they'll be observing and assessing student behaviors consistently.

- Periodically "recalibrate" raters to ensure that they're continuing to observe and assess student behaviors consistently.

Having raters discuss their initial reactions during the training period is important in determining if they have any preconceptions or unstated objectives that may be biasing their observations and adversely influencing the consistency of results. These clarifying discussions can also help the assessment developers eliminate items and create more explicit observation statements, rubrics, and directions. Performing validation studies on the results of a carefully controlled pilot of the assessment can also help ensure that an observational assessment is being implemented and scored reliably. Like the large-scale scoring of student essays described in chapter 7, careful and consistent scoring of observational assessments can reduce subjectivity to the point where observational assessments become a reliable measure of student achievement.

OBSERVING STANDARDS REQUIRING HIGHER-ORDER SKILLS

An example of an objective that's difficult to measure using other assessment options is the collaboration component of the technology productivity tools standard in the NETS•S. One of the eighth-grade performance indicators for this standard states that students at the end of eighth grade should be able to:

Apply productivity/multimedia tools and peripherals to support personal productivity, group collaboration, and learning throughout the curriculum.

If this performance indicator were used as the basis for a test blueprint, the blueprint would need to break the indicator down into a set of measurable objectives:

1. Demonstrate the ability to use technology tools to enhance personal productivity, including:

   a. productivity applications (including a word processor, spreadsheet, presentation program, and database)

   b. multimedia tools

   c. computer peripherals

2. Demonstrate the ability to use technology tools to support group collaboration, including

   a. productivity applications (including a word processor, spreadsheet, presentation program, and database)

   b. multimedia tools

   c. computer peripherals

3. Demonstrate the ability to use technology tools to support group learning across the curriculum, including

   a. productivity applications (including a word processor, spreadsheet, presentation program, and database)

   b. multimedia tools

   c. computer peripherals

Each of these objectives would then be broken down further to include, for instance, specific features of a word processor that enhance personal productivity, such as mail merge; specific features of a shared storage device that enhance group collaboration, such as the use of common folders; or specific features of multimedia programs that enhance learning within the curriculum, such as the use of instructional software to master specific language or math skills.

While an understanding of software program features that enhance productivity can be measured using a variety of techniques, the ability to collaborate effectively is more difficult to measure without watching students interact in a group as they work together on a joint project. Therefore, objectives related to collaboration are well-suited for measurement using an observational assessment.

A collaborative project can be created solely for the purpose of enabling an observational assessment, or assessment rubrics can be created to match an existing lesson or project involving group or classroom collaboration. For example, students can be asked to develop a plan for raising funds for a school project. By requiring students to work in collaborative groups on specific projects in a consistent and controlled environment, the process and outcome can be used as the basis for an observational assessment that measures students' ability to use technology collaboratively. Such an assessment would focus on those specific skills that aid collaborative efforts, such as the ability to

- use a computer and network software to create shared folders.

- use program to create and monitor the use of shared documents.

- communicate group rules for collaborative creation and editing of shared documents

- work on shared documents effectively.

- divide a project into manageable segments and assign those segments to work-group members.

- consolidate information from multiple documents created by individual work-group members into a single shared document.

- manage the editing, review, and approval of the final product.

USING RUBRICS FOR OBSERVATIONS

Constructing a rubric to measure the skills described above requires careful consideration of the behavioral indicators that mark skill progression, from minimally exhibiting the behavior to fully exhibiting the behavior. Rubrics with narratives—written in clear language and illustrated with concrete examples—are the most helpful for observers and can increase inter-rater reliability. Figure 10.1 reproduces a section of the NETS•S Assessment Rubric for Grades 6–8 (the full rubric appears in appendix B).

The portion of this performance indicator that requires direct observation is the student's ability to collaborate with peers to create a group product. Such a rubric provides clear categories for rating different elements of the student's collaboration. Figure 10.2 presents a sample rubric for assessing student participation in a cooperative learning project.

FIGURE 10.1
NETS•S Assessment Rubric for Grades 6–8 (excerpt)

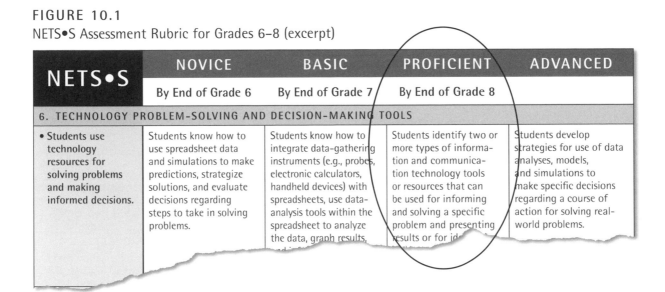

NETS•S	NOVICE	BASIC	PROFICIENT	ADVANCED
	By End of Grade 6	By End of Grade 7	By End of Grade 8	
6. TECHNOLOGY PROBLEM-SOLVING AND DECISION-MAKING TOOLS				
• Students use technology resources for solving problems and making informed decisions.	Students know how to use spreadsheet data and simulations to make predictions, strategize solutions, and evaluate decisions regarding steps to take in solving problems.	Students know how to integrate data-gathering instruments (e.g., probes, electronic calculators, handheld devices) with spreadsheets, use data-analysis tools within the spreadsheet to analyze the data, graph results,	Students identify two or more types of information and communication technology tools or resources that can be used for informing and solving a specific problem and presenting results or for id	Students develop strategies for use of data analyses, models, and simulations to make specific decisions regarding a course of action for solving real-world problems.

FIGURE 10.2
Group Project Rubric

CRITERIA	DOES NOT MEET	APPROACHING	MEETS	EXCEEDS
Initiative Contribution to group by working toward group goals is evident	only when prompted.	but requires occasional prompting.	without prompting.	actively and consistently.
Team role and duties In the division of work to create a work plan	does not fulfill any of the work assigned.	completes some of the work.	performs all work assigned.	completes all work and assists others.
Interaction Quality of interaction with others in support of goal shows	little interaction, disinterest in others, distraction.	attentive listening, some discussion with group.	listening and contributing to discussion, lively interaction, focus on topic.	leadership skills to facilitate others, honoring of others' views, facilitation of consensus.
Contribution To complete the project, the contribution to the end product	was minimal and required considerable prompting.	adequate in terms of the work plan but required work of others.	on target with work plan.	exceeded work plan target and facilitated the infusion of work of others to create an outcome beyond expectations.

The above rubric is not unique to education technology learning situations. Cooperative group projects in technology rich environments often require students to be aware of each other's strengths and weaknesses. While the teacher's role is to assure that each student is actively participating in the project, an ancillary role is to educate students on how they can teach each other and strengthen self-assessed weaknesses. Especially in the area of technology, students find that they can help each other learn quickly by listening and teaching each member of the group about newly discovered skills, resources, and applications.

In addition to rubric criteria that measure general areas of collaboration, such as initiative and interaction, rubrics can also be created that look at specific technology use. An example of such a rubric appears in Figure 10.3.

FIGURE 10.3
Group Technology Use Rubric

CRITERIA	DOES NOT MEET	APPROACHING	MEETS	EXCEEDS
Creates shared folders and work spaces	Student work group does not create shared folders or work spaces for the project.	Student work group makes minimum use of shared folders or work spaces, for example, only creating a single shared folder or document for the entire project.	Student work group creates shared folders and work spaces, but those folders/work spaces are not optimized (i.e., not organized logically or not assigned meaningful or logical names).	Student work group creates shared folders and work spaces, organizes and names folders and work spaces logically, and communicates the organizational and naming structure to all members of the work group.
Uses application software to create and monitor the use of shared documents	Automated document-sharing features of application software are not used for any document created for the project.	Automated document-sharing features of application software are used in a very limited way (i.e., only used for a single document or used by some group members for some documents but not others).	Automated document-sharing features of application software are used by all members of the work group for all appropriate documents created by the group, but the work group does not make effective use of version tracking and other features that could make collaboration more effective and efficient.	Automated document-sharing features of application software are used by all members of the work group for all appropriate documents. The work group makes maximum use of document sharing functionality, including version tracking and control, communicating the use of such features to all members of the work group.

Because an observational assessment allows the observer to view and determine the interaction between group members, this assessment technique is well-suited to measuring complex processes that involve the interplay of many skills (such as the use of networks to enable work groups), abilities (such as the use of shared documents and work spaces), and aptitudes (such as leadership and communication).

USING CHECKLISTS

If you're a teacher, you observe students exhibiting behaviors, skills, and aptitudes all day long. In an effort to create flexible groupings to meet students' learning needs, you may keep a mental list of a student's ability to do a particular task. Or you may have a list of knowledge and skills that you mentally check off whenever a student demonstrates understanding of a topic in your classroom.

While such mental lists may not constitute a formalized assessment, the concept of checking students off on a list of defined behaviors is one way to keep track of student performance on many subjects, including the education technology skills covered in the NETS•S. More formalized checklists have been used as the basis for scoring observational assessments. Such checklists are actually a type of modified rubric, called a "checkbric," and can provide a useful and intuitive way to monitor observed behavior in the context of learning and assessment.

If you work with very young students, employ checkbrics to keep track of how your students are doing. Figure 10.4 shows an example checkbric based on the NETS•S performance indicators for Grades PK–2, which are listed in Figure 1.1 in chapter 1. The target portion of the checkbric has been customized for the K–1 unit "Things that Go on Land" (Kelly & Witherspoon, 2004). Because observation is such a key component of assessing very young learners, you must have a contextualized sense of what the child is doing, both in terms of effort and skill. The five-category observational scale shown in Figure 10.5 can be used to assess a student's developmental competence with any concept or skill.

The following case studies demonstrate how well-constructed rubrics and checkbrics, built on a well-defined series of NETS•S assessment objectives and combining both teacher observation and student products, can be used as the basis for assessing student performance across all grade levels.

HANDHELD HELP

Using a handheld computer or electronic recording device that synchronizes with your computer can save you considerable time compiling student performance information obtained from checkbrics.

FIGURE 10.4
Technology Rubric

This rubric was designed for the "Things that Go on Land" unit in the ISTE book *NETS•S Curriculum Series: Multidisciplinary Units for Prekindergarten through Grade 2*, pp. 38–39 (full unit on pp. 179–188).

1. Student uses input devices and output devices to successfully operate computers, VCRs, audiotapes, and other technologies.	
• Uses Kid Pix	
• Operates Roamer Robot	
• Operates Museum of Buses slideshow	
2. Student uses a variety of media and technology resources for directed and independent learning activities.	
• Uses buttoned Web resources	
3. Student communicates about technology using developmentally appropriate and accurate terminology.	
• Participates in discussions throughout unit	
• Provides directions to Roamer Robot	
4. Student uses developmentally appropriate multimedia resources to support learning.	
• Operates student-created slideshows	
• Listens to Web-played music	
5. Student works cooperatively and collaboratively with peers, family members, and others when using technology in the classroom.	
• Demonstrates cooperative and collaborative behavior at computer center	
6. Student demonstrates positive social and ethical behaviors when using technology.	
• Shows positive social and ethical behavior in large and small group situations	
7. Student practices responsible use of technology systems and software.	
• Behaves responsibly at computer center	
• Takes turn shutting computer down and storing computer software and peripherals	
8. Student creates developmentally appropriate multimedia products with support from teachers, family members, or student partners.	
• Contributes to class slideshows	
• Creates slideshow pages on vehicles—includes writing on pages	
9. Student uses technology resources for problem solving, communication, and illustration of thoughts, ideas, and stories.	
• Creates Web dictionary	
• Visits buttoned Web sites, recording essential learning	
• Uses graphing program to record results of Lego car run down inclined plane. Makes generalizations from results	
• Creates Kid Pix safety poster	

FIGURE 10.5

Rubric for Younger Learners

This checkbric assesses skills of very young learners during the interdisciplinary unit "Things that Go on Land."

CRITERIA	NOT INTERESTED	TRYING IT	WORKING ON IT	GOT IT!	HELPING OTHERS
Vehicle is present and parts are locked.					
Safety rules are clear and appropriate.					
Story includes places to go.					
Computer skills are evident.					
Writing is clear.					

CASE STUDY: DIOCESE OF ALBANY
http://rcdaschools.org/techcomp.htm

The Roman Catholic Diocese of Albany, New York, has created a series of checklists to record student technology competencies as students move from grade to grade. The checklists are passed along each year and retained in students' permanent files. Based on the NETS•S, the checklists provide a consistent format for teachers to record student growth in meeting the standards.

The sample shown in Figure 10.6 from the middle school checklist asks teachers to annually rate students' ability to perform specific tasks on a three-point scale: not evident, developing, or mastered. This checklist is a form of observational assessment in that teachers must identify and score the behavior in terms of meeting each specified standard.

The successful use of such a checklist presumes that teachers are well-versed in the NETS•S and have been trained to score student behaviors consistently, that is, there's high inter-rater reliability). Implementing an observational assessment based on this checklist, or another similar tool, has two beneficial effects:

- Data collected on student performance can be conveyed in a simple way to multiple audiences.

- Teachers realize that to be credible observers they must understand what they're observing.

The second outcome results in raising teachers' awareness of both the technology standards and the necessity for them to master the same technology tasks and skills they're observing in their students.

FIGURE 10.6

Sample of a Technology Checklist

Student Name _____

School Name _____

KEYS TO RATING SCALE:

NE..Not Evident

D ....Developing

M..Mastered

BASIC OPERATIONS AND CONCEPTS	6	7	8
Is able to define and use advanced computer vocabulary.			
Independently operates school computers and uses the software and its special features.			
Is able to retrieve documents and save onto the hard drive or floppy disk.			
With assistance, develops strategies for solving common hardware and software problems.			
Uses correct fingering position on the keyboard.			
Is able to achieve a typing speed of at least 20 wpm with reasonable accuracy.			

SOCIAL, ETHICAL, AND HUMAN ISSUES	6	7	8
Practices responsible use of computer equipment and software.			
Work...			

CASE STUDY: FALLBROOK UNION ELEMENTARY SCHOOL DISTRICT

Fallbrook Union Elementary School District in California has infused technology into their English language arts program to support their large population of English language learners. As part of an Enhancing Education Through Technology (EETT) grant titled Improving Learning through Educational Technology for Staff and Students (iLETSS), the district used trained observers to examine the classroom environment and the technology use by students and teachers (Hayden, et al., 2005). The data were used to validate student-reported competencies as well as teacher behaviors.

Because of the effort and cost of implementing an observational assessment, it's often productive if trained observers use multiple measures within one observation period. In the case of the Fallbrook project, observers used a multipart checklist that covered the following elements of classroom technology use:

- the amount of time (measured in 3-minute intervals) students engaged with technology or focused on teaching and learning, or both
- the technologies used by teachers and students
- how students worked (individually, in small groups, and so forth)
- the learning activities observed (research, writing, and so forth)
- the general extent of technology use in the classroom
- the NETS observed

In addition to collecting checklist or quantitative information, the classroom observation form also provides ways for observers to add qualitative comments to supplement their ratings. The comments provided might be useful to teachers trying to improve their use of technology in the classroom and might also be used to help fine-tune observational ratings when the work of several raters needs to be compared.

Figure 10.7 shows the evaluation form used for this observational assessment.

The successful implementation of this observational assessment program was the result of a commitment to the project by all stakeholders, the use of well-designed tools, such as the form in Figure 10.6, and intensive training of raters to ensure accurate and consistent scoring of observational data.

Program directors made use of scenarios, such as the one illustrated in Figure 10.8, to train those who would be serving as raters in the classroom. This training process included the following steps:

1. Observers read a scenario of a classroom situation. Any questions about the details of the situation were filled in by the trainer and added to the scenario.

2. All observers completed observation forms as a group.

3. A standard completed form was provided by the trainer, and the standards for completing the form were discussed.

FIGURE 10.7
iLETSS Classroom Observation Recording Form

Date:	School:	District:	Observer:
Teacher:	Grade:	Subject:	No. Students:
Main Activities:			
Notes on Students/Setting:			

How many minutes were spent in this observation?	mins.	(No. of intervals from chart below x3)
What % of *that* time were teachers or students engaged with technology?	%	(Engaged intervals / total intervals)
What % of that *engaged* time was technology used for teaching and learning?	%	(T+L intervals / engaged intervals)

START TIME >																				
3' Interval:	1	2	3	4	5	6	7	8	9	10	11	12	13	14	15	16	17	18	19	20
1. Engaged with technology																				
2. Focused on teaching and learning																				
Notes:																				

What technologies were used? (Example)	By Teacher	By Students	Comments
word processing (Word)			
presentation (PowerPoint)			
spreadsheet (Excel)			
database (Access)			
graphics (ImageBlender)			
Web authoring (FrontPage)			
outliner (Inspiration)			
simulation (Geo Sketchpad)			
drill/practice (Accelerated Reader)			
e-mail (Outlook)			
Web browser (Explorer)			
discussion (WebCT)			
videoconference			
CD-ROM			
library database			
digital camera			
video camera			
reading intervention program (Read 180)			
multimedia (MediaBlender)			
ILS (SuccessMaker)			
administrative package (Edusoft)			
Other:			

Teacher Roles		Comments
lecturing		
interactive direction		
discussion		
facilitating/coaching		
modeling		
Other:		

Student Groupings		Comments
individual work		
student pairs		
small groups (3+)		
whole class		
Other:		

Learning Activities		Comments
creating presentations		
research		
information/ data analysis		
writing		
taking tests		
drill and practice		
simulations		
hands-on skill training		
Web site critique		
Other:		

continued

FIGURE 10.7 *continued*

iLETSS Classroom Observation Recording Form

To what extent was technology useful in teaching and learning the context of the lesson?

Check One:		Comments
Technology use was **not essential**; other approaches would be **better**.		
Technology was **somewhat useful**; other approaches would have been **as effective**.		
Technology was **useful**; other approaches would **not be as effective**.		
Technology was **essential**; the lesson **could not be taught without it**.		

NETS for Teachers (NETS•T) Addressed:

(1 = observed, successful; 0 = observed, unsuccessful; NA = not applicable or observable)

			Comments
I. TECHNOLOGY OPERATIONS AND CONCEPTS			
A.	1. operating system procedures		
	2. routine hardware and software problems		
	3. content-specific tools		
	4. productivity tools		
	5. multimedia tools		
	6. interactive communication tools		
	7. curriculum-based presentations/publications		
	8. curriculum-based collaboration		
	9. appropriate technology selected		
III. TEACHING, LEARNING, AND THE CURRICULUM			
A.	1. learning experiences address content standards		
	2. learning experiences address student technology standards		
B.	1. technology supports learner-centered strategies		
C.	1. technology applied to develop students' higher-order skills		
	2. teacher applies technology to develop students' creativity		
D.	1. class management facilitates engagement with technology		
	2. technology integrated as a teacher tool		
	3. technology integrated as a student tool		
	4. student grouping varied as needed to facilitate learning		
IV. ASSESSMENT AND EVALUATION			
A.	1. student learning of subject matter assessed with technology		
	2. teacher assesses student technology skills		
	3. teacher employs a variety of assessment strategies		
VI. SOCIAL, ETHICAL, LEGAL, AND HUMAN ISSUES			
A.	1. teacher models legal and ethical technology practices		
	2. teacher explicitly teaches legal/ethical technology practices		
B.	1. diverse learners enabled and empowered		
C.	1. safe and healthy use of technology promoted		
D.	1. equitable access to technology for all students		

FIGURE 10.8

Classroom Observation Form Scenario for Practice Scoring

Classroom Observation Form Scenario for Practice Scoring

Grade: 8   Subject Area: Language arts

No. Students: 24 (of 27; 3 absent)

Main Activities: Using the Web to look up information about 19th century American authors for use in literature reports.

Setting: Classroom with five computers and teacher workstation. No projection device except for conventional overhead. Computers are networked Pentium IVs, 1GHz, running Windows NT and Microsoft Office. Students = 14 boys, 10 girls. Anglo and Hispanic. Regular class, with one mainstreamed student with a learning disability.

Technologies used: Students use five computers, Web browsers, word processor. Teacher has same software on a teacher presentation station. Would have gone to a lab, but lab was booked on this day.

Classroom organization: Pairs of students working on the computers, with some whole-class instruction. Ninety-minute block class.

Teacher roles: Lecturing and facilitating

Kinds of learning activities: Creating and receiving presentations, research, and analysis.

Notes: Observation starts a few minutes after the bell. Teacher reviews the assignment, how to open the browsers, and writes beginning URLs on the board. The lesson plan is available; this is the 2nd of 2 days devoted to this activity.

Each student is to locate certain biographical and literary information about their chosen authors and enter it into a worksheet that will serve as a template for their written reports. This is the second day of the project, and if they already have the worksheet filled out, the pairs can start to create their reports from handwritten notes.

Students find partners and go to computers in shifts of 20 minutes at a time. One machine is down, and the previously assigned groups don't quite work out because not everyone can be on the machine they worked on before; but because of absences, everyone ends up with a machine. Some individuals from different pairs end up sharing a single machine.

The groups start to work. Some students have their information and are copying notes or writing new material. There's some tension in the groups. More advanced students are frustrated at having to wait for slower ones in their groups, but some of them help others along to speed the process. Some students have worked on home computers but are having trouble importing data from different platforms and word processors.

Students who aren't online consult textbooks or write in notebooks, still working in pairs. Some socialize, one dozes. The teacher circulates, encouraging activity, asking questions, and offering advice. The teacher points out the mainstreamed student to the observer. The student is quiet and lets her partner, another girl, do most of the work. Her level of engagement in this assignment is comparable to that of several other students.

At several points the teacher stops to reteach some elements of literary history as well as computer procedures, such as how to work with multiple Web windows. The worksheet prompts students to cite their sources correctly, but several need encouragement and direct instruction to do so. The activity has to end before the end of the block so that students can complete some readings. At the end of the activity, the teacher extends the deadline for the papers to the next week to allow everyone to finish.

continued

FIGURE 10.8 *continued*

Classroom Observation Form Scenario for Practice Scoring

Time Segments:

START > 10:06	:09	:12	:15	:18	:21	:24	:27	:30	:33	:36	:39	:42	:45	:48	:51	:54	:57	11	:03	:06
3' Interval:	1	2	3	4	5	6	7	8	9	10	11	12	13	14	15	16	17	18	19	20
1. Engaged with technology			X	X	X	X	X	X	X	X	X	X	X	X	X	X	X	X	X	X
2. Focused on teaching and learning			X	X		X	X	X	X	X	X			X	X		X	X	X	
Notes:	Intro to activity.	Transition to activity. Log on. One break for reviewing use of browser windows.							Transition to second shift. Teacher reviews meaning of "themes."						Third shift. Observation ends at 11:05.					

4. Observers, including the trainer, then completed real observations in pairs.

5. Observers met after each observation and resolved rating differences by consensus. The normal practice was to exit each observation a few minutes early so that a consensus form could be prepared immediately after the observation.

Figure 10.8 illustrates one of the training scenarios used for this purpose.

The results of this extensive preparation and training were demonstrated when the teams completed 127 observations of 20 language arts teachers over a 2-year period, with virtually no significant overall differences in observer responses. No one observer pair was more likely than another to rate technology use as essential or to recognize evidence of a particular standard being met. The few anomalous cases tended to occur for observers who had to work solo and thus skipped the debrief-and-consensus stage of the procedure.

The examples in this chapter demonstrate the challenges of implementing a large-scale observational assessment. They also illustrate how such assessments can be creatively developed and implemented in ways that reveal considerable data about students, teachers, and the classroom environment.

It's often noted that observational assessments have a tendency to provide unexpected data that reflect the overall complexity of the classroom situation. These data add context to results obtained under otherwise difficult-to-measure circumstances. Examples of such circumstances include multiple constraints imposed on teachers; the effects of noise, location, and other conditions on the classroom; and special circumstances that occur concerning students and other personnel.

Teaching and learning take place in a complex environment that cannot be judged by a single source of data. Observational assessment can help round out the picture of technology use in the real-world environment of the classroom.

References

Carroll, J., Kelly, M., & Witherspoon, T. (2004). "Things that go on land," *NETS•S curriculum series: Multidisciplinary units for prekindergarten through grade 2*, pp. 38-39, p. 41. Eugene, OR: International Society for Technology in Education.

Hayden, K., Fish, C., Bielefeldt, T., & Stermon, D. (2005, June 28). *EETT: Training + implementation + assessment = increased student achievement in writing.* Presentation at the National Educational Computing Conference, Philadelphia.

CHAPTER 11

Portfolio Assessments

Portfolios have become an important part of many educational programs over the past few decades, and they are increasingly being used as a platform for assessment. Traditional, paper-based portfolios in which students collect work samples documenting their progress through a program of study are typically housed in a single place and organized in a way that demonstrates continual learning and growth. Work samples may include graded tests, writing samples, term papers, projects, and other classroom artifacts. From a learner's perspective, using a portfolio to track growth and progress means, "Let me show you!"

In an ideal situation, an effective portfolio assessment focuses on student development and growth over time, with benchmarks established to examine learning. In a standards-based portfolio, students collect artifacts in a "working" portfolio. Eventually, students select those producs that best demonstrate how they've met the standards, with accompanying reflections that justify their choices and document their learning.

Unfortunately, typical portfolio assessment programs rarely match this ideal. Because so many complex issues and political pressures are related to assessment at the school level, implementing a full portfolio program is difficult and requires careful planning, administrative commitment, and consistent oversight and revision. Coupling a portfolio program with other assessment options can provide a more complete picture of student learning and standards attainment.

With the advent of networking and Internet technology and the decreasing cost of mass computer storage, traditional portfolios are being replaced by electronic portfolios. These allow students to archive multiple versions of document files, record assessment scores, and include multimedia content such as audio and video recordings. Electronic or digital portfolios can be shared and reviewed easily by students, parents, and teachers, and they can travel with students as they move through the year and from one grade or school to another.

Using portfolios for assessment purposes has gained considerable momentum in recent years, especially in the area of teacher candidate assessment and professional portfolios for educators (see *National Educational Technology Standards for Teachers: Resources for Assessment* [International Society for Technology in Education, 2003] for several examples). As with other types of assessment, portfolios turn complex and diverse information into a consistent measure of student performance. Portfolios can be an effective tool for assessment when they're built into a well-defined and comprehensive assessment plan.

PORTFOLIO DESIGN AND FUNCTION

Portfolios, whether paper or electronic, typically consist of the following elements:

Artifacts. Work samples, or reproductions of work samples, such as test results, papers, student projects, and other items that illustrate classroom experiences.

Productions. Work samples created specifically for inclusion in the portfolio.

Attestations. Third-party reviews, recommendations, or comments on a student's work by individuals other than the student creating the portfolio.

Reflections. The student's own commentary on items in the portfolio.

Reflections are a critical part of any portfolio project, allowing the student to analyze how individual items in the portfolio fit into an overarching narrative of development and learning.

Portfolios can serve different functions for students at different stages in their education.

Formative Portfolios. In a formative portfolio students add items, including reflections, as they move through a course of study. The resulting portfolio, usually organized chronologically, reflects the student's growth and learning over time.

Summative Portfolio. Students create a summative portfolio, or reorganize an existing formative portfolio, at a predetermined benchmark in their education to summarize academic achievement at the end of a course of study. Reflections in a summative portfolio allow the student to comment on earlier work based on the understanding the student has gained over the course of study.

FIGURE 11.1

Sample of a Standards-Based Portfolio

1. Basic Operations and Concepts

- **Students demonstrate a sound understanding of the nature and operation of technical systems.**

    Artifact 1:   Test scores from objective classroom assessments of technology basics.

    Reflection 1:   Student analysis of the questions answered incorrectly on these assessments based on summative knowledge at the end of a course of study.

    Artifact 2:   A graded essay describing how workers interacted with computers in 1960 compared with how they interact with them today.

    Reflection 2:   Additional information students now understand is important to this subject that was not included in the original paper.

- **Students are proficient in the use of technology**

    Artifact 1:   Certificate of achievement for passing an IT certification test such as the International Computer Drivers License, the Internet and Computing Core Certification (IC^3), or the Microsoft Office Specialist (MOS) exam.

    Reflection 1:   Student analysis of how the basic skills covered in these certifications was useful in maximizing productivity, collaboration, communication, and learning in the classroom.

    Artifact 2:   A business plan created for a business and technology class that was developed using multiple applications and involved the collaborative use of software and documents.

    Reflection 2:   Student analysis of the required proficiency in computer hardware, software, and research tools needed to create the business plan.

STANDARDS-BASED PORTFOLIOS

Because a portfolio can be used to archive the results of other assessment tools, it can become the central source of information regarding assessment of a wide variety of abilities. For example, a summative portfolio for Grades 9 through 12 that's organized around NETS•S 1, Basic Operations and Concepts, might contain artifacts and reflections for the performance indicators related to those standards, as shown in Figure 11.1.

As with other types of assessment that require a third party to assign an objective score to information that might be considered subjective, it's important that evaluators develop scoring rubrics to assign scores to student artifacts and reflections. This is an essential step if the portfolio is to be used as a basis for effective assessment. See chapter 2 and appendix B for rubrics based on the NETS•S.

Rubrics should assign descriptive categories for work indicating how well the student's work fits the criteria used to evaluate each standard, such as "developing," "approaching," "meets," or "exceeds." Because a well-designed and well-organized portfolio contains information that illustrates multiple dimensions of a student's knowledge, skills, and abilities, this allows the portfolio evaluator to categorize the student more thoroughly than do assessments designed to measure individual dimensions.

Standards-based portfolios can either be organized around the standards themselves or around required artifacts. For example, the matrix shown in Figure 11.2 illustrates how an assessment program can tie standards-based activities and projects to the NETS•S.

Model projects and activities suitable for inclusion in a portfolio can be found in ISTE's publication *National Educational Technology Standards for Students: Connecting Curriculum and Technology* (International Society for Technology in Education, 2000a; see Figure 11.3). The portfolio entries in Figure 11.2, taken from that book, are targeted at an intermediate grade level (Grades 3–5). The first entry, "You Were There!," is primarily a literacy unit focused on teaching point-of-view through reading historical fiction and studying the Revolutionary War. (This activity is also referenced in chapters 2 and 4 as an example of a primary assessment activity for Grade 5.) The activity involves the use of technology to interview historical figures from a specific point of view. A lesson excerpt appears in Figure 11.3. (International Society for Technology in Education, 2000b, [pp. 48–51]). The required portfolio entries include both a news article and a videotaped interview, thereby demonstrating the student's ability to meet the NETS•S while also addressing academic content standards. The matrix verifies that, over time, fifth-graders will eventually be able to meet all the standards by collecting data on a series of academic content activities.

The matrix includes two other activities, also from the book *National Educational Technology Standards for Students: Connecting Curriculum and Technology*.

Million- (Billion-)Dollar Project. Students are given the task of spending $1 million (or $1 billion). The way in which students spend their money is determined by the theme for the unit, such as improving the nation or the world, creating an ideal world, or taking a fantasy trip. Final projects include a spreadsheet of expenses, a narrative description including lessons learned, a chart of how money was spent, and a graphic or class presentation of purchases and rationale. This project was modified to spending a *billion* dollars to give fifth-grade students a connection with the terms being used in the media to describe the federal and state budget issues.

Bird Rap, a Web Guide to Local Birds. Students identify 20 or more local birds by collecting data on their behavior, shape, size, song, color habitat, and food requirements. Students produce a database of birds as well as a Web page to share their work with the community. This project is often modified to identify other wildlife in the region.

The student entries in the portfolio address the standards and performance indicators listed below. Notes that could not be reflected in the portfolio are made on other ways of collecting information during the activity.

The specific tasks listed in the matrix may produce a portfolio that will be used primarily for NETS•S technology assessment, but these tasks may also form part of a larger portfolio aligned with academic-content-area standards. The matrix provides a way for students, parents, and teachers to ensure that the standards have been assessed, and assessed in context.

FIGURE 11.2

Example NETS•S Portfolio Matrix for Grades 3–5

These lessons were taken from *National Educational Technology Standards for Students: Connecting Curriculum and Technology* (International Society for Technology in Education, 2000a).

STANDARDS AND PERFORMANCE INDICATORS*	ENGLISH LANGUAGE ARTS "You Were There!" Videotape	ENGLISH LANGUAGE ARTS "You Were There!" News Article	MATHEMATICS Million- (Billion-) Dollar Project	SCIENCE Bird Rap— A Web Guide to Local Birds
1. BASIC OPERATIONS AND CONCEPTS				
• Nature and operations of technology systems	observe video use	observe computer use	observe	observe
• Proficient in use of technology	video, word processing	word processing	spreadsheet, graphics	database, Web page
2. SOCIAL, ETHICAL, AND HUMAN ISSUES				
• Ethical, cultural, and societal issues	varies	varies	varies	varies
• Responsible use of technology and information	varies	varies	varies	varies
• Positive attitude supporting learning	observe	observe	observe	observe
3. TECHNOLOGY PRODUCTIVITY TOOLS				
• Enhance learning, productivity, and creativity	varies	varies	varies	varies
• Collaborate to create models, publications, etc.	observation and reflection	observation and reflection	can be if collaborative	database, Web page
4. TECHNOLOGY COMMUNICATIONS TOOLS				
• Use telecommunications	NA	if extension activity used	varies	varies
• Variety of media to inform other audiences	presentation	presentation	presentation	Web
5. TECHNOLOGY RESEARCH TOOLS				
• Locate, evaluate, collect information	varies	varies	varies	varies
• Process data and report results	NA	optional	varies	varies
• Locate, evaluate new info sources for tasks	varies	varies	varies	varies
6. TECHNOLOGY PROBLEM-SOLVING AND DECISION-MAKING TOOLS				
• Solving problems and making decisions	observe	observe	observation and reflection	observation and reflection
• Develop strategies to solve real world problems	follow-up discussion	follow-up discussion	dependent on topic	varies

*Note: The language in the performance indicator column has been abbreviated to fit this chart.

FIGURE 11.3
"You Were There!" Lesson

You Were There!
English Language Arts
Intermediate Grades 3–5

Purpose
Students read for point of view (POV) as they study a historical fiction novel, original source documents, and other sources of information. Students produce both a written and visual account of an event that advances their own point of view.

Description
Note: Although the novel selected for this lesson sequence is appropriate for the fifth grade, consider examining the technology-related options to revise the sequence to fit a grade-designated core literature selection.

Using literature to enhance social studies units by adding personal stories is a way to hook students into understanding the point of view of people of a particular time. Students read about the Boston Massacre through the historical fiction novel *My Brother Sam Is Dead* by James and Christopher Collier, factual texts, and other documents related to the event. Students enjoy visiting Web sites to view actual documents from the period. After evaluating, analyzing, and synthesizing the information in the documents and sites, students (1) write an article for publication in a classroom political newspaper; (2) produce a multimedia eulogy for one of the Boston Massacre victims; and (3) develop and present a group video "on-the-scene" report of the Boston Massacre.

Activities

	ENGLISH LANGUAGE ARTS STANDARDS	NETS PERFORMANCE INDICATORS GRADES 3–5
① Begin this activity by reading together Chapter 1 in *My Brother Sam Is Dead* and discussing the characters' POV.	ELA 1, 6, 7, 8, 9, 11	1, 2, 3, 4
② Assign or allow students to select a specific point of view of the incident. Investigate other accounts and documents at predetermined Web sites using each team's assigned POV.	ELA 2, 3, 7, 8	3, 6, 9, 10
③ Teams produce on-the-scene video accounts of the Boston Massacre. Either the "RBC" (Redcoat Broadcasting Company) or the "LTBC" (Liberty Tree Broadcasting Company) sponsors each group. As chair of the editorial review board, join board members (selected students) to screen all videos. The account should be from the POV of the reporter who represents the view selected for the group.	ELA 4, 5, 6, 8, 9, 11, 12	1, 4, 5, 9, 10
④ Have individual or groups of students produce a word-processed newspaper article that supports their political POV. Articles are to be published in one of two class newspapers: *Redcoat Daily Gazette* or *Liberty Tree Press*. The editorial review board will screen all articles.	ELA 4, 5, 6, 12	4, 5
⑤ Students each draw the name of a massacre victim. Using multimedia software (e.g., HyperStudio, PowerPoint, or mPower), students develop several testimonials for their victim from the perspective of survivors who knew the victim well. Each stack should include the following: the victim's name, date of birth and death, image of the grave site (actual or student-visualized and -generated), drawing of the victim, and voice or text testimonials. At least one of the testimonials should be written from the POV of a surviving female (e.g., wife, sister, aunt) to help clarify the role of women in this event. The presentations can be part of a parent evening, shared with another classroom, or shared over the Internet with other students. (The violent nature of the deaths may be a concern to some students. The activity, however, should keep the focus on the humanness of each victim rather than how they died. The activity does involve violence, but when students see the victims as human beings like themselves and not as statistics, they are more likely to see violence for what it really is and less likely to glorify it.)	ELA 4, 5, 6, 8, 12	1, 4, 5, 6, 9

Examples of researched information:

(1) Mr. Samuel Gray, killed on the spot by a ball entering his head; (2) Crispus Attucks, a mulatto, killed on the spot, two balls entering his breast; (3) Mr. James Caldwell, killed on the spot, by two balls entering his back; (4) Mr. Samuel Maverick, a youth of 17 years of age, mortally wounded; he died the next morning.

	ENGLISH LANGUAGE ARTS STANDARDS	NETS PERFORMANCE INDICATORS GRADES 3–5
⑥ Team members present their final products to various audiences (entire class, cross-grade-level classes, parents, interested community members).	ELA 4, 8, 11, 12	
⑦ Consider the following extensions:		
▶ E-mail with a class in the Boston area	ELA 8	
▶ Create a digital walking tour of grave sites	ELA 4, 7, 8	
▶ Do grave rubbings (be sure to get permission)		
▶ Create a market to exchange products	ELA 7	
▶ Write a song to a popular tune that tells the "real" story of the Boston Massacre	ELA 7	

Students can use a matrix such as the one in Figure 11.2 to write reflections on how they've progressed in meeting the technology standards since their most recent portfolio assessment.

For each activity, a unique rubric should be provided that assesses the product on the basis of both academic content standards and the NETS•S. For the activity in Figure 11.3, a rubric was created. It appears in chapter 4 (figure 4.2). Note that the activity is assessed using multiple dimensions. The language in the rubric makes the assessment criteria transparent to students and parents.

CASE STUDY: HENRICO COUNTY SCHOOLS

The Henrico County Schools district in Virginia uses a hybrid assessment model that includes both a checklist and a portfolio of student work. The checklist consists of a list of skills that are assessed using both observational data and the products collected in student portfolios. Each student keeps a technology assessment portfolio throughout the year as a formative assessment tool. At the end of the academic year, teachers assist students in selecting only those work samples that best reflect the NETS•S. These artifacts, as well as each grade-level checklist, become a part of each student's permanent portfolio, traveling with the student across grades as an ongoing benchmark of progress.

Figure 11.4 shows the checklist of technology skills that students are expected to demonstrate by the end of the fifth grade. Figure 11.5 shows the technology scope and sequence chart from which artifacts for the portfolio are drawn. While the list includes many of the skills covered in the NETS•S performance profiles up to Grade 5, not all the standards are represented in this version of the portfolio. In addition, there doesn't appear to be any student reflection on individual artifacts or overall progress made.

The Henrico model, which bases assessment on student work collected in a portfolio, provides real-world evidence of student performance on specific technology tasks. The richness of information contained in the student work samples will allow teachers in subsequent grades to look at how the student has gained skill and knowledge in using technology over time and in context. For example, students might demonstrate how they've developed both their writing skills and their use of technology by including multiple versions of a research paper in their portfolios, from minimally formatted rough draft to professionally formatted final document.

USING PORTFOLIOS FOR NETS•S ASSESSMENT

Ideally, effective portfolio assessment of the NETS•S focuses on a student's development and growth over time, with the portfolio examined at certain benchmarks to demonstrate skills and knowledge obtained in the process of learning. In a standards-based portfolio keyed to the NETS•S, students collect artifacts that best demonstrate how they've met the standards, with accompanying reflections that justify their choices and document their learning. Like observational assessments (discussed in chapter 10), portfolios can demonstrate multiple

FIGURE 11.4
Checklist of Skills for Grade 5

Grade Five

✓ Indicates Mastery

Word Processing	Database	Spreadsheet
_____ Type a 1-2 page document.	_____ Create a database with a minimum of five fields and five records.	_____ Create a spreadsheet.
_____ Edit using a spell check and thesaurus.		_____ Create a chart using the spreadsheet data.
_____ Insert a minimum of two graphics into the document.	_____ Insert a header.	_____ Add a title to the chart.
_____ Create and center a title.	_____ Rearrange information by using the sort feature.	_____ Enter formulas to calculate data.
_____ Insert a header and footer.	_____ Create and use one or more searches to locate information.	_____ Save and **print** a copy of the spreadsheet and chart.
_____ Save and **print** the document.	_____ **Print** a copy of a database sorted by a selected field.	

Keyboarding

_____ Type 20 words per minute with no errors.

_____ Complete and **print** a one-minute timed typing test at the end of the year using selected text.

Multimedia (Select one)

HyperStudio Stack (minimum of eight cards):	iMovie
_____ Include text boxes, buttons, and transitions.	_____ Import video clips and/or still images from multiple sources (camera, Internet, CD, or clip art).
_____ Operate a peripheral device (digital camera or scanner), save images to a folder, and import one or more images.	_____ Create an opening and closing title.
_____ Add graphics from a variety of sources (Internet, CDs, or other software).	_____ Import one or more sound clips.
	_____ Add transitions between clips.
_____ Save and **print** one page of the final project (two or four cards per page).	_____ **Present** the final project to the class.

Information Acquisition

_____ Use electronic encyclopedias, almanacs, indexes, and catalogs to obtain information on a selected topic.

_____ Use appropriate search engines and keywords to search the Internet for information on a selected topic.

_____ Determine the appropriateness and reliability of information obtained from the Internet.

_____ Use CDs and online databases to obtain information on a selected topic.

_____ **Print** a copy of a final research project. Include a bibliography with a minimum of two electronic sources.

Teacher's Signature _____ Date _____

dimensions of student skills and provide compelling, concrete evidence of student attainment of the standards. Portfolios can also be used to measure certain NETS•S, particularly those involved with higher-order thinking skills, that would be difficult to measure using other assessment techniques.

While portfolios are particularly good at demonstrating a student's contextualized knowledge of technology, educators face significant challenges when they try to scale portfolio assessments for use beyond the classroom. If used widely to make comparisons among students in different classes or schools across a district, portfolios face the same major difficulty as observational assessments: how to rate or score assessment material, in this case portfolio artifacts and reflections, in a way that's both objective and consistent. The fact that portfolios can contain a wide range of diverse artifacts, which is what makes them so useful as a record

FIGURE 11.5

K–5 Technology Scope and Sequence Chart

K-5 Technology Scope and Sequence   I = Introduce   M = Master   E = Extend

Objective	KG	One	Two	Three	Four	Five
BASIC CONCEPTS						
Identify the major parts of a computer and peripheral devices: CPU/ hard drive/computer, keyboard and mouse, monitor, disk drive, printer, CD ROM player.	I-M	E	E	E	E	E
Identify desktop icons (hard drive, disk, file server, trash can).	I-M	E	E	E	E	E
Develop technology vocabulary appropriate to grade level.	I/M	I/M	I/M	I/M	I/M	I/M
Demonstrate the safe handling of a disk and CD.	I/M	E	E	E	E	E
Demonstrate the proper use of special keys (return, escape, delete, spacebar, arrows, caps lock, enter, and shift).	I/M	E	E	E	E	E
Utilize the mouse to move and point to a designated location; point and click; point and double click; press and drag; and select options from the menu bar.	I/M	E	E	E	E	E
Select, open and quit programs.	I/M	E	E	E	E	E
Print a document.	I/M	E	E	E	E	E
Start, restart, and shut down computers properly, open and close windows, use the scroll bar.		I/M	E	E	E	E
Explain what a computer is and its basic capabilities.		I	M	E	E	E
Move and resize windows.			I/M	E	E	E
Apply technologies to strategies for problem solving and critical thinking.				I	M	E
Select and use technology appropriate to tasks.				I	M	E
KEYBOARDING						
Type a minimum of 10 wpm with no errors as demonstrated on a timed typing test.					I/M	
Type a minimum of 15 wpm with no errors as demonstrated on a timed typing test.					M	
Type a minimum of 20 wpm with no errors as demonstrated on a timed typing test.						M
COMMUNICATIONS						
WORD PROCESSING						
Use a word processing program to:						
Create, name, save, and print documents which include text and graphics.		I/M	E	E	E	E
Insert and delete text.		I/M	E	E	E	E
Modify font, style and size of text.		I/M	E	E	E	E
Edit work using a spelling checker; center the title of a document; highlight text to modify and delete.			I/M	E	E	E
Cut, copy, and paste text and graphics; edit text using a thesaurus.				I/M	E	E
Import graphics from a variety of sources (scanned images, digital camera pictures, internet graphics, CD resource discs).					I/M	E
Resize and crop graphics; use tab, margin and alignment settings in text.					I/M	E
Cut, copy, and paste text and graphics between two documents.						I/M
Create headers and footers.						I/M
Use the "save as" feature to create new versions of documents.						I/M
Create a 1-2 page document using word processing skills, writing process steps, and publishing programs.					I/M	E
Save documents in a personal folder on the file server.				I/M	E	E
DATABASE						
Define a database as a collection of information with two or more categories.		I/M	E	E	E	E
Explain the purposes of a database.			I/M	E	E	E
Add data to an existing database.		I/M	E	E	E	E
Participate in database sorting activities.		I/M	E			
Use a database to locate information.				I/M	E	E
Create a database; sort records in a database.				I/M	E	E
Filter records in a database.					I/M	E
SPREADSHEET						
Identify the parts of a spreadsheet; explain the purposes of a spreadsheet (charting and calculating).				I/M	E	E
Create a simple spreadsheet; create a chart (graph) from a spreadsheet.				I/M	E	E
Enter a simple formula to calculate information in a spreadsheet.					I/M	E
INFORMATION ACQUISITION AND MANIPULATION / MULTIMEDIA						
Use a variety of multimedia programs.		I/M	E	E	E	E
Participate in the creation of a multimedia class project.			I/M	E	E	E
Create a multimedia presentation with teacher assistance.				I/M	E	E
Create a multimedia presentation.					I/M	E
Operate a digital camera or other peripheral device.					I/M	E
Send and retrieve data on a local area network (county electronic mail).				I/M	E	E
Use electronic mail to participate in collaborative projects.		I/M	E	E	E	E
Use CDs and online databases for search and retrieval of information.		I/M	E	E	E	E
Determine the usefulness, appropriateness, and reliability of information.					I/M	E
Use Boolean logic as appropriate in keyword searching.					I/M	E
Use effective strategies to send and retrieve data on a wide area network (VaPen, Internet).					I	M	E
Use electronic encyclopedias, almanacs, indexes, and catalogs.					I	M	E
Describe advantages and disadvantages of various computer processing, storage, retrieval, and transmission techniques.					I/M	E

of an individual student's learning, further increases the challenge of using portfolios for comparative assessment purposes.

Despite these challenges, portfolios remain an attractive option for broader assessment projects that go beyond measuring the progress of individual students. If portfolio assessment is to be used as the basis for making comparisons among students, classrooms, or schools, all the elements of a professional assessment project that we've discussed in previous chapters—standards, documentation of assessment content and structure, careful construction of scoring rubrics, training of raters to ensure consistent scoring, and so forth—must be in place for the assessment to yield valid, reliable results.

References

Fogerty, R. (1998). *Balanced assessment.* Arlington Heights, IL: Skylight Professional Development.

International Society for Technology in Education. (2000a). *National educational technology standards for students: Connecting curriculum and technology.* Eugene, OR: Author.

International Society for Technology in Education. (2000b). "You were there!" In *National educational technology standards for students: Connecting curriculum and technology.* Eugene, OR: Author.

International Society for Technology in Education. (2003). *National educational technology standards for teachers: Resources for assessment.* Eugene, OR: Author.

CHAPTER 12

Automated Assessments

Both the No Child Left Behind (NCLB) legislation (Cradler & Cradler, 2002) and the National Educational Technology Plan (U.S. Department of Education, 2004) specify goals for nationwide computer literacy skills. Most states have now either adopted the NETS•S or adapted them to create their own technology standards and support the development of a technology-teaching curriculum. Few, however, have designed a statewide assessment program to demonstrate progress on these national goals.

To provide the kind of accountability data required by NCLB—for technology literacy as well as for all the core academic content areas—individual districts and states are now faced with the challenge of developing or choosing assessments that can be efficiently implemented on a district- or statewide scale. Automated assessments—assessment instruments that are delivered and scored by stand-alone computers, over a network, or through the Internet—offer planners a number of advantages for doing assessments on a large scale.

Businesses and schools, especially the employment industry and higher education, have used automated testing for years to assess core computer skills. Automated assessments offer consistent test delivery and immediate data reporting as well as flexibility in format and design. In many cases, the technology for delivering these assessments is fairly mature. However, automated technology testing used at the K–12 level to deliver high-stakes assessment has yet to be used on the same wide scale as state-mandated exams in subjects such as English and math.

Automated assessments can be used to measure a wide range of competencies in computer and technology literacy. All the test item types described in chapter 7 can be delivered on a computer, including performance-based items that incorporate interactive simulations, concurrent applications, and similar technologies. The ability to deliver these performance-based items to large groups of students and score them automatically makes automated assessments a particularly promising option for assessing those NETS•S performance indicators that focus on objectively measurable knowledge and skills. They can be delivered and scored as easily and efficiently as standard linear assessments.

This chapter explores some of the types of automated assessments that have been developed in recent years and addresses implementation issues that should be considered when planning or choosing automated assessments for a particular testing program.

AUTOMATING LINEAR ASSESSMENTS

As noted in chapters 7 and 8, well-constructed linear test items are an excellent way to measure knowledge-based objectives. They can also be used to measure objectives related to problem solving or other higher-order elements of the NETS•S. A variety of inexpensive and easy-to-use software tools are available for automating linear item construction. These tools allow you to create linear test items by inputting the elements of a question—question stem, distracters, and correct answer—into the appropriate fields in an on-screen form. When delivered to students, the questions are displayed on a computer screen or Web page in a way that makes it easy for your students to answer the test items and navigate between questions.

In addition to allowing for easy creation of familiar linear test item types, such as multiple-choice or multiple-response, test automation tools provide ways to automate complex linear items, such as those illustrated in Figures 12.1 and 12.2.

Figure 12.1 shows a matching item being created with the SkillCheck ItemWriter tool. This tool allows test developers to add graphics to drag-and-drop matching items. In this item, test takers are asked to match images of common hardware items with typical specifications for that hardware, such as Monitor—300 dpi and Processor—500 MHz.

Figure 12.2 shows a "click area" item being created using the assessment module of Blackboard's classroom automation suite. In this case, the item requires a student to click on a specified part of the map to get the question correct. This demonstrates a type of item that might be difficult to implement in a pencil-and-paper format.

FIGURE 12.1.

An Automated Drag-and-Drop Matching Item

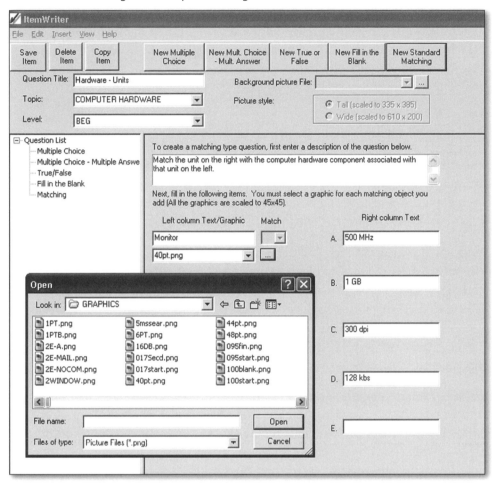

FIGURE 12.2

An Automated "Click Area" Item

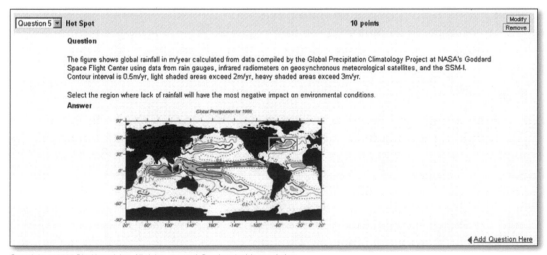

Linear test items delivered in either pencil-and-paper or automated formats can include exhibits such as reading passages and graphics to enhance a question. Automated assessments can also make use of more complex exhibits, such as movies and animations, to create rich contexts for standard linear test items. The addition of media can significantly enhance the context of the NETS•S assessment, allowing students to more readily provide responses that demonstrate their knowledge, skills, and understanding.

AUTOMATING PERFORMANCE-BASED TESTS

Chapters 10 and 11 focused on the use of classroom observations and portfolios to assess student performance in real-world classroom environments. These types of performance assessments are ideal when assessing complex abilities such as collaboration and problem solving, which are best measured in the context of classroom learning.

At the same time, a wide variety of specific skills, such as the ability to use word processing, database, or spreadsheet software to perform discrete tasks, can be objectively measured using automated performance-based assessment questions. Performance-based test items are particularly helpful in assessing the skills needed to meet particular performance indicators for NETS•S 3, such as "Students use technology tools to enhance learning, increase productivity, and promote creativity," and NETS•S 4, such as "Students use telecommunications to collaborate, publish, and interact with peers, experts, and other audiences."

A performance-based test item might measure the skill aspects of NETS•S 3 by first placing students into a real software program, perhaps WordPerfect or Microsoft Word, or a simulation of such a word processor. Students then might be asked to perform one or more functions, such as saving a document, setting margins, or printing. The students' ability to perform the function as specified would determine whether they've answered the question correctly or incorrectly. Similarly, performance-based items can be used to determine if a student knows how to use such communication tools as an e-mail program (NETS•S 4) or a Web browser (NETS•S 5).

As you look at automated performance assessments, keep in mind that you can use automated assessment tools in several ways to measure software skills. The two most common methods are known as *concurrent testing* and *simulation-based testing*.

Concurrent Testing

Testing within a live software program application, known as concurrent testing, uses software tools to control the application and measure what students do when interacting with the software program. Figure 12.3 shows an example of this type of test item. Here, a Microsoft Office Specialist test question—in this case, to test editing of a business document—is being delivered in a concurrent environment.

Concurrent test items place your students inside the software and provide instructions to perform a specified set of operations. Because students are inside a real software application, they have access to all of the software program features and can try different commands and

FIGURE 12.3

Sample of a Concurrent Test Item

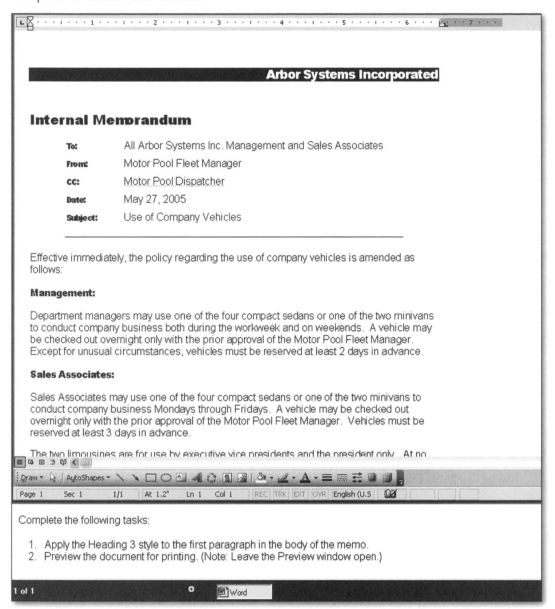

even use online help before submitting a final answer. The concurrent testing program either monitors the user's activity to see if the correct commands have been given or reviews the final state of the application to determine if the task has been performed correctly or incorrectly.

Simulation-Based Testing

Simulation-based test items look and feel much like concurrent items, since they ask students to perform specific tasks or functions in a software application environment. While in this case the application is only simulated, it still requires students to select from menu options and use toolbar buttons or keyboard commands to perform the specified operation, as shown in Figure 12.4.

Figure 12.4 illustrates a Course Technology SAM (Skill Assessment Manager) test question being delivered in a simulated software application environment. The level of functionality in a simulation-based item will vary depending on how much of the application has been simulated. Some simulations may ask a student to perform only a single step in a process (using a question such as "Give the command that will allow you to change margins"). Others, like the one shown above, are based on more complete simulations that provide multiple routes to the correct answer. They ask a student to perform a complete task from beginning to end.

FIGURE 12.4
Sample of a Simulation-Based Test Item

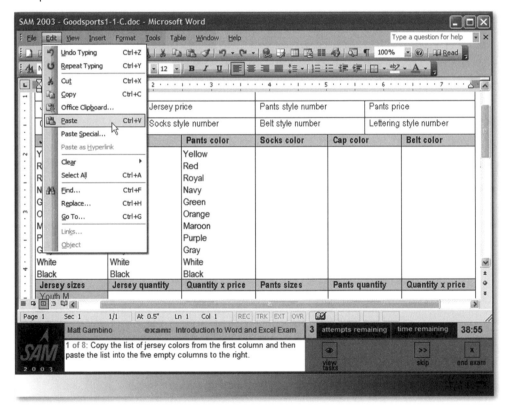

Some simulation-based testing products go further in trying to emulate the real software application, providing access to simulations of both correct and incorrect answers and even access to online help when answering a question.

Concurrent versus Simulation-based Testing

Both concurrent and simulation-based testing have advantages and disadvantages. Because concurrent testing uses the real software application, it provides access to all the features and functionality of the software product. However, developers of concurrent tests are often limited in the kinds of questions they can ask based on what elements of an application can be controlled or monitored.

Concurrent tests also require that each user have access to the application being tested, which can add expense to a testing program and introduce issues of stability and scaling when running a concurrent test on a network or other large-scale deployment. Developing concurrent assessments for software applications that must have access to outside resources, such as an e-mail program or a Web browser that interacts with networks or the Internet, or that must access critical files on a local computer, such as a computer operating system, adds another layer of complexity and potential limitation to concurrent testing.

Unlike a concurrent test that runs one or more control or monitoring programs on top of the software application being tested, a simulation-based test will usually run a single program, the simulation engine, which allows for greater stability and scaling potential. Simulation-based products also represent a safe way to test skills on software applications that are difficult to secure or control, such as operating systems, network tools, e-mail, and Web browsing programs.

However, simulation-based test items provide only the level of fidelity to the real software application that the test developer has chosen when programming the items. For example, in a concurrent test, both correct or incorrect answers may lead to a response from the program, such as a dialog box appearing. In a simulation test, on the other hand, nothing may happen unless and until the student performs the correct operation to answer the question. If the student takes a wrong step, the simulation either may not respond or may end. It's difficult for a test developer to incorporate into the simulation every possible method your students might try, especially the more creative, indirect routes.

Research has shown that performance-based testing using both concurrent and simulation technology can be used to create highly reliable test items with excellent performance statistics. The decision to either use one technology over the other or a combination of both should be based on practical considerations, such as the availability of products for the assessment goals you have in mind. Implementation and deployment issues—cost, scaling, and the ability to work with your school's existing technology infrastructure—also need to be considered.

DEVELOPING PERFORMANCE-BASED ASSESSMENTS

The automation of linear test items can be carried out by individual educators filling out simple forms in an online item-development tool. But performance-based items—based on either concurrent or simulation technology—require development efforts by programmers specializing in performance-based testing. Unless you're willing to undertake a significant development project to create your own concurrent or simulation-based test, the use of commercial, third-party products that provide access to performance-based test content is usually necessary.

Points to consider when reviewing commercial performance-based testing products include:

- How well do the test items resemble the real-world applications, features, and situations being tested? How much effort has gone into giving students access to all correct answers, including both the most direct method as well as indirect methods for performing a specific function?

- Does the test cover all the objectives necessary to meet your assessment requirements? Do you have the ability to change questions included in a test or to customize the test in other ways, such as incorporating your own questions?

- Can the technology behind the test be supported in your testing environment? Does your computer lab have enough copies of a software product to consider concurrent testing? Will a simulation-based testing product run on your school network? How fast does the product perform when running over the network or the Internet in your lab?

TEST DEPLOYMENT AND SCALING

Once a test has been created or purchased, it needs to be able to perform on one or more of the following platforms:

- stand-alone computers
- computer networks
- the Internet

Delivery of performance-based content involves either running and controlling a live software application (concurrent testing) or running a simulation engine that may use numerous graphics or large amounts of data to display a simulation of an application on screen. While the technology to deliver performance-based testing items on stand-alone computers has been available for many years, some products face performance issues, even when running on moderately sized networks in school classrooms or computer labs. If a simulation-based test item, however well-programmed, runs too slowly on a student's computer, the test item may not seem "real" to the student or might frustrate a student trying to answer as many questions as possible during a timed test.

Running a performance-based test over the Internet may pose quite a few technical problems, both for users and test developers. For example, the need for access to adequate bandwidth to run a performance-based test over the Web can present a significant challenge in a computer lab or classroom that may have dozens of computers sharing a single access line to the Internet.

Developers of performance-based tests have turned to a variety of technologies to allow complex content to run over the Internet with adequate performance, including

- programming languages or frameworks, such as Java or Microsoft .NET, that provide capabilities beyond standard HTML for creating interactive tests that run over the Internet

- multimedia authoring systems, such as Macromedia Authorware or Flash, that provide development capabilities for creating interactive testing content

- thin-client systems that effectively create a virtual computer within a Web browser capable of running high-quality testing applications at acceptable performance and speed

These technologies have been used for years to provide Internet-delivered performance-based testing for business environments. Schools, however, face unique challenges in implementing Internet-based testing, notably the need to have many students taking the same test at the same time. Even in testing situations that don't involve complex test items, access to hardware can be a limiting factor in trying to implement automated versions of standardized tests. This is why most high-stakes NCLB-inspired tests are still delivered on paper. Online performance-based tests that may require large amounts of Internet bandwidth are also susceptible to hardware and connectivity limitations.

Some performance-based testing products solve this problem by taking a "hybrid" approach to test deployment. Such hybrid products may install the test on a stand-alone computer, allowing all the processing power of that computer to be used to run the complex test content instead of streaming the content over a network or the Internet. Once a test is completed, test scores and student information are uploaded to a centralized database. By storing important, dynamic information—such as student registration and test scores—centrally on a network or Internet database, the test itself can be installed on local computers on the school's network, erased, and installed again as needed.

OTHER CONSIDERATIONS

Data Consolidation and Reporting

If you're considering launching a large-scale assessment project, such as a district- or statewide assessment, it's important to have the ability to store scores centrally for easier consolidation and analysis of information. This also permits you to produce the customized reports often requested by teachers, schools, districts, and states to support planning and improve student achievement. While locally delivered software-based assessments are adequate for classroom or even school-level test deployment, the larger the project, the greater the need for a testing system that makes use of networks or the Internet for score centralization and report generation.

Timing and Scheduling

You often hear the phrase "testing window," a reference to the time allotted by the district or state for administering large-scale assessments. This window can be anywhere from a few days to an entire month or more, depending on the type of assessment and how the test is being deployed. To minimize some of the hardware and bandwidth resource issues mentioned earlier, some schools have used assessment models that don't require all students to take the same test at the same time. This can include "on demand" testing, in which students can take a test at any time, or "sequencing" test schedules, so that different classrooms, schools, or districts take the test at different times. Building multiple equivalent test forms for a testing program can provide enough variety to ensure that test integrity is not compromised by exam overexposure.

Security

Performance-based testing programs provide another means of protecting exam security within a flexible exam-scheduling environment. Unlike a linear exam that can be severely compromised if the questions in the exam are revealed before everyone has had the chance to take a test, performance-based exams require students to be able to perform specific functions correctly. Thus, cheating on a performance-based exam would still require students to learn and understand the objectives of the exam to successfully answer test questions, even if those questions have been exposed to the public before a testing program is completed. Randomizing test questions is another way to ensure that each student's testing experience is slightly different, minimizing the opportunity for item memorization and cheating.

As with any automated assessment project, several factors—convenience of test delivery, convenience of scoring, availability of computer hardware and connectivity, and test security considerations—have to be carefully weighed and balanced to ensure that a technology assessment program can be practically and successfully implemented.

DYNAMIC TESTING METHODS

Computer- or Internet-based testing, whether linear or performance-based, or both, can be used to deliver dynamic assessments that aren't possible with a pencil-and-paper format.

For example, adaptive testing is a type of assessment that automatically adapts to the skill level of the user. This type of test quickly pinpoints a user's skill level by presenting a more difficult question whenever the user answers a question correctly, and presenting an easier question whenever a question is answered incorrectly. The dynamic nature of adaptive testing means it can only be performed by an automated assessment.

While adaptive testing has been used successfully for many years in programs such as CompTIA's A+ certification, the technology depends on complex models based on Item Response Theory (IRT) that require a significant amount of data and professional analysis to be used successfully. While statewide educational exams generate more than enough data to create adaptive tests based on IRT principles, this technique has yet to be widely used in education. This is due, in part, to the perception that it's unfair to compare the scores of students who may have answered different test questions during the course of an assessment.

While advanced, dynamic testing models, such as adaptive testing, offer promise for creating accurate, efficient assessments in a variety of subjects, such options need to be reviewed in the context of all the goals and requirements of an institution's testing program.

CASE STUDY: NORTH CAROLINA TECHNOLOGY ASSESSMENT PROGRAM

North Carolina has led the nation in setting and assessing standards for computer and technology literacy. In May 1991 the State Board of Education established computer proficiency as a requirement for graduation from North Carolina high schools. In June 1992, the board approved a computer and technology skills curriculum that defined grade-level competencies for Grades K–12.

An assessment based on this curriculum was administered to eighth-grade students in the 1995–96 school year as a local option. Since 1996, all eighth-grade students have been required to pass the computer skills test before high school graduation. Students first take the test in eighth grade, but they may repeat the test at least once per year until the proficiency requirement is met. In North Carolina, technology literacy is viewed as a "new basic skill," and the proficiency requirement is designed to ensure that students have sufficient computer skills for use in high school, at home, and in the workplace.

The computer and technology skills curriculum was revised in 1998, and students who entered the eighth grade in 2000 were required to demonstrate proficiency based on the revised curriculum. Results from the eighth-grade computer skills test were added to the performance composite in the statewide accountability system beginning in the 2000–01 school year. However, North Carolina does not include computer skills proficiency in its calculations of adequate yearly progress.

The computer skills curriculum was revised again in 2004 to clarify the competencies for Grades K–12, as well as to reflect current technologies and incorporate future technological developments. The 2004 revision also aligned the computer and technology skills curriculum to the NETS for Students. Although the North Carolina computer skills curriculum and assessment program have evolved since 1991, the three main competency goals have remained unchanged.

> **Competency Goal 1.** The learner will understand important issues of a technology-based society and will exhibit ethical behavior in the use of computer and other technologies.
>
> **Competency Goal 2.** The learner will demonstrate knowledge and skills in the use of computer and other technologies.
>
> **Competency Goal 3.** The learner will use a variety of technologies to access, analyze, interpret, synthesize, and communicate information.

North Carolina takes the view that these competencies should be integrated with the core curriculum because computer and technology skills enable students to improve and enhance their learning of other basic skills, particularly reading and mathematics. The state recommends that classroom teachers, technology specialists, and media specialists collaboratively introduce the computer and technology skills curriculum at each grade level. The goal is for students to develop computer and technology skills over time in all content areas so that they'll be equipped for lifelong learning as critical seekers and synthesizers of information and as effective communicators and problem solvers.

Assessment Design

North Carolina's computer and technology skills curriculum and testing standards are based on six "strands":

- societal and ethical issues
- database
- spreadsheet
- keyboard use, word processing, and desktop publishing
- multimedia and presentation
- telecommunications and the Internet

The state has developed a 70-item, pencil-and-paper, multiple-choice test to assess all six strands. It's designed to take 90 minutes to complete, although students are to be given sufficient time to complete the test and schools are urged to adjust scheduled testing times if necessary. The assessment also includes a performance-based component that requires students to create or modify documents or other types of files using application software. Artifacts generated during this part of the test, such as printouts of word processing documents created by following a list of instructions, are provided to human graders for manual scoring.

Scoring the Assessment

The multiple-choice part of the computer skills test is scored and aggregated by school districts, and the results are reported to the State Board of Education. The performance tests are scored by a contractor the board selects through a competitive bidding process. Students must print their responses to performance items, and these are sent to the contractor. The contractor scores the performance tests using rubrics developed by the board of education and reports scores to the board and the school districts.

The 70 multiple-choice items are scored by computer, giving 0 for an incorrect answer or 1 for a correct answer. Correct responses are added together to produce a raw score (the total number of questions answered correctly). The raw score is then converted to a scale score by the school district based on instructions provided by the state board. Scores for individual students are reported on a scale ranging from 20 to 80. The passing score for the computer skills multiple-choice test is a scale score of 47 or higher. If a student fails the multiple-choice test by 1 point, the test is graded by hand to ensure accuracy.

Each performance item is scored by at least two scorers, using a rubric provided by the state board. The rubrics produce a raw score that may range from 0 to 4 for each performance item. The raw scores for each of the three parts of the performance test are then added together to create an overall, weighted raw score for the test. The contractor then converts the overall raw score to a final scale score based on instructions provided by the state board. This score

INTEGRATING AUTOMATED ASSESSMENTS

Nancy Goth moved from training adults in computer technology to teaching in the Computer Internet Technology program at the Middle Bucks Institute of Technology, a career and technical high school in Jamison, Pennsylvania. In her new role, she discovered her high school students were struggling with subjects such as relational databases that her adult students grasped far more quickly. Said Goth: "For 20 years, I worked in industry, where my duties included training coworkers in computer applications. It amazed and discouraged me from the very beginning that a subject I personally found fascinating and critically important in the work place completely frustrated my high school students. Adult students seemed to grasp instruction on relational databases almost immediately and eagerly began the process of application. What was going on in my high school classroom?"

Goth suspected that her adult students' ability to put such applications as databases immediately into practice to accomplish job-related functions was what was missing from her high-school students' experience. She was pursuing a master's degree in applied technology at the time and decided to study this problem for her thesis.

The study began with traditional tutorial-based teaching in relational database theory. To assess her students' ability after tutorial instruction, Goth used Course Technology's Skills Assessment Manager (SAM) software. SAM is an automated assessment program that allows teachers to create assessments using either the teacher's own test content or linear and performance-based assessment items that Course provides as part of the SAM product.

Goth created an assessment to measure her students' understanding of three principal areas of databases: database design, organizing data, and defining relationships. After obtaining assessment data from her students, she immediately immersed the same students in a problem-based learning unit so they could put their new knowledge into practice. Goth says, "Students were given raw data in the form of customer invoices, a company catalog, 3 months of an accounts receivable journal, and a list of questions regarding the current state of a fictitious business. They had to examine and find logical groupings in the data, design and build the database, and answer the questions—a process that would take the average student 3–4 weeks."

After exposing students to this real-world project that required the use of the relational database concepts they'd studied, Goth used the same SAM exam to measure the students' database skills. Goth reports that assessment indicated an increase in skill mastery in all three of the primary areas—defining relationships increased by 38.8%, organizing data by 6.4%, and database design by 8.4%. The overall increase was 22.2% across all relational database skill sets taught at the introductory level. "While I expected to see a rise in mastery," she says, "I was surprised and delighted at the increased levels I was able to measure."

The results of this study show the importance of incorporating real-world projects in the classroom, especially in areas such as relational databases where theory becomes far more understandable when put into the context of concrete experience. This study also demonstrates how automated assessments can be integrated into the learning process and help teachers and students put their learning into practice.

is then converted into the final scale score. Scores for individual students are reported on a scale ranging from 18 to 82. The passing score for the computer skills performance test is 49 or higher. If a student fails the performance test by 1 point, the test is scored by a third person to ensure accuracy.

To meet the graduation requirement for computer skills proficiency, students must pass both the multiple-choice test and the performance test. School districts must administer each test at least once per year, beginning in eighth grade. Students may take the tests as many as three times in one year by participating in test administrations in the fall, spring, and summer. If students pass one of the tests and fail the other, they're not required to retake the test they passed. High school seniors who have not passed either the multiple-choice or performance tests may have one additional opportunity during the last month of school prior to graduation. Students who do not graduate may retake the test until age 21.

Assessment Results

During the 2000–2001 school year, 75.9% of 8th-grade students passed both the multiple-choice and performance tests. Overall, 80.8% of 9th-grade students, 89.9% of 10th-grade students, 92.1% of 11th-grade students, and 92.5% of 12th-grade students had met the computer skills proficiency requirement by passing both the multiple-choice and performance tests.

Achievement gaps occurred among Hispanic (50.2%), black (60.2%), and American Indian (64.9%) 8th-grade students compared to 8th-graders who were multiracial (78.6%), Asian (80.2%), or white (85.0 %). However, these gaps were narrowed, and in some cases closed, by 12th grade. By 12th grade almost as many Hispanic (88.0%), black (88.3%), and American Indian (90.8%) students had met the computer proficiency requirement as students who were multiracial (91.8%), Asian (91.9%), or white (94.4%).

Achievement gaps also occurred among students with disabilities and limited English proficiency. Of 12,781 8th-grade students with disabilities, 42.0% met the computer proficiency requirement. Of 1,795 limited-English-proficiency 8th-grade students, 27.8% met the requirement. These gaps seemed to persist into 12th grade, where 76.6% of students with disabilities and 81.5% of limited-English-proficiency students met the computer skills proficiency requirement.

Students are asked to provide some background information when they take the computer skills test, and this data reveals some interesting trends. Female students have higher passing rates than male students: 80.2% to 71.% in 8th grade and 94.0% to 90.8% by 12th grade. Fewer students who use computers in a laboratory (73.3%) met the requirement than those who use computers in the media center or library (77.0%) or classrooms (78.2%). Students were also more likely to meet the computer skills requirement if they had access to computers outside of class (85.2% to 49.9%), indicating that the digital divide continues to be a serious consideration for school districts.

In addition to providing a benchmark that ensures students are graduating with adequate technology skills, the North Carolina assessment program has generated valuable data upon which to make decisions related to education technology across the state.

Into the Future

North Carolina continues to explore innovative ways to assess student technology competency. The state is developing an online computer skills test that will replace the existing paper-based linear assessment and the manually scored performance assessment. The online assessment will be enabled by a collection of small Java programs, called NCDesk (http://ncdesk.ncsu.edu/ncdesk/), which provide students the ability to answer performance-based questions within a simulation of common application software. Rather than simulate a specific software, such as Microsoft Word, the NCDesk assessments place students into a generic software environment to perform specified tasks. The generic environment may be word processing or spreadsheet software with common interface elements such as menus and icons.

The automated performance assessment capabilities provided by NCDesk holds promise for more accurately assessing the basic computer skills of students, including important NETS•S standards covering the legal and ethical use of technology. Because the automated performance assessment cannot examine collaborative work or complex student work, the North Carolina assessment program will continue to require observational and portfolio evidence to provide a more complete picture of student attainment of the NETS•S.

CASE STUDY: MICROSOFT ASSESSMENT
www.iste.org/resources/asmt/msiste/

With the assistance of a team of ISTE NETS collaborators, Microsoft developed a free online eighth-grade assessment designed to provide teachers and students immediate, formative feedback on students' ability to use common technology tools to address some of the NETS•S. The purpose is not to provide high-stakes, standardized data. Rather, the assessment is a criterion-referenced instrument that uses activities designed to measure progress in meeting the NETS•S outlined in Figure 12.5.

The Microsoft assessment is a concurrent test delivered over the Internet. The assessment consists of a series of activities designed to resemble real-world student projects. For example, an activity titled Day in My Life presents students with a spreadsheet outlining the various ways in which they may allocate their time during the day. The student is asked to analyze the information on the spreadsheet and create a presentation that communicates what they've learned and decided. Each task in the activity (performing a spreadsheet operation, creating a presentation file, and so forth) is a discrete objective, measurable by a performance-based test item. Figure 12.6 shows how the user works within the software application to accomplish the task.

Because the Microsoft assessment is not used for high-stakes purposes, students are provided feedback at the end of each question indicating whether they have answered it correctly or incorrectly. The student then has the opportunity to try the question again, allowing the test to be used as a basis for both assessment and learning.

The following blueprint for the Day in My Life assessment module illustrates the types of skills that can be assessed using this performance-based testing platform:

FIGURE 12.5

Microsoft Assessment for Eighth-Graders

ACTIVITY	TOPIC	STANDARDS CATEGORIES ADDRESSED
Business Letter	Word processing, e-mail	NETS•S 1, 3
A Day in My Life	Presentation, spreadsheet	NETS•S 1, 5
In the News	Word processing	NETS•S 1
Track Team	Word processing, database	NETS•S 1, 5
Olympic Runners	Word processing, spreadsheet	NETS•S 1
Olympic Champions	Presentation, spreadsheet	NETS•S 1, 6
What's the Weather	Web browser, spreadsheet	NETS•S 1, 6
Birthstones	Web browser, spreadsheet	NETS•S 1, 5
The Planets	Word processing	NETS•S 1, 3
The Nine Planets	Presentation	NETS•S 1
Skateboarding	Web page authoring	NETS•S 1, 3
Music Survey	Web page authoring	NETS•S 1, 5, 6

a. Assesses NETS•S 1, second item, and NETS•S 5, second item

b. Application Skills Assessed

    i. **Presentation**

        1. Enter text into a title slide

        2. Insert clip art into a slide

        3. Insert several different types of slides

        4. Change the size of a graphic

        5. Insert bulleted text into slides

        6. Select a background color and apply it to all slides

        7. Set the transition type

        8. Set the timer to automatically advance through slides

    ii. **Spreadsheet**

        1. Enter cell values

        2. Use the SUM function

        3. Use data to create pie graph

        4. Change font style in a graph

5. Change font size in a graph

6. Copy a graphic and paste it into a slide

As with other performance-based assessments designed to measure objective skills, such as the ability to use software products, the Microsoft assessment is best used to assess those NETS•S objectives that are skill-based and discrete. The use of live-application, concurrent testing delivered over the Internet provides teachers a unique way to include formative technology assessment into various parts of their curricula.

FIGURE 12.6
Microsoft Assessment

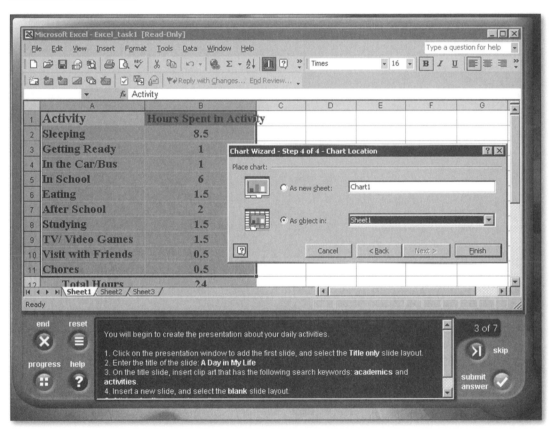

A VALUABLE OPTION

Automated assessment tools provide a way to easily create and deploy linear assessment items, from simple multiple-choice questions to complex items that include graphics, animation, and video. Automated assessments also provide a way to deploy performance-based test items to assess discrete skills. Thanks to their ability to present students with authentic tasks in which multiple ways to achieve the intended result occur, automated assessments hold great promise for assessing the NETS•S.

Automated assessments also represent a good option for districts and states looking for a high-volume, secure, and automatically scored assessment for high-stakes testing. Part 4 of this book provides three examples of how automated assessments have been used in unique ways to provide assessment on the district, state, and national levels. Each case study illustrates the content, development, validation, and deployment issues that go into any standardized assessment project that makes use of the automated assessment tools available today.

References

Cradler, J., & Cradler, R. (2002). NCLB poses challenges: New federal programs suggest an expanded role for technology. *Learning & Leading with Technology, 30*(2), 46–49, 56–57.

U.S. Department of Education, Office of Educational Technology. (2004). *Toward a new golden age in American education: How the internet, the law and today's students are revolutionizing expectations.* Washington, DC: U.S. Government Printing Office. Available: http://www. nationaledtechplan.org

PART 4

Large-Scale Assessment Initiatives

The greatest obstacle
even to discovery is not
ignorance—it is the illusion
of knowledge.

—K. P. GERLACH

In contrast to part 3, which focuses on classroom-level assessments that teachers can design and implement on their own, the chapters in this section focus on large-scale assessment initiatives at the district, state, and national levels. In each case, the assessment basics introduced in chapter 7 were used to formulate and develop the assessment plan.

Although none of the initiatives described in this section completely addresses all the NETS•S performance indicators, each covers a significant range of technology skills and knowledge. When coupled with other measures of technology performance, the data generated by these large-scale assessments can go a long way toward completing a student's performance profile.

CHAPTER SNAPSHOTS

CHAPTER 13
District Assessment Initiative— Chicago Public Schools

In 2003 Chicago Public Schools embarked on an initiative to provide individual, school, and district-wide data on what students know and are able to do with technology at the NCLB-mandated eighth-grade benchmark. This chapter describes in detail the planning and development of an automated technology assessment instrument and provides the results from the instrument's pilot test.

CHAPTER 14
State Assessment Initiative—Utah

Chapter 14 outlines the testing options offered to students in Utah schools as a way to opt out of the state-mandated technology course required for high school graduation. The chapter focuses on the creative use of IT certification exams for assessing student technology skills.

CHAPTER 15
National Assessment Initiative—Australia

Australia has set itself the challenge of creating an automated assessment that will benchmark the ICT literacy of Australian 6th- and 10th-grade students. The exam is being developed and will be used to provide evidence that students are meeting Australia's National Goals for Schooling in the Twenty-First Century.

CHAPTER 13

District Assessment Initiative—Chicago Public Schools

In 2003 the Chicago Public Schools (CPS) Office of eLearning initiated a project to assess technology literacy in eighth grade using funds from the district's Enhancing Education Through Technology (EETT) grant. The 5-year technology plan adopted by the state of Illinois for 2002–2007 incorporates the NETS in its state technology standards for students. Therefore, the district decided to base its technology literacy assessment on the NETS•S.

The goal of the eLearning project was to measure school and district progress in meeting the No Child Left Behind (NCLB) Act's eighth-grade technology literacy requirement. To achieve this goal, CPS determined that it would be necessary to compare the technology literacy of students in different schools in the district and to track changes in students' aggregate achievement in relation to the NETS. In addition, eLearning wanted to design an assessment that would support data-driven decision making in CPS's delivery of professional development and curriculum resources.

To ensure their assessment would meet high standards of validity and reliability, comply with the spirit of NCLB, and inform the district's use of EETT resources, CPS contracted with Learning Point Associates (LPA) to help them design the assessment. LPA is a nonprofit organization, founded in 1984 as the North Central Regional Educational Laboratory (NCREL). LPA assembled a team made up of experts in education technology content and in education measurement. The team included individuals from both the ISTE NETS leadership team and the Measurement, Evaluation, Statistics, and Assessment Laboratory at the University of Illinois at Chicago.

ASSESSMENT CONSIDERATIONS

CPS is a large urban district with nearly 500 elementary schools and more than 275,000 elementary students, including more than 33,000 eighth-graders. As a result, testing options were constrained by the need to deliver the assessment to large numbers of students and generate results as quickly as possible. Because the assessment would not be used to make decisions concerning individual students, ease of delivery and scalability were determined to be more important than test security. Given the priority of these scaling considerations, test developers decided that an automated, online assessment made up of linear multiple-choice items would be the most appropriate option for the district's needs.

During the test development process, it became apparent that additional data would be needed to help contextualize and interpret assessment results. These data would also better inform the delivery of more effective professional development and curriculum resources. As a result, permission was secured from the Consortium on Chicago School Research to use survey items that had been developed and validated for a previous study on student technology use (Hart, Allensworth, Lauen, & Gladden, 2002).

PLANNING THE ASSESSMENT

The key elements of the test construction plan for this project included

- Internet delivery (for widespread testing and centralized deployment)
- multiple-choice items (so that the test could be given in schools with minimal bandwidth and limited technical resources and could be scored automatically)
- a 40-minute time limit for the test (to ensure the test could be completed at school and within one class period)

To ensure the assessment would integrate well with the NETS-aligned Illinois state technology plan, test planners decided to use the NETS•S as the basis for item development. First, however, they would have to turn the high-level NETS•S domains into a test blueprint that could serve as the basis for item writing.

After a careful review of the NETS•S and performance indicators, it became apparent that more specific and measurable objectives would be needed to guide item writers. CPS also wanted to define multiple levels of achievement to chart students' progress toward the eighth-grade technology literacy standards. They turned to NCREL, which, in conjunction with an expert panel of ISTE NETS leaders, was in the process of drafting for each of the standards an extended assessment rubric that would do just that. This rubric, reproduced in appendix B, was designed to serve two purposes:

1. to provide a blueprint for item writers that would specify discrete, measurable objectives tied to each content domain (that is, the six NETS•S categories)

2. to provide scoring guidelines in the form of clearly defined achievement levels for each domain

Originally, this rubric defined three levels of achievement—basic, proficient, and advanced. As the rubric took shape, however, CPS decided that adding a lower level (below basic) would help measure the achievement of those students with little prior exposure to education technology. LPA consequently added a novice level, and the resulting four-level rubric was presented to the expert panel and revised based on their feedback. The revised rubric served as the blueprint for the assessment project, providing specific, measurable objectives and criteria to guide item writing.

ITEM WRITING

Typically, when a test is being developed, many potential test items must be eliminated because of redundancy, failure to meet content requirements, or failure to perform—as determined by statistical analysis of items during piloting and field trial. For tests consisting entirely of multiple-choice items, the number eliminated during validation can be more than 50 percent of the total item pool. Since the 50-minute time limit requirement meant that the final test could include no more than 60–70 multiple-choice questions, the expert panel recommended that three times this number of questions be drafted.

At this point, LPA, in collaboration with ISTE, selected a writing team of three members drawn from the NETS project leadership. Each member was asked to write three items at each of the four achievement levels for each of the six NETS•S categories. Together, the writing team drafted a total of 216 multiple-choice questions. Items were written based on the team's expert knowledge of the NETS•S, as well as on many of the design principles for linear test items described in chapter 8. After 26 of the 216 items were removed because of redundancy, the remaining 190 items were included in a pilot test to collect preliminary data on how well each item would perform statistically.

THE VALIDATION PROCESS

The data generated from the pilot were analyzed using methods derived from the Rasch analysis model of Item Response Theory, or IRT (see below for explanation of the Rasch IRT model). As expected, a large number of items didn't perform well enough to be included in the final test. Because they didn't fit the expectations of the Rasch, 103 test items were eliminated. These items failed for one of two reasons: difficult items were answered correctly by a disproportionate number of low-ability students, or easy items triggered an unexpected number of incorrect answers from high-ability students. Typically, this kind of result can be attributed to wording that students find ambiguous or otherwise confusing.

After items that didn't fit Rasch model expectations were removed, 78 of the remaining 87 questions were selected to provide the best coverage of the six NETS•S categories and to ensure that the final assessment would include at least 60–70 items, with the expectation that additional items would be removed in subsequent validation activities.

THE RASCH IRT MODEL

To understand how the Rasch IRT model works, it's important to first understand the concept of a *test construct* and *construct validity* (see chapter 7).

The construct represented by the NETS•S is known formally as a *latent construct* because it cannot be directly measured. Instead, the assumption is made that a test, based on a carefully designed rubric such as the ones in appendix B, represents an accurate means of determining if someone possesses the range of knowledge, skills, abilities, and aptitudes represented by the high-level NETS•S.

IRT assumes there's a correlation between the score gained by a test taker on a given test item and the person's overall ability with regard to the latent trait that underlies test performance. Rasch item analysis makes the latent trait operational by providing an item hierarchy and evaluating how each test item functions based on quality control fit statistics. To learn more about IRT and Rasch model analysis, see http://edres.org/irt/baker/.

These 78 questions were assembled and field-tested in May and June 2004. Sixty Chicago public schools were randomly selected for the field test—10 schools from each of six geographic areas. Schools were contacted by eLearning and asked to administer the technology literacy assessment to their eighth-grade students.

A total of 1,217 students in 25 schools participated in the field test, including students from at least 3 schools in each of the six geographic areas. This stratified random sample of 1,217 students (out of a total of 33,000-plus eighth-grade students district-wide) provided accurate results within a margin of error of plus or minus 3%. As expected, analysis of the field test data indicated that 9 of the 78 questions didn't fit Rasch model expectations. These were subsequently eliminated from consideration as well, leaving a total of 69 questions for the final assessment instrument.

CONTENT ANALYSIS

To provide evidence of content validity for the assessment, an expert panel of NETS leaders was convened and given the original rubric that served as the assessment blueprint, a printed copy of the 69 questions that fit Rasch model expectations, and an item hierarchy from the Rasch analysis specifying the difficulty of each item. The panel examined each question using the rubric and the item hierarchy and rated it for alignment with the NETS•S. Panel members first examined each item independently and then discussed their ratings as a group until a consensus on the best items was reached.

During this process, the expert panel removed seven additional items for one of two reasons:

1. the question either did not represent the content of the standard it was intended to assess or was not sufficiently consistent with the content of the standard, or

2. the question was either more difficult or less difficult than intended for reasons not related to the content of the standard, such as ambiguous wording or implausible distracters (Rothman, et al., 2002).

Finally, the panel set cut points for the remaining 62 items based on the rubric and item hierarchy (Figure 13.1). A *cut point* is the space between the most difficult question at one level and the easiest question at the next.

CUT SCORE DETERMINATIONS

A cut score determination based on the judgment of test developers and subject matter experts is a frequently used technique for test score analysis. For example, test developers frequently use the Angoff (1971) method for generating cut scores for a test such as a standardized educational test or certification exam.

The Angoff method, and other variations and techniques, asks test developers to judge test items based on such criteria as "What is the probability that a candidate with minimal mastery of this material would answer this question correctly?" Analysis of this probability input from multiple experts is used to generate a cut score for the test.

ASSESSMENT RESULTS

Figure 13.1 illustrates the item hierarchy for the questions that survived both construct validation by the Rasch item analysis and content validation by the NETS expert panel.

The left side of the figure depicts the overall technology literacy of students, based on the distribution of scores of all students taking the test. The right side depicts the difficulty of the questions. This figure also shows the mean ability level of students on the left and the mean

FIGURE 13.1
Student Item Hierarchy

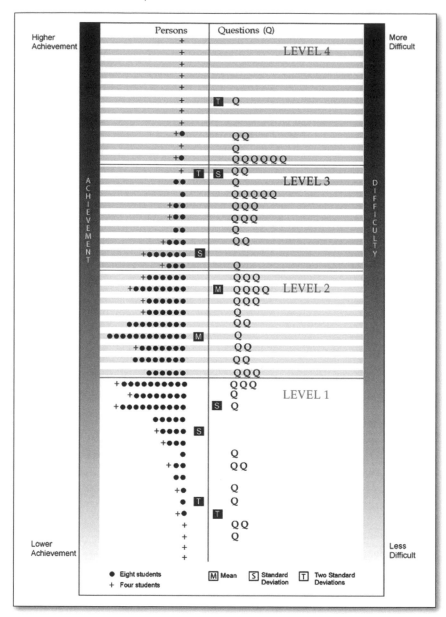

difficulty level of questions on the right, which indicate that the mean ability level of students was below the mean difficulty level of the questions.

Although the questions were somewhat more difficult overall than the ability level of the students who participated in the field test, the overlap between the distribution of students and questions shown in Figure 13.1 is generally very good for a standards-based assessment. The item reliability for the assessment was 0.98, indicating that items were very well distributed across the four achievement levels. The person reliability for the assessment was 0.79, indicating that students were reasonably well spread out on the technology achievement continuum.

Future test development will be focused on generating more questions at the lower end of the difficulty scale and closing gaps in the item hierarchy. A gap is a space in the hierarchy where no question matches the exact ability level of one or more students.

The cut scores established by the expert panel categorize students into four levels of achievement in relation to the NETS•S. Figure 13.1 shows that an overwhelming majority of students scored in the novice (n=558) or basic (n=473) range on the field test. Only 40 of 1,217 students achieved at the advanced level, while 143 scored in the proficient range. Figure 13.2 illustrates the achievement levels of all 1,217 students who participated in the field test.

FIGURE 13.2
NETS Achievement of Students

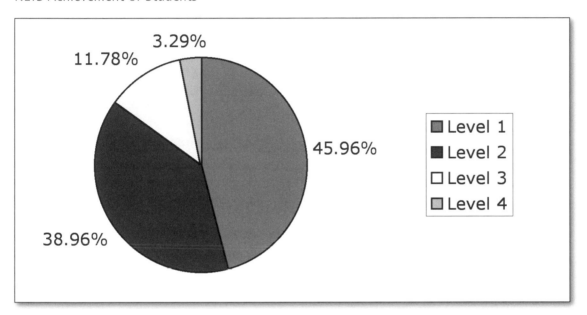

These empirical data provide evidence to support the assumption that student attainment of the NETS•S could be represented by the four achievement levels defined in the rubric. They demonstrate that item writers were able to understand the rubric and write items at each of the four achievement levels. For example, the easiest question on the field test was:

What is the best thing to do when you cannot log in to a school computer with your password?

• Break the computer

• Ask a teacher for help

• Use a friend's password

• Make up a new password

This question was constructed to assess the novice level of the rubric and survived both Rasch fit and content validity evaluation, meaning that it performed as intended. In contrast, the most difficult question on the field test was:

> Which of the following features of many word processors provides the best way to include the same information on each page of a document?
>
> - Track changes
>
> - Copy and paste
>
> - Header or footer
>
> - Bullets and numbering

This question was constructed to assess the advanced level of the rubric and survived both Rasch fit and content validity evaluation. Again, this means that the question performed as intended and can help provide empirical support for the validity of the technology literacy assessment.

To provide some preliminary evidence of criterion validity, LPA asked eLearning to convene a panel of three CPS teachers known for their mastery of education technology. The teacher panel followed the same rating process used by the NETS panel and arrived at almost identical results. Specifically, the members of the teacher panel reached a consensus that the results of the field test were generally consistent with the levels of technology literacy they had observed in their students.

SURVEY RESULTS

Additional data were collected through a survey to provide information to help contextualize the results of the pilot test. The survey was completed by 617 males and 597 females, with 3 students not providing a response. A large majority of the students who completed the survey reported they were either African American or Latino. Those who completed the survey included 83 white students, 547 African American students, 45 Asian students, 5 American Indian or Alaska Native students, 7 Native Hawaiian or other Pacific Islander students, and 513 Latino students. Seventeen students did not provide their ethnicity. Figure 13.3 illustrates the percentage of students in each subgroup who completed the survey.

Most students (n = 619) had a positive attitude toward technology, with 146 having a very positive attitude. Figure 13.4 summarizes the attitudes toward technology of students who completed the survey.

A large majority of the student sample (n = 946) said they had a computer in their home, while 243 reported not having a computer in their home. Most students (n = 782) reported having Internet access at home. Most students also said they used the computer almost every day (n = 450), or once or twice weekly (n = 263), while 228 students said they never used a computer at home. Figure 13.5 shows students' computer use at home.

FIGURE 13.3
Ethnicity

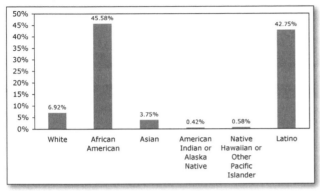

FIGURE 13.4
Student Attitudes toward Technology

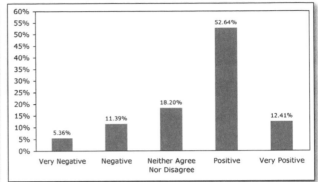

FIGURE 13.5
Computer Use at Home

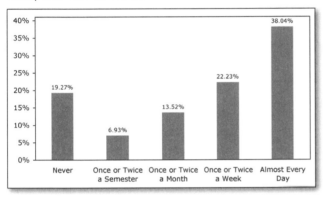

FIGURE 13.6
Student Access to Computers at School

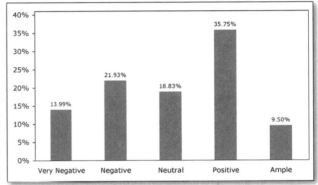

FIGURE 13.7
Computer Use at School

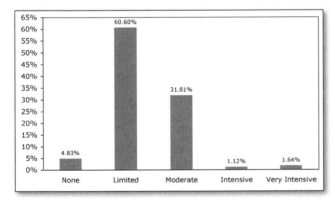

A considerable number of students (n = 414) reported their school had computers readily available, with an additional 110 reporting ample access. Figure 13.6 illustrates student perceptions of computer access at school.

Although students generally felt they had good access to computers at school, a vast majority reported limited (n = 703) to moderate (n = 369) use of computers at school for a variety of activities, including practice drills, word processing, Internet research, and presentations. Very few students reported intensive (n = 13) to very intensive (n = 19) use of computers, while 56 students said they never use computers at school. Figure 13.7 shows that a majority of students reported limited or no use of computers at school.

FIELD TEST RESULTS

The field test of the CPS technology literacy assessment may have been the first time that both survey and assessment data have been collected simultaneously from a large group of students. When taken together, the two sources of data paint a compelling portrait of education technology in a large urban district. In addition, they provide valuable data the district can use to inform the development and delivery of professional development and curriculum resources.

Most students in the field test had a positive attitude toward technology. They indicated that technology was generally available to them in their schools, but they also reported limited or infrequent use of that technology. In addition, very few students demonstrated mastery of either proficient or advanced questions. One plausible interpretation of this data is that while students have ready access to technology in school, most are not given enough opportunities to use it to develop technology literacy.

The fact that a majority of students also reported they have a computer and Internet access at home, and use both fairly frequently, suggests that use of technology at home doesn't necessarily enable students to meet the NETS•S. Home use doesn't seem to prepare students to use technology tools for productivity, research, communication, problem solving, and decision making. This data could also help explain why most students had positive attitudes toward technology despite their limited and infrequent use of it at school, especially if home use is focused on entertainment rather than education.

RISING TO THE CHALLENGE

Based in part on the field test data, CPS subsequently contracted with LPA to develop instructional materials to improve the technology literacy of seventh- and eighth-grade students. The objective was to provide more and better opportunities for CPS students to become technology literate. The strategy was to provide CPS teachers with curriculum and assessment resources that would make it easier for them to integrate technology. So as not to burden teachers with anything that would be perceived as additional content, it was important to ensure that the technology literacy materials were clearly aligned to existing curriculum objectives.

CPS assembled a team of teachers known in the district for their mastery of education technology. In turn, LPA assembled a team of curriculum writers, instructional designers, measurement experts, and evaluators. The two teams worked in close collaboration to develop a scope and sequence for the technology literacy curriculum. The teams decided to develop a series of project-based learning materials that would enhance the existing curriculum and provide structured support for both teachers and students to become more technology literate. The teams designed a series of four technology literacy curriculum enhancement projects, two for seventh grade and two for eighth grade. The projects consist of four activities each, with four distinct tasks per activity. Each of these projects was designed to be completed over the course of one semester, with two 40-minute class periods of instruction per week.

The two teams based the scope and sequence on three foundations:

- the ISTE NETS•S and performance profiles for sixth through eighth grade
- the rubric created as a blueprint for the multiple-choice assessment
- the Illinois Learning Standards, performance descriptors, and rubrics provided by the Illinois State Board of Education.

The teams employed strategies from *Understanding by Design* (Wiggins & McTighe, 2000) to develop essential questions for each of the NETS•S. The essential questions were grouped to form a scope and sequence, which provided a foundation for the development of both a set of performance assessments and the four technology literacy curriculum enhancement projects.

Each of the four activities in a project has one performance assessment; the fourth performance assessment is the culminating performance for the project. Each of the performance assessments includes a rubric; the seventh- and eighth-grade series has 16 rubrics. A sample of these performance assessment rubrics is presented in Figure 13.8.

The performance assessments are a critical part of the CPS strategy because they provide an explicit link—through the NETS•S—between the multiple-choice assessment and the technology literacy projects. These rubrics provide formative assessment data for teachers in the classroom, library, and computer laboratory, while the multiple-choice assessment provides summative data for the district.

LPA determined through needs assessment that the technology literacy projects would be implemented in three basic models:

1. by computer teachers or librarians independently
2. by classroom teachers independently
3. by computer teachers and librarians in collaboration with classroom teachers

Although CPS preferred the third implementation model, it was clear from the needs assessment that most schools wouldn't be able to use that model without significant support and

FIGURE 13.8
Performance Assessment Rubric for Project 8.1, Activity 4, "Publishing a Web Site"

SKILLS	NOVICE	BASIC	PROFICIENT	ADVANCED
Purpose	The purpose of the site may be implied but is not clearly stated.	The purpose of the site is clearly stated, but some content seems unrelated to the purpose.	The purpose of the site is clearly stated, and all content is clearly related to the purpose.	The purpose of the site is clearly stated, and all content enhances the purpose of the site.
Architecture	Most content is not logically organized.	Most content is logically organized, but some pages seem out of place.	All content is logically organized, and all pages seem to be in the most appropriate location.	All content is logically organized, and a site map is provided to improve usability.
Layout	Page layouts are disorganized or cluttered.	Page layouts are well-organized but may sometimes distract the reader from the content.	Page layouts are clean and attractive and do not distract the reader from the content.	Page layouts are clean and attractive and enhance the experience of reading the content.
Navigation	Navigation is inconsistent or does not provide links to the home page and main sections of the site.	Navigation is consistent and provides links from most pages to the home page and main sections of the site.	Navigation is consistent and provides links from every page to the home page and main sections of the site.	Navigation is consistent, shows the reader's current location, and provides links from every page to the home page and main sections of the site.
Copyright	Fair-use guidelines have not been followed for most content and media.	Fair-use guidelines have been followed for most content and media.	All fair-use guidelines have been followed, and written permission has been secured when required.	Written permission has been secured for all content and media.
Collaboration	Students do not agree on roles or do not collaborate with other team members.	Students agree on roles but must be reminded or coached to collaborate with other team members.	Students agree on roles, collaborate with other team members, and share responsibilities fairly.	Students agree on roles, collaborate with other team members, share responsibilities fairly, and show respect for all members of all teams.
HTML	HTML code does not include basic formatting, image, hyperlink, or table tags.	HTML code includes basic tags and most code displays and works correctly.	HTML code includes basic tags and all code displays and works correctly.	HTML code includes advanced tags and all code displays and works correctly.
Writing Mechanics	Misspelled words, incomplete sentences, punctuation errors, grammatical errors, or broken links are numerous. Technology to check spelling and grammar is not used.	Misspelled words, incomplete sentences, punctuation errors, grammatical errors, or broken links are few. Technology to check spelling and grammar is sometimes used.	There are no misspelled words, incomplete sentences, punctuation errors, grammatical errors, or broken links. Technology is always used to check spelling and grammar.	Vocabulary, sentence structure, punctuation, grammar, and links are correct and varied to engage the reader. Technology is used to improve word choice and sentence structure.
File Management	Work is lost because files are not clearly named or consistently saved to the correct location.	Work is not lost, but files are not clearly named or consistently saved to the correct location.	Files are clearly named and consistently saved to the correct location but are not well-organized in folders.	Files are clearly named, consistently saved to the correct location, and well-organized in folders.

professional development. LPA was charged with developing a framework that would support all three of these implementation models. The framework has four fundamental characteristics.

1. A series of curriculum enhancement projects provides authentic opportunities for students to legally and ethically apply technology tools for productivity, communication, research, problem solving, and decision making.

2. A companion set of step-by-step tutorials provides just-in-time support for students—and teachers—to build their basic technology skills. Every task includes hyperlinks to the skills needed to complete the task. When a task requires a technology skill that a student or teacher doesn't have, he or she can follow the link to the relevant tutorial.

3. All the projects and tutorials are based on an instructional design template developed specifically for CPS in collaboration with teachers. The template is modular so that teachers can adapt the scope and sequence of the technology literacy projects to the specific needs of their students and the specific context of their school.

4. All the projects employ multiple instructional strategies to support different teaching and learning styles. Teachers are encouraged to model technology literacy for their students, provide direct instruction in technology skills, facilitate student use of technology tools, and allow students to apply technology tools independently.

The framework is designed to provide enough curriculum support for computer teachers, librarians, and classroom teachers to implement projects independently, even though, as stated previously, the ideal would be for computer teachers and librarians to implement them in collaboration with classroom teachers.

It's expected that one of the most important benefits of the technology literacy projects will be that teachers' collaboration on technology integration issues will increase significantly. The framework is expected to reduce barriers to collaboration because

1. the projects and tutorials are aligned to the NETS•S and employ the same basic instructional design template, and

2. the projects and tutorials are explicitly connected by a system of hyperlinks.

As a result, it will be easy for computer teachers and librarians to know how students are applying technology tools in the classroom and for classroom teachers to know what technology skills students have and what skills need to be developed.

CONCLUSION

The field test results appear to support the need for research-based strategies to address gaps in student technology literacy by means of a targeted technology literacy curriculum, even when students have access to technology at home. As a consequence, in the 2005-2006 school year CPS will implement throughout the district an integrated technology literacy curriculum for Grades 7 and 8. The curriculum is based on performance assessments derived from the NETS•S through a backward design process.

The district's strategy is to provide formative assessments and curriculum enhancements for the classroom and a valid and reliable summative assessment at the district level. Although this strategy is supported by the field test data, further research is needed to monitor the effectiveness of the technology literacy curriculum and identify factors that have the greatest effect on student attainment of the NETS•S.

References

Angoff, W. H. (1971). Scales, norms, and equivalent scores. In R. L. Thorndike (Ed.), *Educational Measurement* (2nd ed.). Washington, DC: American Council on Education.

eLearning: Produced for the Chicago Public Schools Office of Technology Services by Learning Point Associates. Copyright June 2005, Board of Education of the City of Chicago. All rights reserved.

Hart, H. M., Allensworth, E., Lauen, D. L., & Gladden, R. M. (2002). *Educational technology: Availability and use in Chicago's public schools.* Chicago, IL: Consortium on Chicago School Research.

Rothman, R., Slattery, J. B., Vranek, J. L., & Resnick, L. B. (2002, May). Benchmarking and alignment of standards and testing. (CSE Technical Report 566). Los Angeles: National Center for Research on Evaluation, Standards, and Student Testing. Retrieved October 10, 2003, from http://www.cse.ucla.edu/CRESST/Reports/TR566.pdf

Wiggins, G. & McTighe, J. (2000). *Understanding by Design.* Arlington, VA: Association for Supervision and Curriculum Development.

CHAPTER 14

State Assessment Initiative— Utah

In 2002 Utah became the only state in the country to require that every student pass a high school-level information and communication technology (ICT) requirement to graduate. Basing this requirement on the ICT references in the NETS•S, state officials have mandated that beginning with the class of 2006 all students must either

- pass a high school-level computer technology course based on the state's technology curriculum

- pass an equivalent course offered by Utah's Electronic High School or applied technology colleges, or

- pass an authorized opt-out exam (www.usoe.k12.ut.us/ate/Skills/bus/ ComputerTechnology/ComputerTechFAQ.htm)

In 2002, only a third of Utah's high school students enrolled in Information Technologies Essentials courses. By 2006, all 35,000 high school students will be required to meet the state's ICT education requirement, placing a tremendous strain on school districts to increase course capacity. Consequently, the state has an official policy of encouraging alternative methods of fulfilling the requirement.

One locally developed alternative is Utah State University's Computer Information Literacy Assessment. This pencil-and-paper assessment is required of all University of Utah students and has been offered as an opt-out option for the 2006 ICT education requirement (http://cil. usu.edu/comptech/). Utah also turned to commercial IT certification to offer an opt-out option through Certiport's The Internet and Computing Core Certification (www.certiport. com). IT certification programs are increasingly being used to assess technology skills at the school and district level.

INFORMATION TECHNOLOGY CERTIFICATION

Certification programs became a major factor in the growth of technology companies in the 1980s and '90s. Technology training programs proliferated as the job market for IT development and maintenance specialists exploded. However, hardware and software manufacturers soon discovered what trainers and educators have long known: without an agreed-on set of standards, it's difficult to create a high-quality training program. Enter the first IT certifications.

IT certification programs such as Novell's Certified Network Engineer (www.novell.com/ training/certinfo/cne/index.html) program and the Microsoft Certified Professional program (www.microsoft.com/learning/mcp/default.asp) defined standards upon which trainers and educators could build their curricula. These standards were accompanied by high-stakes certification exams to validate skills and "license" candidates.

Like the high-stakes tests used for academic and professional purposes—such as the SAT, GRE, or the NCLEX exam for nurse licensure—IT certification exams were built using rigorous test-development procedures, including

- a well-defined set of standards that could be used as a basis for education, training, and exam development

- careful item and content validation analysis

- security provisions to ensure exams were taken in secure, professionally proctored environments

As the popularity of IT certification grew, certification programs began to target a broader range of computer technology capabilities. CompTIA, a trade association of computer hardware and software manufacturers, launched the A+ program to certify entry-level PC hardware and software maintenance professionals. Similarly, Microsoft began the Microsoft Office Specialist program to certify professional users of its suite of desktop applications.

THE INTERNET AND COMPUTING CORE CERTIFICATION

In 2002, two companies partnered to create an IT certification that would cover a broad range of basic-level computer literacy skills. Certiport, Inc., of Utah, manages the Microsoft

Office Specialist program, and SkillCheck, Inc., of Massachusetts is a specialist in ICT assessment for business and education. Together, they developed a basic skills assessment called the Internet and Computing Core Certification, or IC[3] (SkillCheck, 2002, June).

Test development began with fundamental research on the foundational IT skills required of anyone wanting to be an effective user of modern computer technology. This research included a thorough review of the NETS, as well as the work done by individual states that have created student education technology standards. This U.S. information was supplemented with research from overseas, including the eSkills initiative in the United Kingdom (www.e-skills.com), the ICT Literacy Progress Map (see chapter 15), and similar work from educational researchers and governments in European and Asian countries. Individuals involved in creating these state and national standards were recruited to join the Global Digital Literacy Council (www.gdlcouncil.org), a team of senior educators and industry professionals that helped guide the development of standards used for IC[3] certification.

Interestingly, this research uncovered an emerging, worldwide consensus regarding the definition of ICT literacy, a definition that combined contextualized knowledge, skills, and aptitudes with an understanding of ethical and responsible uses of technology.

Test Planning

This basic research led to the development of a detailed list of measurable objectives that would be used for creating a valid assessment instrument. Two sets of planning documents were created:

- exam blueprints providing detailed objectives that would be covered in the exam
- a test construction plan spelling out all requirements for the exam beyond content coverage, including practical considerations such as the time available to take the test in an academic or commercial setting

As a result, it was decided that IC[3] would consist of three separate 45-minute exams.

Computing Fundamentals. Covers fundamental knowledge of computer hardware and software, as well as basic skills in the use of a computer operating system.

Key Applications. Covers common features of software applications and specific skills related to word processing, spreadsheet, and presentation programs.

Living Online. Covers networks, electronic mail, the Internet, and the impact of computers and the Internet on society.

With guidance and support from the Global Digital Literacy Council, the IC[3] development team created three exam blueprints, one for each of the three exams (Figure 14.1). (For more on test blueprints, see chapter 7.) Because IC[3] is a computer-scored exam, every objective is measured using an automated test item, either linear or performance-based.

FIGURE 14.1

IC³ Key Applications Assessment Blueprint

DOMAIN 2.0 WORD PROCESSING FUNCTIONS

This domain includes the knowledge and skills required to perform functions specific to creating documents with a word processor (as opposed to common functions such as those identified in Domain 1: Common Program Functions). Elements include paragraph formatting (including line spacing, indenting, and creating bulleted or numbered lists), document formatting (including headers and footers), applying styles and other automatic formatting options, creating tables, applying borders and shading to text and tables.

CONTENT LIMITS

2.1 Be able to format text and documents, including the ability to use automatic formatting and language tools

Content may include the ability to perform the following:

2.1.1 Identify on-screen formatting information, including
- Breaks, including line, page, and section breaks
- Paragraph markers
- Tab markers
- Indent markers

2.1.2 Select word, line, paragraph, document

2.1.3 Change spacing options, including
- Line spacing
- Paragraph spacing (before and after a paragraph)

2.1.4 Indent text

2.1.5 Create and modify bulleted and numbered lists

2.1.6 Use outline structure to format a document

2.1.7 Insert symbols/special characters

2.1.8 Insert date and time

2.1.9 Insert, view, and print document comments

2.1.10 Display the ruler

2.1.11 Use tabs, including
- Insert tabs
- Modify tab style (left, right, center, decimal)
- Move and position tabs
- Delete tabs

2.1.12 Insert and delete a page break or section break

2.1.13 Insert, modify, and format page numbers

Blueprint Validation

Once input from exam developers and the Global Digital Literacy Council was incorporated into the blueprints, the blueprints were turned into a preliminary online survey. This survey was sent to several hundred subject-matter experts in 19 countries, many of them IT trainers and educators. The subject-matter experts were asked to rate the importance and frequency of use of each set of objectives, using the 1–5 scale reproduced in Figure 14.2.

FIGURE 14.2

Online Survey Sent to Subject-Matter Experts

SURVEY

This questionnaire is designed to solicit your review and analysis of individual test objectives as they relate to (1) the IMPORTANCE of an objective in assessing the literacy or competency of a candidate, and (2) the FREQUENCY with which a competency-based objective is performed.

2.1 Identify how software and hardware work together to perform computing tasks and how software is developed and upgraded

Content may include the following:

2.1.1 Identify how hardware and software interact, including

- How data is input into a computer (keyboard, mouse, scanner, microphone, etc.)
- How users interact with software by giving commands
- How software applies rules (algorithms) to process data
- How software outputs the result of data processing to output devices such as a monitor or printer

2.1.2 Identify simple terms and concepts related to the software development process, including
- Programming
- Debugging
- Beta review
- Quality control
- Upgrades

2.1.3 Identify issues related to software upgrades, including
- Reasons behind upgrades (adding new features to products, fixing problems, such as bugs or compatibility with new hardware, operating systems, or other types of software)
- Methods of upgrading software (by installation floppy or CD, or by automatic online updates)
- Benefits of upgrades (access to new functionality, ability to use new hardware and software)
- Drawbacks of upgrades (incompatibility with older hardware and software, risks of being an "early adopter" of new technology, conflicts with existing programs)
- Staying up-to-date and informed about product upgrade availability and issues

IMPORTANCE OF THIS OBJECTIVE

1 = Not important
2 = Of little importance
3 = Of modest importance
4 = Very important
5 = Critically important

FREQUENCY OF PEFORMANCE OF THIS OBJECTIVE

1 = Never
2 = Rarely
3 = Often
4 = Very often
5 = Always

COMMENTS:

The experts also provided feedback on each objective which was used to refine the blueprints. The two sets of ratings provided quantitative data used to determine the number of exam questions needed. Statistical analysis of the ratings indicated that the Computing Fundamentals exam should include almost twice as many items covering basics of computer hardware (40%) as software (25%). Similar content validation analysis was performed for the other IC[3] exams.

Given a 45-minute time limit for each exam and an estimated 1 minute per question pace, developers began writing the test items with a firm understanding of what the final product would look like.

Item Development

Because the IC[3] would be an automated, computerized assessment, developers were able to take advantage of numerous item types, including linear test items—multiple-choice, multiple-response, and matching items, with and without exhibits—and interactive, performance-based items.

Items were developed and reviewed by a team of subject-matter experts, and they were supervised by a professional psychometrician with years of experience in the IT certification field. After a final set of items was selected, specifications for the content were forwarded to item programmers for automation and compilation into six 60-item beta tests, each with one third more items than needed for the final 45-question exams.

Because performance-based items tend to demonstrate better measurement statistics than linear test items, it was decided that a beta test could be created with just 33% more items than would be needed in the final exam. This is in contrast to pure linear exams in which two or three times the number of needed items need to be created for a beta exam to ensure enough questions survive the validation process and can be used in the final test (see chapter 13).

Exam Validation

Each of the six beta tests were delivered to 400 candidates under carefully controlled and proctored test-administration environments. Unlike the content validation phase, which made use of subject-matter experts, the beta test was delivered to individuals of all skill levels and backgrounds. Test results and survey information were analyzed using a variety of statistical models to determine

- the difficulty and reliability of individual items in each beta exam
- the reasons behind the poor performance of some items
- the overall reliability of each test
- the likelihood that test items would adversely influence the performance of any protected groups

As expected, a large percentage of items in each pool performed well enough to be included in the final set of exams. The team's psychometrician determined the makeup of two forms for each IC^3 module that would

1. meet the content balance requirements of content validation

2. include the best items based on their performance in the beta trial

3. have identical cut (pass/fail) scores, so that each IC^3 module would be represented by parallel forms that were statistically equivalent

Once the final exam forms were determined, SkillCheck and Certiport released the exams, which were then translated into 12 languages for worldwide distribution. Given the prevalence of Macintosh computers in U.S. academic environments, an exam form was also created that included performance-based items simulating the Macintosh operating system and applications.

THE IT CERTIFICATION ALTERNATIVE

While many schools, districts, and states have created their own ICT assessments, the use of IT certifications for academic purposes has a long history of success. Many vocational and technical schools have built their computer maintenance programs around CompTIA's A+ standards, using the actual A+ certification exam as a final exam. Many school districts, including several in Virginia and South Carolina, have integrated IC^3 into their ICT literacy programs.

IT certifications provide a number of advantages to educators, not the least of which is the ability to build on rigorous test-development work that has already been done. This saves both the time and expense it takes for test-development and validation efforts that might have little value outside a particular district or state.

As a graduation requirement, certifications such as IC^3 also provide students with benefits they might not get from a locally created assessment. These benefits include college credit from the many universities that allow students to apply recognized certifications toward graduation requirements and job opportunities with organizations that recruit from pools of certified personnel.

Fundamental questions about the role of ICT certification exams and their relationship to students' ability to use technology for learning should be carefully explored by educators who are considering adding them to their technology assessment program. While certification exams can provide valuable data on knowledge and skills related to computer hardware and software, they are external to the academic context and the application of technology concepts to learning. However, coupled with other forms of technology assessment, ICT assessment can provide a detailed picture of student skill development.

References

SkillCheck, Inc. (2002, June). *The Internet and computing core certification (IC^3): Building a dynamics standard and IC^3: 2005 standard white paper addendum* (2004, December). Available from Certiport, Inc.

CHAPTER 15

National Assessment Initiative— Australia

In the United States, education is the responsibility of the states, and the U.S. Department of Education cannot set standards for curriculum content. Consequently, it has been left to professional societies such as ISTE to create and disseminate national standards that can then be used or referenced by individual states to determine student outcomes.

Initiating a nationwide effort in the United States to reach a common set of standards would be a difficult undertaking, not easily fitting the country's decentralized education system. Fortunately, we can look to our international counterparts in nations with more centralized education systems, such as Australia. This chapter describes Australia's National Assessment Initiative. While the initiative is a work in progress as this book goes to press, it has already succeeded as a useful model for nationwide implementation of student performance standards and assessments.

In 1999 education ministers from Australia's state, territory, and Commonwealth-level governments drafted the *National Goals for Schooling in the Twenty-First Century* (Ministerial Council on Education, Employment, Training and Youth Affairs [MCEETYA], 1999). This document serves as a planning document designed to provide "broad directions to develop in all Australian students the knowledge, understanding, skills and values they need for a productive and rewarding life in an educated, just and open society." As part of this agreement, a Performance Measurement and Reporting Taskforce (PMRT) was charged with developing a plan for determining that these national goals were being met.

For some academic content areas, such as mathematics and language arts, standardized written assessments were subsequently developed and delivered on a state level to entire student populations at various grade levels. For other subjects, however—including science, civics and citizenship, and information and communication technology—the government contracted with the Australian Council for Educational Research (ACER) to develop methods for benchmarking student achievement.

ACER is a nonprofit organization that conducts research and development projects in early childhood education, learning processes and contexts, and the economics of education. ACER was chosen for this task because of its extensive experience directing student assessment projects and national and international educational surveys (see www.acer.edu.au). Despite this experience, ACER faced a tough assignment: building a valid, effective assessment instrument that could be used to measure Information and Communication Technology (ICT) literacy levels for students nationwide.

As we saw in the previous chapter outlining Utah's assessment initiative, ICT literacy encompasses many of the elements of the NETS•S, but not all. In Australia's case, the *National Goals for Schooling* specified ICT literacy as one of the nation's primary educational goals:

> When students leave school they should be confident, creative and productive users of *new* technologies, particularly information and communication technologies, and understand the impact of those technologies on society. (DETYA Goal 1.6)

In 2002 education ministers also endorsed the PMRT's *Measurement Framework for National Key Performance Measures* (Performance Measurement and Reporting Taskforce [PMRT], 2002, June). This publication determined that ICT literacy would be monitored at the 6th- and 10th-grade levels, with a national assessment administered every 3 years to measure growth in student ICT knowledge, skills, and abilities. ACER's challenge was to turn these high-level goals and requirements into a practical set of objectives that could be measured through advanced assessment technology.

DEFINING INFORMATION AND COMMUNICATION TECHNOLOGY (ICT) LITERACY

The first job was to settle on a definition of ICT literacy that could be used to develop assessment domains and objectives. The PMRT led this process in consultation with ACER and other experts and key stakeholders. The accepted definition was based on national and international research, drawing heavily on the 2003 Framework for ICT Literacy developed by the International ICT Literacy Panel and the *OECD PISA ICT Literacy Feasibility Study of 2003* (Lennon, et al., 2003). This research defined ICT literacy as "the ability of individuals to use ICT (information and communication technology) appropriately to access, manage, and evaluate information, develop new understandings, and communicate with others in order to participate effectively in society."

This definition was further refined into a set of educational and assessment domains—which are very close to the NETS•S—that included the following:

Accessing Information. Identifying what information is needed and knowing how to find and retrieve it.

Managing Information. Organizing and storing information for retrieval and reuse.

Evaluating. Reflecting on the design and construction of ICT solutions and making judgments on the integrity, relevance, and usefulness of information.

Developing New Understanding. Creating information and knowledge by synthesizing, adapting, applying, designing, inventing, or authoring.

Communicating with Others. Exchanging information by sharing knowledge and creating information products to suit the audience, context, and medium.

Using ICT Appropriately. Making critical, reflective, and strategic ICT decisions and using ICT responsibly by considering social, legal, and ethical issues.

While technology, including ICT, can be broadly defined to include a range of tools and systems, the decision was also made that the first benchmark assessment would focus primarily on the use of the computer.

The ICT Literacy Progress Map

The domains derived from this definition of ICT literacy were further elaborated in an ICT Literacy Progress Map that tied specific, measurable objectives to three "strands" derived from the six original domains:

Strand A. Working with Information

Strand B. Creating and Sharing Information

Strand C. Using ICT Responsibly

Each strand is defined by six levels of proficiency, with specific performance indicators associated with each level. The six levels of the progress map represent a cumulative proficiency, one level leading to the next. For example:

Working with Information. Students progress from using key words to retrieve information from a specified source, through identifying search question terms and suitable sources, to using a range of specialized sourcing tools and seeking confirmation of the credibility of information from external sources.

Creating and Sharing Information. Students progress from using functions within software to edit, format, adapt and generate work for a specific purpose, through integrating and interpreting information from multiple sources with the selection and combination of software and tools, to using specialized tools to control, expand, and author information that can be used to represent complex phenomena.

Using ICT Responsibly. Students progress from understanding and using basic terminology and uses of ICT in everyday life, through recognizing responsible use of ICT in particular contexts, to understanding the impact and influence of ICT over time and the social, economic, and ethical issues associated with its use.

The indicators associated with each strand at each level provide a set of objectives that can be measured in an assessment, providing a structured blueprint for content development. In addition to its usefulness for assessment-planning purposes, this progress map will also be used to describe the national benchmarks for 6th- and 10th-graders.

DESIGNING THE ASSESSMENT

ACER's extensive experience with student assessment initiatives encouraged the organization to think outside the box on this project. As a consequence, the instrument designed combines a number of assessment techniques. For example, the assessment makes use of a wide variety of item types, including

- linear test items (primarily multiple-choice and multiple-response) to assess specific knowledge
- performance-based items to assess skills using software products and tools
- live application items that require students to create artifacts that will be scored manually using human graders working with predetermined scoring rubrics

Most of the artifact-creation exercises require students to make use of information from multiple sources and in different formats to solve a problem or accomplish a goal. In one assessment module, students are required to take information from Web pages and other electronic documents and spreadsheets and integrate them into a presentation on a particular subject. The resulting artifact (the presentation file) is saved and later scored using a rubric that measures both the students' technical competence while using software tools and their demonstration of higher-order thinking skills in creating, working with, and communicating information.

Other outputs from the assessment are also subject to human scoring. Students are asked to provide keywords for an information search on the Internet by interacting with a simulated version of a Web browser. The students' ability to use the search engine is measured automatically, but the keywords chosen for the search are manually reviewed and scored for relevance and likelihood of success.

This combination of linear, simulation-based performance items and live-application, artifact-generating exercises serves as the basis for a unique hybrid assessment that combines many of the best features of an objective, machine-scored test and a portfolio assessment (see chapters 11 and 12). Like a computer-based test, the ACER ICT assessment measures knowledge and skills using appropriate, automatically scored item types. Like a portfolio assessment, the test requires students to create a set of technology-rich artifacts that demonstrate both their technical and higher-order information-processing skills. By integrating artifact creation into a consistently delivered assessment, the ACER product overcomes one of the biggest challenges facing portfolio assessments: how to ensure that artifact generation takes place within similarly controlled environments, allowing a fair comparison of student outputs over a large population.

The decision was also made to create theme-based modules for Grades 6–10 structured to emulate real-world exercises or projects. These modules include

DVD Day. Students make use of online information sources to help a school select a film for a school DVD Day event and write a letter to the school's principal that recommends a Web site where the film can be rented.

Video Games and Violence. Students review and evaluate online information sources concerning the link between video game violence and real-world violence and present their findings in a classroom presentation.

Help Desk. Students answer a series of e-mails regarding problems students are encountering with computers.

Conservation Project. Students prepare a report on how to implement in their own school a conservation-related project undertaken by another school.

Photo Album. Students make use of information from a travel site and other sources to create a photo album of a specific tourist location.

Flag Design. Young students design a new flag for one of the Australian territories.

The assessment also includes a General Skills module, the only part of the assessment to be scored entirely by computer. This module determines whether a student's foundational computer skills are high enough to allow him or her to advance to the theme-based modules described above. Students who score below the cut level of the General Skills module are allocated the two least difficult thematic modules: Flag Design and Photo Album. The cut level of the General Skills module was established according to the substantive task demands of the items in the module and was informed by data from the national trial. Approximately 90% of Grade 6 and 95% of Grade 10 students achieve or better the cut level. The modular structure of the entire assessment is illustrated in Figure 15.1.

Note that the assessment also includes a survey designed to capture the students' important demographic information, as well as details about their exposure to and use of computers at home, work, and school.

FIGURE 15.1
Modular Structure of the ACER ICT Assessment

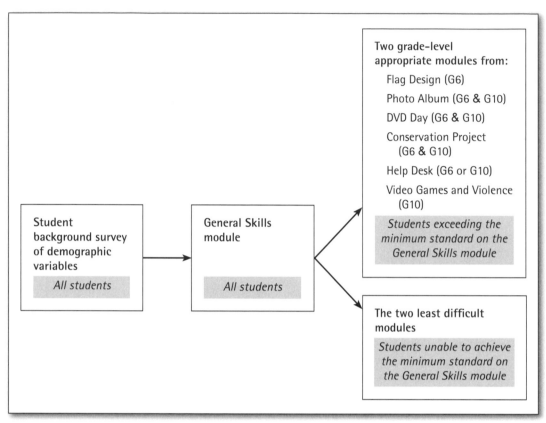

CREATING THE ASSESSMENT

Automation of the assessment was completed as a collaboration between ACER and the technology assessment designers at SkillCheck, Inc., of Massachusetts. SoNet Systems, a Melbourne company, developed the software that linked the live-application, artifact-creation exercises to the simulated platform.

To ensure the assessment will be given in a consistent environment, ACER has decided to deliver a software-based—rather than an Internet-based—test that will be run on networked laptop computers managed by ACER-trained proctors working at different schools. While this will require dozens of traveling proctors to manage portable testing labs in hundreds of school locations, the software-based design will ensure consistency from one testing location to another, increasing the likelihood that all data collected as part of this project will be comparable and of high quality.

Development proceeded through the following stages:

Automation. SkillCheck automated test modules as specified in detailed design documents provided by ACER.

Internal Review. ACER test specialists reviewed the automated material and requested modifications and updates.

Qualitative Trialing. The assessment was taken by small groups of students, with ACER test specialists reviewing the candidates' interaction with the assessment to make final recommendations for changes to the automated modules.

Product Integration. The modules were integrated into an automated test-delivery mechanism, developed by SoNet systems, that controlled the test-module flow illustrated in Figure 15.1.

Field Trial. The test was given to more than 500 students at the 6th- and 10th-grade levels to obtain data that will be used to perform test validation.

Validation. The data from the field trial will be analyzed using IRT validation techniques (see chapter 13) to determine the final configuration of the assessment modules and an appropriate cut score for the automatically scored General Skills module.

Final stages for the project include

Deployment. The assessment will be given to 8,000 students to serve as the basis for benchmarking ICT skills for the entire country.

Reporting. ACER will analyze the results of all 8,000 candidates to determine a benchmark of skill level—based on the ICT Progress Map—and report their findings back to the state and national ministries of education.

Continuing Benchmarking. The process will be repeated on a 3-year basis to analyze ongoing progress in ICT literacy for Australia.

Representative versus Comprehensive Sampling

Benchmarking student assessments in language arts and mathemathics is accomplished by providing written assessments to entire student populations. However, the ACER ICT assessment will be handled differently; the assessment will be provided to a representative sample of students to determine a benchmark for the country. In this case, the assessment will be delivered to 15 randomly selected students at each of more than 500 schools, with these students serving as a representative sample of all 6th- and 10th-graders in the country.

Part of the decision to use a statistically representative sample (rather than testing all 6th- and 10th-graders in the country) is based on the practicality of delivering and scoring such a complex assessment. As Julian Fraillon, a research fellow at ACER, notes:

> Given the complexity of the skills we are assessing and the need to provide a test that is consistently delivered and scored, we prefer high-quality data from a representative sample, rather than collecting test scores from tens or hundreds of thousands of students who might end up taking the test in different environments, diminishing the quality of results and of the subsequent analysis (personal communication, December 2004).

The use of random sampling, the cornerstone of most survey-based research, also fits the over-all goal of the assessment project, which is to benchmark the country's 6th- and 10th-graders as a whole rather than provide accountability information at the student or school level. While many ICT literacy assessment projects in the United States have a similar goal of state- or district-level benchmarking, many of these projects also involve providing teachers and administrators with detailed information at the student, classroom, and school level, requiring all students be tested. Testing on this scale presents issues of cost and practicality that are different from those involved with the Australian project.

AN INTERESTING PERSPECTIVE

While unique in the context of other ICT literacy assessment projects going on in other locations, the ACER project fits the model established by the Organization for Economic Cooperation and Development (OECD) Program for International Student Assessment (PISA) (www.pisa.oecd.org) and other institutions that routinely benchmark national student populations in academic areas such as languages, mathematics, and sciences. The Australian project provides an interesting and valuable perspective for those looking to make the best use of the many testing practices described in part 3.

References

International Information and Communication Technologies (ICT) Literacy Panel. (2002). *Digital transformation: A framework for ICT Literacy.* Princeton, NJ: Educational Testing Services (ETS). Retrieved October 21, 2004, from http://www.ets.org/research/ictliteracy/ictreport.pdf

Lennon, M., Kirsch, I., Von Davier, M., Wagner, M., & Yamamoto, K. (2003, October). *Feasibility Study for the PISA ICT Literacy Assessment.* Retrieved October 18, 2004, from http://www.pisa.oecd.org

Ministerial Council on Education, Employment, Training and Youth Affairs (MCEETYA). (1999). *National goals for schooling in the twenty-first century (the Adelaide Declaration).* Melbourne, Australia: Author. Available: http://www.mceetya.edu.au/nationalgoals/natgoals.htm

Performance Measurement and Reporting Taskforce (PMRT). (2002, June). *A measurement framework for national key performance measures.* Melbourne, Australia: Ministerial Council on Education, Employment, Training and Youth Affairs (MCEETYA).

PART 5
Making Decisions

We are now at a point where we must educate our children in what no one knew yesterday, and prepare schools for what no one knows yet.

—MARGARET MEAD

This section takes a step back from the details of test development and focuses on the larger implementation issues you'll need to address to create a viable assessment plan for your school, district, or state. Unless an assessment is designed solely for an individual teacher in a single classroom, important programmatic considerations—such as how to scale exam delivery, how to report the results most effectively, and how to garner broad-based understanding and support for the assessment plan—need to be taken into account within a broader context before decisions are made.

CHAPTER SNAPSHOTS

CHAPTER 16
Implementation Guidelines

This chapter returns to the fundamental questions that should be asked at the start of any new assessment planning:

WHAT? What do stakeholders (teachers, school and district administrators, board members, and the public) really want to know?

WHY? Why is the assessment plan being developed? What purposes will it serve?

HOW? How will test data be generated, collected, and reported?

WHO? Who are the consumers of the information? How will the data be communicated in a way that makes sense to these consumers and at the same time meets the purpose(s) of the assessment?

Chapter 16 discusses how to go about answering these questions within the context of the education technology goals of your school, district, or state. It also addresses issues of scaling, scoring, and communicating assessment data.

CHAPTER 17
Looking Ahead

Looking at NETS•S implementation from a broad, future-focused perspective, chapter 17 revisits the "essential conditions" discussed in chapter 1. Technology, education policy, and teaching methodology are always changing, and this chapter discusses where NETS•S assessment fits within these larger trends.

CHAPTER 16

Implementation Guidelines

This book began with a set of fundamental questions that should be asked by everyone who wants to implement a program to assess achievement of the NETS for Students (NETS•S). Now that we've looked more closely at various types of assessment and the different kinds of data they can generate, it's time to go back and reexamine the set of questions posed in part 1. Before you make any decisions or plans with regard to education technology assessment, it's crucial that you and your school, district, or state come to some consensus on these basic what, why, how, and who questions.

Among other goals, a NETS•S assessment program may be designed to map the progress of individual students over time; compare the performances of classes, schools, or districts; or determine the relationship between teacher technology resources and student performance. As with any far-reaching assessment initiative, it's important to involve multiple stakeholders from the outset and seek answers to the fundamental questions outlined in chapter 1.

WHAT DO YOU REALLY WANT TO KNOW?

When employers test potential job candidates, they want to know if the individual they might hire has the skills required for a particular job. When universities require students to take college entrance exams, they want to know if the students possesses the knowledge and skills the university believes relate to success in higher education. When teachers give final exams, they want to know if students have mastered the material they've been taught over the course of the semester.

FIGURE 16.1

What Do You Really Want to Know?

IF YOU WANT TO KNOW...	THEN CONSIDER THIS OPTION:
...how well each of your students has mastered the technology skills specified in the NETS•S performance indicators for their grade range,	Your assessment program will be trying to capture a "snapshot" of student skills at a particular point in time. This suggests that you should consider creating or obtaining a benchmark assessment that provides data on individual student mastery of skills derived from the NETS•S grade-range performance indicators. Such benchmark assessments can take the form of objective exams with linear or performance-based test items, hands-on assessments such as observational and portfolio assessments, or a combination of both.
...how well individual students are progressing in their mastery of technology skills over time,	Your assessment program must be able to deliver a consistent assessment, such as an objective assessment or survey, to the same student over a given period of time. Alternatively, your assessment program could use tools such as student portfolios, which allow a student to demonstrate his or her progress by assembling artifacts showing growth in technology skills.
...the level of technology skill throughout your school or across several schools in your district or state,	Because you're trying to discover the skill level of students as a group rather than tracking individual students' current skill level or growth over time, you should consider assessment instruments—surveys, linear assessments, and performance-based assessments—that provide aggregate rather than individual student data.
...how well new technology, or a professional development program designed to increase teacher use of technology in the classroom, is improving student performance across the curriculum,	Because you're trying to discover the impact of technology in the classroom rather than students' mastery of technology itself, you may want to consider tools such as observational assessments that measure the use of technology in complex environments like the classroom. Data from such assessments—or self-reported surveys from students and teachers—can be compared with other data, such as student performance in statewide language or math exams, to see if technology is having an impact within the general curriculum.

As these examples make clear, with any assessment project, large or small, testing is not an end in itself but a means to an end. The general purpose of any NETS•S assessment is to measure a student's ability to use technology for learning, but it's crucial to understand at the outset what aspect of that broad purpose a particular assessment is meant to inform. As an assessment planner, educator, administrator, or other stakeholder, what do you really want to know? Figure 16.1 provides potential answers to this question and presents options you may want to consider in each case.

Your answer to this fundamental question can also help you determine whether you want an assessment that measures only some of the NETS•S or all of them. For example, if you're primarily interested in what students know about technology and are able to do with it, objective tests measuring the NETS•S performance indicators related specifically to technology use may be the best assessment method. For example, you might want to test for NETS•S 1, basic operations and concepts. If you want to look at higher-order thinking skills, such as research and problem-solving skills, in relation to the use of technology, you may want to fold the assessment of NETS•S 5 and 6 into a test also designed to assess content area standards (see part 2).

Above all, you must be clear about what it is you want to know, for this will define the scope of your assessment plan.

WHY IS THE ASSESSMENT BEING DEVELOPED?

It's clear that the purpose of implementing state technology standards is to give educators a set of agreed-on guidelines for building curricula, professional development programs, and other educational resources. However, the purposes for building an assessment based on those standards can vary widely and are likely to be informed by a number of different institutional goals—educational, financial, and political.

Figure 16.2 provides potential answers to the question of just why the assessment is being developed, and it presents options you may want to consider in each case. These are just a few of the many potential purposes for implementing a NETS•S assessment program. Clearly identifying the purpose for the assessment will define the type of questions that should be asked and show how the data from the assessment should be reported.

FIGURE 16.2
Why Is the Assessment Being Developed?

IF THE ASSESSMENT IS BEING DEVELOPED TO...	THEN CONSIDER THIS OPTION:
...create a graduation requirement in technology literacy,	This purpose implies that the assessment must be able to demonstrate that individual students have mastered standards-based technology skills and knowledge by a certain point in their schooling if they are to be allowed to graduate. Such an assessment can vary in type, from objective (linear or performance-based) to hands-on (portfolio). However, if such an assessment is to be used as a graduation requirement, it's critical that it be implemented consistently to ensure fairness.
...demonstrate that students are meeting the No Child Left Behind Act requirement for technology literacy by the end of the eighth grade,	If you want to ensure that each student has mastered specific technology skills by the end of the eighth grade, you may want to consider some kind of standardized exam to serve as an eighth-grade technology literacy benchmark exam. If you're more interested in assessing general levels of knowledge and skill for groups of students rather than individuals, surveys, observational assessments, and portfolio assessments can also be considered.
...provide evidence for the effectiveness, or lack of effectiveness, of increased spending on technology and professional development in technology integration,	If you're trying to demonstrate that investments in computer technology and teacher training have increased the level of student technology skill, providing benchmark assessments before and after the new technologies—or the new methods of instruction—have been introduced can help measure that effect. If you're interested in measuring how these new resources are affecting the behavior of students and teachers in the classroom, tools such as surveys and observational assessments can provide the needed data.

HOW WILL THE TEST DATA BE GENERATED, COLLECTED, AND REPORTED?

The collection and reporting of data will depend on what types of assessments are being considered. The resources and organization needed for assessments that can be scored automatically on a computer or over the Internet are vastly different from assessments that require observers to visit the classroom or review a portfolio. Similarly, the scale on which an assessment is to be delivered—within a class versus across a school, district, or state—will dictate how data can be collected and reported.

Answering the following questions will be critical to the decision-making process during the creation of an assessment plan that can actually be implemented:

1. How will the assessment be deployed and administered?
2. Who will score the assessment, and when and how will they score it?
3. How large is the group of students you want to assess?

Test Deployment: How will the assessment be deployed and administered?

Test deployment is a key component of a test construction plan and dictates many elements of the test design. If a test is to be deployed in traditional pencil-and-paper format, the types of items will be restricted to those that can appear on a printed page. Similarly, if tests are to be deployed as software or over the Internet, a wider variety of item types can be used. But the need for adequate computer hardware and reliable connectivity must be taken into account to ensure that everyone who requires access to a test will have it at the appropriate time. Figure 16.3 illustrates the different ways tests are typically deployed, the types of questions used, and the strengths and weaknesses of each option.

Scoring: Who will score the assessment, and when and how will they score it?

Scoring depends on the type of deployment chosen for a particular assessment. Human graders will score most pencil-and-paper and hands-on assessments, while computers will score software-based and Internet-based assessments. Bubble sheets can be scanned to automate part of the scoring process for paper-based linear assessments, but human scoring is still required for complex test items, such as essays or other student work. These require a flexibility only the human mind can provide.

Whether an assessment is scored by humans or machines, the process of grading can be simple, such as calculating the percentage of correct answers and assigning a grade based on that raw percentage. Or, it can be complex, such as assigning each score to a norming category or applying a customized rubric to assessment results. Most software-based and Internet-based test development and delivery tools have mechanisms both for performing simple calculations on test scores and for generating reports, including score reports that can be presented to students at the end of a test to indicate their grade. However, in the case of large-scale assessments, such as statewide standardized tests, scores are usually collected and analyzed. Results may be provided to students and other stakeholders within several days, but sometimes it takes weeks or months after testing has been completed before results are available. How quickly the results are reported will often determine how the data can be used.

FIGURE 16.3
Test Deployment Options

DEPLOYMENT TYPE	BENEFITS	DRAWBACKS
PENCIL AND PAPER The vast majority of testing is still done with traditional pencil and paper. This includes quizzes and tests given in individual classrooms, as well as college entrance and other types of standardized educational exams given to large populations. Pencil and paper tests typically use linear test items, although survey-style and observational assessments may also collect information in pencil-and-paper formats.	• Convenience • Ability to deploy in any location • Availability of scoring technology (form scanning, optical character recognition)	• Limits test items to those that can be displayed on the printed page (notably, linear and survey items) • Requires manual handling of the grading process (less of a problem when using scanned forms) • Creates security issues (particularly on high-stakes tests that must be duplicated and passed through several hands) • Calls for tracking of numerous test booklets or answer sheets after testing is completed
SOFTWARE-BASED TESTING Several software products allow teachers to use or create a variety of computer-delivered tests that may include linear, survey, and performance-based test items. These systems combine pre-created test content and test creation capabilities with powerful test-management tools, including the ability to control access to tests and centralize test scores by means of school networks or the Internet.	• Ability to make use of tests that include a wide range of item types, including linear, performance-based, and survey-style test items • Ability to allow the computer to directly score exams, eliminating the need for "double input" or other forms of manual scoring	• Means each student being tested must have access to a computer—a potential limit to the number of students that can be tested simultaneously • Causes testing workstations to become islands of data that must be centralized manually unless a testing system centralizes test scores on a server or Internet database • Limits ability to assess complex tasks, such as higher-order thinking skills
INTERNET-BASED TESTING In many ways, Internet testing is the ideal solution for managing the delivery and grading of tests on both a small and large scale. Numerous tools are available for automating linear test content for delivery over the Internet. In addition, recent technologies have enabled the delivery of highly complex content (including performance-based content) by means of a Web browser. Internet testing is equally capable of deploying linear, survey, and performance-based assessments.	• Use of diverse content (linear, performance-based, and survey) • A means to score tests automatically, eliminating the workload (and subjectivity) of human graders • Centralization of data and content in a single location, allowing for easier updating of tests, consolidation and analysis of scores, and management of access to exams for security purposes	• Requires each candidate to have access to a testing workstation. • Requires significant server resources from a test provider, and adequate connectivity on test takers' workstations for online delivery of complex test content (such as performance-based or multimedia content) • Needs careful consideration of security implications when designing a testing program that will make tests available anywhere in the world by means of the Internet • Limits ability to assess complex tasks, such as higher-order thinking skills
HANDS-ON TESTING Hands-on testing refers to those assessment options in which teachers or other graders review actual student behaviors and products for scoring purposes, such as observational assessments or portfolio assessments	• Can be used to demonstrate student skills, such as collaboration and problem-solving skills, that are difficult to measure using other assessment options	• Grading can be labor intensive, often requiring human graders who have been trained to score work samples in a consistent manner • Requires that tests be carefully constructed to minimize ambiguity regarding what the student is being asked to demonstrate • Makes automating and scaling difficult

The need for multiple individuals or organizations to have access to various views of test data is an important consideration for a testing program. In most statewide academic exams, the following individuals or groups may request access to different types of information:

Students. May receive access to their score and, if used in the assessment, a pass/fail mark.

Teachers. May receive access to pass/fail and score information for every student in their classes.

School/District/State. May receive access to "roll-up" data that includes statistics on test performance based on school, district, or the entire state. Because of professional and legal requirements, this roll-up data may include only score summaries, not information on individual students.

Even a simple automated test delivered by an individual teacher in a single classroom may have to generate results that can be incorporated into a teacher's grade book or other information source. The ability of automated testing tools to integrate with other testing data or to create outputs, including reports or transportable data files, needs to be taken into account when evaluating the tools that will be used to implement any kind of testing program.

Some of the performance assessment projects outlined in chapters 3 through 6 demonstrate issues related to scoring integrated assessments that combine both content area and technology. Other projects demonstrate the use of such hands-on methods as classroom observation and portfolios. Scoring performance assessments such as these can be time-consuming, and if such assessments are to be used to make comparisons among students in different classrooms (across a school or across a district or state), they must be carefully constructed to ensure consistent scoring against a well-defined rubric.

Several states have tried using portfolios that require a standardized scoring process, although each has encountered challenges with regard to resources and implementation. Large-scale assessments of student essay-writing skills have been implemented successfully, and some education organizations, such as the Board for Professional Teaching Standards, continue to conduct nationwide hand-scored assessment programs. This demonstrates that large-scale scoring of complex assessments can be accomplished when resources are adequate.

Scalability: How large is the group of students you want to assess?

Throughout this book, reference has been made to the scale on which particular types of tests can be implemented. At the smaller end of the scale, an individual teacher can either hand score or use automated tools to simplify the testing process in the classroom. The teacher can be the observer or the portfolio grader using a rubric. All are common tasks completed at the classroom level.

At the other end of the scale, statewide testing programs often require testing of large numbers of students at the same time to minimize exam overexposure, which can lead to cheating. If such a large-scale assessment is delivered with pencil-and-paper assessments, teachers will encounter all the benefits and challenges of similar wide-scale paper assessments, such as those for math or English.

The logistics of scaling a test for a large number of students magnifies the issues that emerge during a pilot or field test. For example, if computers are difficult to access and time is of the essence, imagine the same sets of problems with hundreds of students at multiple sites. If scoring performance tasks or portfolios is time intensive for one grade level, imagine the magnitude of the problem when hundreds, or even thousands, of student products need to be evaluated in a timely manner.

To deliver a large-scale exam on computers, districts must have access to a great many of them. They must be loaded with appropriate testing software or connected to the Internet, or both, and all must be operational at the same time. The availability of such equipment is often the limiting factor for automated assessments. This necessitates strategies such as "on-demand" testing, where students can take an assessment any time they're ready, or testing delivered to different groups of students at different times, which may necessitate multiple equivalent-test forms to minimize cheating.

For hands-on assessments, such as observational assessments or portfolios, observing large numbers of students or scoring numerous portfolios within a short period of time can create enormous logistical and reliability issues. Some forms of assessment become unrealistic on a large scale.

Large-scale deployment and scoring of assessments is already part of the testing landscape. The temporary employment industry tests hundreds of thousands of job candidates worldwide every day. Popular certification and licensure exams are delivered to hundreds, and sometimes thousands, of candidates simultaneously, as are standardized academic exams. However, educators interested in large-scale deployment of assessments based on the NETS•S, especially those considering advanced testing methods such as automated assessments and portfolios, face a unique set of challenges: the need to test large numbers simultaneously, often within difficult-to-manage environments such as school labs, and with limited budgets.

WHO ARE THE PRIMARY CONSUMERS OF THE ASSESSMENT DATA?

Understanding the particular audiences that will ultimately be reviewing the data generated by a NETS•S assessment will help determine what kinds of data need to be collected and how results should be presented.

Identifying the needs of these consumers will inform the types of assessments you may choose for your project and determine how the data generated will be packaged to provide answers to all the questions discussed in this chapter. Figure 16.4 identifies potential primary consumers and presents options you may want to consider in each case.

The answer to the question of who the primary consumers of the assessment data are brings us right back to the first question: What do we really want to know? When creating an assessment plan, it's important to keep the consumers of the information in mind: What type of data are they expecting to see? What data would be most useful to them? What data will provide them with the best information to support decision making?

FIGURE 16.4

Who Are the Primary Consumers of the Assessment Data?

IF THE PRIMARY CONSUMERS ARE...	THEN CONSIDER THIS OPTION:
...students (and their parents) who want to make sure they have the technology skills they need to succeed in school and in the workplace,	This implies the need for a standards-based, objective assessment that can be used to benchmark student skills at particular points in their schooling. This may require the development of a standardized assessment that can be delivered across a school, district, or state grade range. Such assessments may include a pass/fail grade and be tied to graduation requirements to ensure that all students are demonstrating an equivalent level of mastery. Data derived from such an assessment can provide parents and students information about individual student performance. Aggregated data, such as overall pass/fail rates for a school, can be derived from such an assessment to help analyze school performance and trends across a district.
	Alternatively, multiple forms of assessments—such as objective tests, classroom observation, and portfolios—can be used to collect information about individual student performance at a particular benchmark. This information can be used by teachers, parents, and students to help guide a student's educational program. However, information derived from measuring individual student achievement using diverse testing methods might be difficult to use as a basis for drawing broad conclusions about students in the aggregate or about general trends over time.
...teachers who want to see how their students are progressing in their learning of technology skills, or how well they're using technology to improve their performance in core curriculum areas,	In this case, teachers may want to use such tools as observational assessments or portfolios. Portfolios assess abilities such as higher-order thinking skills and collaboration, which are difficult to measure using objective assessments such as multiple-choice tests.
	Teachers have latitude in their classrooms to implement assessment projects and derive information from assessments using creative tools such as those described in chapters 3–6. However, if teachers will be using that data to make comparisons among students in different classrooms, efforts need to be made to standardize assessment projects and scoring methods to ensure that comparison of students is done consistently and fairly.
...administrators who want to measure the level of student technology skills throughout an entire school, district, or state,	If the audience is interested in group performance data rather than individual student performance, a wide variety of assessment tools can be used. Self-reported surveys that allow students and teachers to assess their own level of technical skill and their opinions about the usefulness of technology in the classroom have been used widely for educational purposes (see chapter 8). Similarly, objective tests delivered to total student populations or representative samples can be used to gauge overall student ability at the classroom, school, district, and even national level (see part 4).
	Assessments that collect aggregated data can allow students to provide information anonymously. This is an advantage for self-surveys, but not for standardized tests that students perceive as not counting toward a grade or graduation requirements.
...teachers and administrators who want to understand how investments in technology and education technology are affecting classroom performance,	In this case, multiple sources of information may be needed to demonstrate how well broad technology goals are being met by specific investments in technology and teacher training. Survey assessments can be used to gauge student and teacher responses to technology use in the classroom. Similarly, observational assessments can directly review what teachers and students are doing with technology in the classroom.
	If information is available regarding performance in subject areas beyond technology, such as pass rates on state-mandated academic exams, it can be correlated with information related to the use of technology in the classroom. This will provide a review of trends that can help teachers and administrators evaluate the success of new technology or new technology-driven teaching methods.

THE BOTTOM LINE: HOW MUCH WILL IT COST?

How much will it cost to assess achievement of the NETS•S? That depends on your overall goals. Creating and implementing a high-quality NETS•S assessment will entail spending, either on exam development or purchase of a commercial product to measure student technology literacy. The scale of deployment, the complexity of the assessment, and the level of professional test development applied to the project will all contribute to cost.

At the same time, the mission and vision driving an assessment will help determine the costs or cost savings. For example, we saw in chapter 14 how Utah is using an opt-out exam program to provide students with an alternative to the state-mandated computer literacy course. Whatever the cost of the assessment, the cost of putting every student in the state through a semester-long technology course is likely to be significantly higher. Similarly, chapter 13 described how the Chicago Public Schools used a district-wide assessment to measure general student technology ability at the eighth-grade benchmark to inform decision making regarding the need for curriculum development and teacher training.

Keep in mind that the development or purchase of an assessment is only one part of the overall cost for an assessment project. Each step of implementing an assessment—delivering it to students, scoring it, collecting and analyzing data, and communicating the results to stakeholders—represents either *hard costs* in terms of budget dollars or *soft costs* related to teacher training and the administration time needed to support the project. The aggregated cost of a complete testing program should be compared with the benefits from the information obtained. Examples throughout this book have illustrated how district, state, and federal money has been used to fund assessment-related projects. In each case, educational planners have determined that the information that will derive from the assessment is valuable enough to justify not only the cost of the assessment, but also the costs related to creating and implementing a complete assessment program.

Another important issue to keep in mind is consistency of funding. If you're envisioning an assessment program that will measure student progress over time—either individual student progress or the progress of groups of students—it's critical that the funding needed to support the assessment be available over the life of the project. The goals of a multiyear study in which assessments will be used each year to measure student progress in one or more areas of technology literacy can be met only if resources are available to support the assessment during each year of the study. If such funding cannot be guaranteed, you may want to consider alternative assessment strategies that fit your projected budget.

ASSESSMENT PROGRAM DEVELOPMENT PLAN

Creating and implementing an assessment program requires the collaboration and support of many players, all of whom will be critical to its success. To generate and manage an assessment development plan such as the one modeled in Figure 16.5, all players will need to be given room to contribute their expertise, with a common purpose in mind.

FIGURE 16.5

Assessment Program Development Plan

	TASK	DESCRIPTION
STAGE 1	Establish a technology assessment committee	The makeup of this leadership group will vary depending on the nature of the assessment project. To develop a statewide standardized exam, a state-level assessment coordinator and test development and validation experts will likely be involved at a high level. If technology assessment will be part of a multidisciplinary academic program, such as the senior project program described in chapter 6, the technology assessment committee may be a subcommittee of a larger planning group.

For most assessment projects, the core decision makers on a planning committee will include

• teachers, preferably at the grade level(s) where the assessment will be implemented

• administrator(s), preferably at the system level—school, district, or state—where the assessment will be implemented

• parents

• technology coordinator(s)

• experts—assessment professionals or professional development coordinators drawn from the institution or community or brought in as paid consultants for the project |
| **STAGE 2** | Answer fundamental questions: what, why, how, and who | This chapter discusses some of the ways these fundamental questions can be answered and the types of decisions that may result.

The committee established in stage 1 will need to include individuals with enough expertise and authority to answer these questions based on a clear understanding of the resources needed to implement their decisions. The committee's answers will define the goals that will drive the rest of the process. |
| **STAGE 3** | Determine grade-level expectations for meeting the ISTE NETS•S | At this stage, the assessment committee will need to determine which standards and grade-level performance indicators will be used as the basis for the assessment.

Depending on the project, the NETS•S grade-range performance indicators themselves may be adequate as the basis for an assessment. In other cases, more detailed objectives, such as those modeled in the NETS•S assessment rubrics in appendix B, or objectives defined by the state's technology standards, may be needed. |
| **STAGE 4** | Determine benchmarking criteria | The committee will determine how the goals for the program (decided in stage 2) and the standards selected for assessment (determined in stage 3) fit together to specify general benchmarking criteria for the assessment.

For example, a statewide graduation requirement based on the NETS•S 8th- or 12th-grade performance indicators implies the need for an objective exam with a well-defined cut score to determine who can graduate and who has failed and needs to take the assessment again. Conversely, a program that will rely on self-reported data from students concerning how they perceive their own technology skill implies the need for benchmarking that will track changes in this data over time.

Once the planning group has reached consensus on the overall program goals, the standards to be assessed, and the benchmarks that students will be measured against, members will be ready to review the many assessment options available. |

continued

FIGURE 16.5 *continued*
Assessment Program Development Plan

	TASK	DESCRIPTION
STAGE 5	Review and select appropriate instrument(s)	This book has introduced a wide variety of assessment options, such as self-reported surveys, multiple-choice exams delivered on paper, automated exams delivered over computers, and complex projects and portfolios scored by human graders. Some of these assessments can be readily developed by schools and districts, while others are available commercially. Each option has its advantages and drawbacks, and each has a particular utility for certain types of student assessment. At this stage in the process, the planning group will consider all the options for assessment and determine which are the most appropriate for their needs and resources. If a district is interested in deploying a commercially developed standardized technology test, for example, careful analysis of the test development and validation process used to create the exam will be needed. If a district wants to make use of a self-rated survey, a review of existing instruments and development tools (described in chapter 9) will help clarify the options.
STAGE 6	Train teachers and develop the infrastructure	Assessment does not take place in a vacuum. Teachers must be trained to prepare students for assessment, and they may also be involved with the implementation and grading of the assessment. Adequate professional development time and resources will need to be made available to support the project. School and district IT resources will also need to be in place to support the program. If hundreds, or even thousands, of students across the district will simultaneously be taking a standardized exam over the Internet, those responsible for supporting school networks and Internet connectivity must be involved in the planning process to ensure a chosen technology assessment can be implemented successfully.
STAGE 7	Launch the assessment program	Once the assessment instrument(s) have been selected and the human and technology infrastructure is in place, the assessment program will be launched, the students assessed, and the scoring data collected for analysis.
STAGE 8	Analyze the data	Because the goals for the program have been determined early on in the process and all subsequent decisions have flowed from these well-defined goals, the data generated by the assessment should provide a basis for analysis consistent with these goals. For example, if the assessment goal is to benchmark student achievement at the eighth-grade level with an objective exam, pass/fail rates can be used to analyze student performance at the student, classroom, school, district, or state level. If understanding students' experience and comfort level with technology is the goal of the assessment, the survey data will be analyzed accordingly.
STAGE 9	Make decisions	The purpose of any assessment is to help guide and measure the effectiveness of educational programs and initiatives. The data resulting from a NETS•S assessment program can be used to develop or modify a technology curriculum, provide evidence of successful integration of technology in the classroom, or drive data-driven decision making regarding future resource allocation and professional development.

Because assessment projects and goals vary so widely, no single development plan will be applicable to all situations. While informed by real-world projects, the sample plan in Figure 16.5 is a composite that should be modified based on the particular needs and goals of your school, district, or state. It's designed to show you the typical stages of development of an assessment program, from planning to implementation.

The plan in Figure 16.5 requires collaboration and cooperation between the district office and individual school sites. The inclusion of parents on the committee adds community-level input, while the number of teachers on the committee provides a mechanism for ensuring there's a classroom-informed reality check to make sure the development of the assessment and implementation plan is grounded in fact. While many details are left out of this composite plan, it clearly embodies many of the principles we've discussed in this book, such as multiple measures for triangulating data. An assessment program should be reviewed annually to ensure that it's effectively meeting the needs of all stakeholders and adjusting to changes in technology, funding, and the learning needs of students.

CHAPTER 17

Looking Ahead

This final chapter returns to the Essential Conditions introduced in chapter 1 for implementing the NETS•S in teaching, learning, and assessment. It also addresses the economic, political, and educational contexts in which technology assessment programs will be developed and deployed in the coming decade.

As a tool and delivery method for learner-centered instruction, technology is transforming our school environments and changing the way students learn both inside and outside the classroom. However, plans for assessing student technology skills will not be formulated in a vacuum. In an era when schools are struggling to balance competing needs, technology assessments will be competing for time and resources with high-stakes tests in English, math, and science. In addition, the technology itself will always be changing. So any assessment program you decide on today will need to be flexible enough to meet the changing needs of tomorrow's student.

TECHNOLOGY ASSESSMENT IN THE AGE OF ACCOUNTABILITY

The current national emphasis on student, teacher, and school accountability—supported by rigorous standards and high-stakes tests—means that technology assessment planning is taking place in a context in which testing is already receiving considerable attention and resources.

This current state of affairs is not without controversy, of course; the focus on standardized testing embodied in No Child Left Behind (NCLB) legislation has generated both criticism from educators and legal challenges from districts and states. While a debate on the merits and disadvantages of standardized testing is beyond the scope of this book, all parties to such a debate would agree that accountability has transformed the educational landscape, requiring schools to find ways to make preparation for high-stakes academic exams a major part of the learning process. This means that any attempt to introduce a new technology assessment program at the school or district level will face competition for resources from high-stakes assessments in other disciplines. Such challenges, however, also present opportunities for creating new kinds of assessments.

In his May 2000 *New York Times* editorial, "The Tyranny of Standardized Testing," Bard College president Leon Botstein, an education reform advocate and outspoken critic of standardized tests, discussed important ways that technology could assist in breaking the deadlock in which advocates and critics find themselves concerning testing as a basis for accountability:

> [W]e now possess the means to change testing fundamentally. Rapid advances in computers and declining costs make powerful new technologies, once reserved for government and industry, accessible: technology involving complex computer simulation, as in pilot training, and manipulation of data. We can design tests that are interactive in a way that both helps learning and raises the standards of education. Even for young children, it would be possible to throw away the No. 2 pencils and machine-scanned answer sheets, and have the student tested at the computer itself (Botstein, 2000, May 28).

If there's one discipline where innovations such as "complex simulations," "tests that are interactive," and easy "manipulation of data" are already being implemented, it's in the field of technology assessment. This book contains numerous examples of performance-based testing that can be used to assess real-world skills. In some cases, this performance testing takes the form of complex automated simulations delivered on computers or over the Internet. In other cases, it involves hands-on projects completed in the classroom, with assessment built around teacher observation and student portfolios and rigorous, rubric-based scoring methods. Besides offering better ways to measure student technology skills in the context of learning, these new forms of assessment may one day form the basis for new testing paradigms in other academic disciplines.

We're certainly not at a point yet where the multiple-choice test and bubble sheet are about to be replaced entirely by performance-based assessments. In fact, testing programs still struggle with how to scale current statewide academic exams for computer delivery rather than paper delivery. And yet, if and when such innovations are introduced broadly into the educational assessment process, technology assessment will have blazed the trail and made it easier to apply these new forms of testing across the curriculum.

TECHNOLOGY AND THE TRANSFORMATION OF STUDENTS

Just a few years ago, the notion of high-speed Internet access in every school was just a dream. Today, it's a reality. While schools continue to struggle with providing students adequate computer hardware and software and integrating those resources more broadly into classroom learning, the day will surely come when this technology gap will be closed as well.

At the same time, students today come to school already accustomed to dwelling in virtual worlds—even if they're the somewhat dubious game worlds of Doom and Grand Theft Auto—and they're comfortable communicating through virtual means, such as chat rooms and instant messaging. This multitasking, "plugged-in" generation of students enters the classroom with different expectations than we had about how information can and should be received and processed. Noted educational futurist Chris Dede has typified these new expectations and learning approaches as follows:

> Today's students have been described as having an information-age mindset, being Millennials or members of the Net Generation. While this portrayal of generational learning styles can be oversimplified, the technology and media used by children during their formative years do have an influence on how they learn, as do the media used by adults. However, technology is no more static than people. The Internet is a constantly evolving infrastructure that now supports many media, including such disparate applications as "groupware" for virtual collaboration, asynchronous threaded discussions, multi-user virtual environments, videoconferencing, and mobile, location-aware wireless devices such as personal digital assistants (PDAs) with embedded global positioning system (GPS) capabilities (Dede, Whitehouse, & Brown-L'Bahy, 2002). Research indicates that each of these media, when designed for education, fosters particular types of interactions that enable—and undercut—various learning styles (Dede, 2005).

Dede goes on to suggest that over the next several years, "three complementary interfaces will shape how people learn":

The familiar "world to the desktop." Provides access to distant experts and archives and enables collaborations, mentoring relationships, and virtual communities of practice. This interface is evolving through initiatives such as Internet2.

"Alice in Wonderland" multiuser virtual environments (MUVEs). Participants' avatars (self-created digital characters) interact with computer-based agents and digital artifacts in virtual contexts. The initial stages of studies on shared virtual environments are characterized by advances in Internet games and work in virtual reality.

Ubiquitous computing. Mobile wireless devices infuse virtual resources as we move through the real world. The early stages of "augmented reality" interfaces are characterized by research on the role of "smart objects" and "intelligent contexts" in learning and doing.

The emerging Net Generation has experience in virtual environments and remote relationships that aren't yet a part of most current formal educational experience. As we examine the educational implications of emerging technologies and become cognizant of the changes they're inspiring in student learning styles, we must ask ourselves: Are we doing enough as educators to help students take full advantage, or are we simply assuming that students exposed to technology at an early age will enter the classroom fully prepared to use the latest education technology?

Research has shown that exposure to technology at home and at an early age doesn't necessarily translate into an understanding of that technology or into the ability to use the technology to learn. (This finding is echoed by the Chicago Public Schools case study detailed in chapter 13.) The ability to communicate through e-mail, instant messaging, blogs, and chat rooms doesn't mean students are ready to use technology tools to learn and work collaboratively. The ability to play in complex networked environments, such as multiuser online games, doesn't mean students can find information on the Internet or evaluate the quality of that information. The ability to master hardware devices such as MP3 players doesn't mean students understand the legal and ethical dimensions of their use of technology, such as copyright infringement and piracy.

In other words, unless we can find ways to ensure that all students have the knowledge, skills, and dispositions to use technology ethically and effectively, a lack of technical capability will be the limiting factor in implementing some of the high-technology tools already finding their way into our classrooms.

In this context, education technology programs based on rigorous standards, such as the NETS•S, and supported by well-designed and well-implemented assessments, such as those discussed in this book, are critical. They're critical not just for preparing students to use such familiar tools as word processors, spreadsheet programs, or Internet browsers—important as these tools are—but also for instilling in students the critical-thinking skills they'll need to understand and use tomorrow's new technology.

Without these skills, the resources already available for linking students across the country and around the world in rich, collaborative learning environments will never be used to their full potential. They'll remain islands of technology-rich learning located in those few schools that have committed themselves to preparing students and teachers to use these tools.

We still have a long way to go in addressing the needs of the have-nots so as to close the digital divide and ensure that technology resources are available to all students who lack adequate access to them. We must nevertheless simultaneously address the needs of the "know nots," those students who haven't yet mastered the essential technology learning skills embodied in the NETS•S.

TECHNOLOGY AND THE TRANSFORMATION OF CLASSROOMS

The technology tools used in today's classrooms are too diverse to characterize in detail, much less paint a picture of what's to come. Yet, a series of transformations—many of them made possible by technology—that can be captured in a set of general trends are taking place in schools today. Traditional educational practices no longer provide our multitasking, plugged-in, Net Generation students with the knowledge, skills, and dispositions they need to survive economically in the global marketplace. Teachers must embrace new strategies that will help their students develop problem-solving skills and use the most appropriate tools for learning, collaborating, and communicating.

Figure 17.1 summarizes this movement from traditional teaching practices to a new type of learning environment that has been demonstrated in research studies to support improvements in student learning. The elements of this new learning environment represent a set of transformational goals for teachers as they reflect on their own practices and adjust them to fit the way students learn today.

FIGURE 17.1
Establishing New Learning Environments

ESTABLISHING NEW LEARNING ENVIRONMENTS

Incorporating New Strategies

Traditional Learning Environment	→	New Learning Environments
Teacher-centered instruction	→	Student-centered learning
Single-sense stimulation	→	Multisensory stimulation
Single-path progression	→	Multipath progression
Single media	→	Multimedia
Isolated work	→	Collaborative work
Information delivery	→	Information exchange
Passive learning	→	Active/exploratory/Inquiry-based learning
Factual, knowledge-based learning	→	Critical thinking and informed decision-making
Reactive response	→	Proactive/planned action
Isolated, artificial context	→	Authentic, real-world context

Given that experiments in teaching methodology have been going on for decades—some enabled by technology, some not—many of the trends in Figure 17.1 have been underway for some time. Yet technology has helped to accelerate the move toward learning environments that mirror the multitasking, multimedia, communication-intensive computing environments in which many of us currently work.

To take one example, the move from the single media of traditional learning (exemplified by a single teacher writing on the blackboard) to multimedia (filmstrips, video, molecular models, and so forth) was already happening long before computers entered the classroom. However, the advent of new technology has dramatically expanded the range of multimedia tools available to teachers, including computer-based training, interactive Web sites, virtual classrooms, digital microscopes, and probeware, to name just a few. These tools don't simply enhance a teacher's presentations; instead, they transform the learning environment from one in which media are used to make traditional lectures and activities more interesting, to one that enables students to interact in new ways with teachers, other students, and the content itself.

When the NETS Project was started, the goal was to determine what knowledge, skills, and abilities were required by students and teachers to work effectively in the new learning environments described in Figure 17.1. Some of the standards, such as those in NETS•S 1, Basic operations and concepts, were based on the understanding that a certain foundational level of skill with basic technology tools was needed to take part in these new learning environments.

Working with multimedia and online collaboration tools can only happen when students and teachers have an understanding of these fundamentals. Someone untrained in the basic use of a computer's operating system, for example, won't be able to use this crucial technology for education or any other purpose. Other standards, such as those in NETS•S 6, technology problem-solving and decision-making tools, focus on those skills that enable students to choose the most appropriate current technologies to make informed decisions in authentic, real-world contexts.

Eventually, we hope, the teaching of technology skills in the classroom will seem as unremarkable as teaching pencil skills in preschool and kindergarten. Do we have a subject in school called "pencil lessons"? No. Teachers in preschool and kindergarten simply pass out pencils and teach each child how to hold one and put pressure on the lead to make marks on paper. When a pencil's either being held inappropriately or misused, the teacher coaches the child on how to correctly hold and use it.

Very quickly, the pencil becomes an assumed tool in the classroom. While classroom teachers may assess student handwriting in the early grades, we don't assess pencil capabilities on the district or state level. We don't have a rubric for assessing to what degree the pressure is applied, the angle at which the pencil is held, or the number of marks made by the pencil. We just assume the technology is there and that students are using it effectively.

Of course, the pencil is a tool with limited functions—basically, write and erase. While learning *how* to write requires both handwriting instruction (how to acquire a correct and legible technique for forming the letters) and time for physical development, the ultimate goal of teaching these skills is to enable students to focus on *what* they write. What they are eventually able to write and erase is, of course, infinitely broad and multidimensional, because the pencil will be used for subject area, quantitative, illustrative, and creative applications. The application of technology as a learning tool is, in the end, not so different from the ways we use a pencil across subject areas, and our technology assessment programs should reflect this.

The ultimate goal for the NETS•S is to facilitate the move to learning environments in which all students easily meet the standards without necessarily having to verify it with an assessment. But we're still in the preschool and kindergarten stage of education technology. It's easy to get stuck in the write-and-erase mode of technology use—the initial level of learning how to operate the hardware and software. To realize the potential of technology for teaching and learning, these basic skills need to lead to the next level of application: using the tools instinctively to develop products that can be interpreted and used by others. As students develop facility in creating materials that others can interpret, it's critical, as with the pencil, that they're encouraged to explore the infinitely broad and multidimensional ways technology can be used to support subject area, quantitative, illustrative, communicative, and creative applications.

When it comes to technology assessment, the kinds of transformations you want to take place in your classrooms may drive your goal setting. Do you want to ensure that your students have the foundational skills they need to work productively in these new learning environments so that you can focus on the content of their courses and not on teaching basic computer skills? That suggests the need for a benchmarking assessment that will measure student readiness to function effectively in a computer-equipped classroom. Do you want to ensure that students are using the technology tools available to them to collaborate, explore, and think critically? If so, tools such as portfolio assessments can allow students to document their work and progress in a technology-rich environment.

Of course, assessing students' ability to use technology for learning is only appropriate when the technology is actually available to the students and has become an integral part of the assumed operations of their classroom. This brings us back to the larger question of what else is necessary for education technology to be successful. We all know that just placing hardware in a classroom will not guarantee successful, appropriate uses of technology, just as placing pencils in the classroom will not guarantee that learning takes place. What are the *essential conditions* for successful integration of technology in education?

ESSENTIAL CONDITIONS FOR IMPLEMENTING THE NETS•S

In chapter 1, we introduced the Essential Conditions needed for implementing the NETS•S. These Essential Conditions constitute a set of broad, consensus guidelines that describe the fundamental structures, policies, and attitudes that must be in place for the effective integration of technology in schools.

The list of Essential Conditions shown in Figure 17.2 grew out of a series of discussions among thousands of teachers and administrators during the original NETS Project. This list was intended to provide a snapshot of how the NETS•S could be implemented within existing school structures. It's crucial that education leaders revisit these Essential Conditions when planning a technology assessment program, because assessment doesn't take place in a vacuum; it is, instead, deeply integrated into the educational process. To succeed, all stakeholders in the process—students, teachers, administrators, parents, school board members, politicians, and partners in higher education, government, and industry—must be encouraged to buy into a vision of the appropriate use of technology as a force for enhancing student learning.

With the subsequent development of two other sets of technology standards, the NETS for Teachers (NETS•T) and the NETS for Administrators (NETS•A) , the original list of Essential Conditions has been modified to also include the Essential Conditions needed for meeting the NETS•T and NETS•A. Figure 17.2 presents a composite chart showing the interrelationships among the three sets of Essential Conditions.

FIGURE 17.2
Essential Conditions for Implementing NETS•S, NETS•T, and NETS•A

NETS•S (NETS for Students)	NETS•T (NETS for Teachers)	NETS•A (NETS for Administrators)
VISION The education system provides support and proactive leadership.	**SHARED VISION** The entire education system provides proactive leadership and support for the implementation of technology in teaching and learning.	**SHARED VISION** The school board and administrators provide proactive leadership in the development of a shared education technology vision among school personnel, parents, and the community.
ACCESS Students have access to contemporary technologies, software, and telecommunications networks.	**ACCESS** Educators have access to current technologies, software, and telecommunications networks.	**EQUITABLE ACCESS** Students, teachers, staff, and administrators have equitable access to current technologies, software, and telecommunications resources.
SKILLED EDUCATORS Students have access to educators skilled in the use of technology for learning.	**SKILLED EDUCATORS** Educators are skilled in the use of technology for learning.	**SKILLED PERSONNEL** District leaders and support personnel are skilled in the use of technology appropriate for their job responsibilities.
PROFESSIONAL DEVELOPMENT Educators have consistent access to professional development to support technology use in teaching and learning.	**PROFESSIONAL DEVELOPMENT** Educators have consistent access to professional development to support technology use in teaching and learning.	**PROFESSIONAL DEVELOPMENT** District leaders and support personnel have consistent access to technology-related professional development pertinent to their job assignments.
TECHNICAL ASSISTANCE Technical assistance for maintaining and using technology resources is provided.	**TECHNICAL ASSISTANCE** Educators have technical assistance for maintaining and using technology.	**TECHNICAL ASSISTANCE** Personnel have technical assistance for maintaining and using technology.
CONTENT STANDARDS AND CURRICULUM Content standards and curriculum resources are provided.	**CONTENT STANDARDS AND CURRICULUM RESOURCES** Educators are knowledgeable in their subject matter and current on the content standards and teaching methodologies in their discipline.	**CONTENT STANDARDS AND CURRICULUM RESOURCES** Instructional personnel and school leaders are knowledgeable about content and technology standards, related curriculum resources, teaching methodologies, and the use of technology to support learning.
STUDENT-CENTERED LEARNING Student-centered approaches to learning are followed.	**STUDENT-CENTERED TEACHING** Teaching in all settings encompasses student-centered approaches to learning.	**STUDENT-CENTERED TEACHING** Teaching in all settings includes the use of technology to facilitate student-centered approaches to learning.
ASSESSMENT The effectiveness of technology for learning is assessed.	**ASSESSMENT** Assessment of the effectiveness of technology for learning is continuous.	**ASSESSMENT AND ACCOUNTABILITY** The school district has a system for the continual assessment of the effectiveness of technology to improve student learning.

continued

FIGURE 17.2 *continued*

Essential Conditions for Implementing NETS•S, NETS•T, and NETS•A

NETS•S (NETS for Students)	NETS•T (NETS for Teachers)	NETS•A (NETS for Administrators)
COMMUNITY SUPPORT Community partners provide expertise, support, and real-life interactions.	**COMMUNITY SUPPORT** The community and school partners provide expertise, support, and resources.	**COMMUNITY SUPPORT** The district maintains partnerships and communications with parents, businesses, and the community to support technology use within the district.
SUPPORT POLICIES 1. Ongoing financial support for sustained technology use is provided. 2. Policies and standards support new learning environments.	**SUPPORT POLICIES** School and university policies, financing, and reward structures are in place to support technology in learning.	**SUPPORT POLICIES** The district has policies, financial plans, and incentive structures to support the use of technology in learning and district operations. **EXTERNAL CONDITIONS** Policies, requirements, and initiatives at the national, regional, and state levels support the district in the effective implementation of technology for achieving national, state, and local curriculum and technology standards.

As you plan improvements in your implementation of education technology, it's important to periodically reassess where you are in meeting these Essential Conditions. Identifying the gaps and developing an action plan to address those gaps is vital to success. Context, culture, and the level of collaboration among district, school, and classroom leaders will all affect how easily and adequately the conditions are met. Technology assessment that takes place in an environment where there's a shared commitment to the principles summarized in Figure 17.2 is far more likely to produce valid, useful results that will serve the needs of all stakeholders.

Let's take a moment to look more closely at the individual elements of these Essential Conditions.

Shared Vision

Shared vision means the commitment to technology is systemic. From the highest level of administration to support personnel, the implementation of technology is understood and committed to. Teachers, school administrators, collaborating university personnel, and district school board and administrators must develop a shared vision for technology use in the classroom, with a focus on students' use of technology to learn. School personnel, parents, and the community at large can all contribute to a common understanding of both the benefits technology can bring and how those benefits can be realized.

When the implementation of a technology initiative is problematic, a major reason often cited is the breakdown in this shared vision among those who hold the decision-making power. This can occur over something as simple as unlocking the door to a lab or as complex as modifying existing operational budgets to provide allocations for technology funding. Facilitating the integration of technology may require a change in policy or rules, and decision makers have to be willing to forge compromises when necessary and ensure communication among all parties to sustain this common vision.

Equitable Access

Access to current technologies, software, and telecommunications networks must be consistent throughout the educational environment, both at school and at home. Funding for the resources to make this happen varies greatly from district to district and state to state, and creative partnerships are often required to facilitate equitable access.

Leaders should review access needs in context so that resources most appropriate to particular subject areas—for example, a word processor and Internet access in English classrooms, or a spreadsheet program and digital microscopes for science classes—are readily available when they're the best tools for the concepts being taught. Access should be provided in classrooms as well as lab and library settings, and accommodations must be offered for students with special needs.

Looking to the future, the notion of equitable access will extend beyond the classroom and the school day, as affordable, ubiquitous access gradually becomes the expectation for all students, teachers, administrators, and community members.

Skilled Personnel

District leaders, support personnel, classroom teachers, teacher candidates, and teacher educators must all be skilled in the use of technology for learning. They must be able to apply technology in the presentation and administration of their jobs and facilitate the appropriate use of technology by others. Standards for education technology should be one of the criteria used when reviewing applications for hiring new teachers, administrators, and support personnel.

Professional Development

Consistent access to professional development for teachers, administrators, teacher educators, and other support personnel is crucial for timely response to the constant changes in technology. When planning professional development venues and delivery mechanisms, leaders should take into consideration issues of time, location, distance, credit options, and so forth. Professional development is not a one-time event; it should be focused on the needs of each individual and sustained through coaching and periodic updates. The district plan should clearly outline professional development opportunities and expectations for teachers, district leaders, and support personnel to learn job-specific technology skills.

Technical Assistance

Like workers in any other industry, educators must rely on technical assistance to use and maintain the increasingly complex technology available to them. The focus of administrators and teachers should be on teaching and learning, not on maintaining and repairing the technology infrastructure beyond basic troubleshooting procedures. When a technology doesn't function well, learning opportunities are lost, and skepticism and frustration grows.

Timely technical assistance is imperative for students, teachers, administrators, and support personnel to feel confident that technology can reliably support their everyday work. It's critical that leaders understand the negative effects that an unanswered need for technical assistance can have on attitudes toward technology use.

Content Standards and Curriculum Resources

Those working with students and teachers in education technology must be knowledgeable about the content, standards, and teaching methodologies specific to each discipline. Teachers and teacher candidates must learn to use technology to teach content in powerful, meaningful ways. Technology can bring relevant resources from the real world into the classroom, provide tools for analyzing and synthesizing data, and convey content through a variety of media and formats.

All teachers should learn to use technology in ways that simultaneously meet the content standards of their discipline and the NETS•S and NETS•T. Administrators must keep up to date on the variety of technology applications available for teaching, learning, and management, and expect technology to be used to support learning in all curriculum areas.

Student-Centered Teaching

Research has consistently shown that student-centered approaches to teaching and learning are most effective for all developmental levels. Although current demonstration technologies—presentation software, DLP (digital light processing) projectors, and so forth—can be very useful as an enhancement to traditional overhead projectors or blackboards, this capability does not significantly alter traditional teaching practices. To support the move to the new, student-centered learning environment discussed earlier in this chapter, hands-on use of technology by students must become an integral part of regular classroom activities.

Technology empowers students to take control of their own learning process: identifying problems, collecting and analyzing data, drawing conclusions, and conveying results using electronic tools. Teachers and teacher preparation faculty should model the use of technology to demonstrate its usefulness and appropriateness for collaboration, acquisition of resources, analysis and synthesis, presentation, and publication.

Administrators must also recognize the effectiveness of student-centered, collaborative learning for improving student achievement. As many project evaluations have noted, administrators are key to the successful use of technology in classrooms; when administrators recognize promising strategies for technology use and commend teachers who successfully apply those strategies, the benefits are realized immediately in improved student performance.

Assessment and Accountability

When developing an assessment plan for education technology, keep in mind that every link in the teaching-learning chain should be assessed and held accountable for outcomes. This includes students, teachers, school site councils, administrators, district policy makers, and teacher education programs. The data obtained from this comprehensive assessment will

1. inform the learning strategies used,

2. create and maintain a shared vision for technology use throughout the organization,

3. pinpoint potential problems, and

4. provide data for altering policies and instructional strategies, or for acquiring resources.

In an era of data-driven decision making, changes made over time in response to technology innovation should exemplify informed decision making.

Community Support

The visioning process should include the community as well as school partners who provide expertise, support, and resources for technology implementation. Members of the community must be encouraged to see that technology is a valuable tool for students, teachers, administrators, and teacher candidates so that they'll be willing to support technology politically, from the boardroom to the state house. It's much easier to garner support when all players are informed and participating in the process. Community leaders are often far more vocal and effective in the political process than educators are, and they can provide a needed boost for crucial new initiatives.

Support Policies and External Conditions

Policies can either support or hinder the implementation of technology. As decision makers develop new policies, they must consider how policies affect technology acquisition and access for teachers and students. For example, a laptop for every student may be a commendable school- or district-wide goal, but what are the system-wide repercussions of putting a personal computer into the hands of every student? What infrastructure, professional development, and technical support components need to be in place to support such a deployment? Anyone advocating for broad change should make sure that all stakeholders are brought into the process to ensure that bold vision unaccompanied by thoughtful implementation doesn't lead to unintended consequences.

Policies related to technical assistance should also support the use of technology rather than obstruct it. For example, although firewalls are essential to the security of network environments, policies must provide teachers, administrators, and students with remote access while maintaining the security of school servers. Likewise, policies must provide ways to control and filter students' access to objectionable Internet content without discouraging exploration, inquiry, and progressive self-responsibility.

External conditions that may affect an individual school district include policies and programs initiated at all levels of the educational and political system. Since district leaders are responsible for implementing these programs at the local level, they should remain vigilant concerning the potential implications of well-meaning policies that may inadvertently make it difficult for students and teachers to access and use technology resources.

TOOLS FOR ASSESSING THE ESSENTIAL CONDITIONS

When creating a technology assessment plan, take the time first to examine all the conditions that are necessary for its success. A number of tools are available for use in assessing one or more of the Essential Conditions, including

> **Essential Conditions Rubric.** Found in appendix A, this rubric may be used in conjunction with the STaR Readiness Chart to self-assess your organization's progress on the Essential Conditions.

> **STaR Readiness Chart.** This simple, self-report survey allows teachers, administrators, students, parents, and others to rate their school environment on each of the Essential Conditions using a 1–5 scale.

> **PETI Tools.** This tool kit identifies common data elements for evaluating education technology within and across states.

The Essential Conditions Rubric

This rubric examines the typical developmental stages of the Essential Conditions for ease of discussion with constituent groups. It can be used as a planning and development activity for teachers, administrators, and community members. Ask individuals to mark where they believe your district or school is with regard to each of these elements. The discussion that ensues will be instructive in itself.

Discussing why an Essential Condition is being met or not met encourages everyone in the process to come to a common understanding of the situation at hand. Action plans can be made to remedy deficits, or agreements can be reached that some conditions can only be met at less-than-optimal levels. Figure 17.3 shows an excerpt of an Essential Conditions rubric that's been marked up during a district-level discussion. Appendix A also contains an Essential Conditions scorecard for engaging school and district personnel in self-assessment of where they are with regard to the Essential Conditions.

STaR Readiness Chart

The STaR Readiness Chart, accessible at www.iste.org/starchart/, is an interactive tool developed by the CEO Forum. The tool identifies Essential Conditions for schools and provides a self-assessment tool for schools to use in evaluating their readiness for technology. These needs-assessment data are critical to informing decision making and education technology planning efforts. The tools are typically used for

- **Setting benchmarks and goals.** Schools, districts, and states have used the STaR Chart to identify current education technology profiles, establish goals, and monitor progress.
- **Applying for grants.** The STaR Chart has helped schools and school districts identify their education technology needs as they apply for grants.
- **Determining funding priorities.** Education administrators and policy makers have used the STaR Chart to determine where to allocate funds.

- **Creating individualized assessment tools.** Education administrators and policy makers have used the STaR Chart as the basis for statewide technology assessments.

After you complete a 20-question online survey, a profile based on your responses is created. Figure 17.4 is a sample results chart noting that the respondent's school is at the "mid tech" level.

PETI Tools

Developed by the State Education Technology Directors Association (SETDA), the Profiling Education Technology Integration (PETI) Tools (available at www.setda-peti.org) are designed to use common data elements to assess technology integration. SETDA's purpose for creating these tools is "to provide technical assistance and encourage the use of validated tools that incorporate common, agreed-upon definitions to help all education stakeholders better assess technology in their schools." SEDTA (in collaboration with the Metiri Group) has created statistically validated instruments for

1. survey instruments, including a teacher survey (20–25 minutes), a school administrator survey (30–40 minutes), and a district administrator survey (35–45 minutes);

2. site visitation protocols for classroom observations, focus groups with students and teachers, teacher and principal interviews, school walk-throughs, artifact reviews, sample communiqués, and strategies for ensuring inter-rater reliability;

3. recommended report structures; and

4. sampling strategies for reducing the data collection burden on schools.

FIGURE 17.3
Marked Up Rubric

TABLE 2 *continued*

NETS Essential Conditions Rubric

ESSENTIAL CONDITION	INITIATING (Attempting)	APPROACHING (Working)	MEETS (Achieving)	EXCEEDS (Leading)
TECHNICAL ASSISTANCE Educators have technical assistance for maintaining and using technology.	Technical assistance for PK–18 faculty, teachers, teacher candidates, and students is viewed as inconsistent or inadequate by faculty, teachers, teacher candidates, and students. Issues of access and quality are unresolved.	Technical assistance for PK–18 faculty, teachers, teacher candidates, and students is readily available but is limited to troubleshooting hardware. Technical assistance for supporting teaching and learning is not a clearly defined role or is understaffed and, therefore, not useful.	Technical assistance for PK–18 faculty, teachers, teacher candidates, students, staff, and administrators is readily accessible. It includes mentoring to enhance skills in managing classroom hardware and software resources as well as instructional strategies to support teaching and learning.	Technical assistance for PK–18 faculty, teachers, teacher candidates, students, staff, and administrators is available 24/7. The technical assistance includes paid staff, identified peer and student mentors, and and pedagogy supporting in teach
CONTENT STANDARDS AND CURRICULUM RESOURCES Educators are knowledgeable in their subject matter and current in the content standards and teaching methodologies in their discipline(s).	Educators are beginning to feel comfortable in implementing the content area standards and understand which teaching methodologies are most appropriate. Knowledge of the NETS is limited. NETS is viewed as a separate subject from content area standards of t	Educators are comfortable with how to meet content area standards and teaching methodologies in their discipline. Although aware of technology use and integration, access technology-based res	PK–18 faculty, teachers, and teacher candidates are edgeable in th they t	

FIGURE 17.4
Sample of STaR Readiness Report

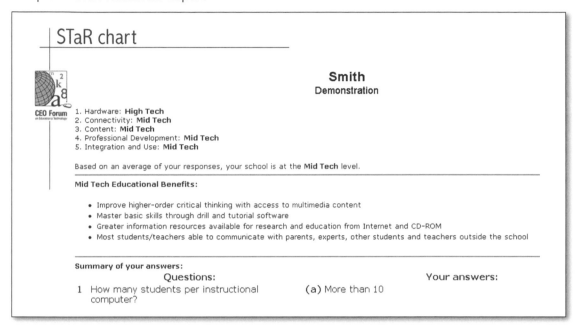

The common data elements built into these instruments enable school districts and states to aggregate and compare data with a common metric. These common data elements were derived by examining questions that meet the NCLB Title II, Part D, requirements, and they provide valid data for tracking change over time. The framework includes the following elements:

1. student impact
2. conditions essential for effective technology use:

   a. effective practice in teaching and learning with technology

   b. educator proficiency in effective practice with technology

   c. robust access anywhere, anytime

   d. digital age equity

   e. vision, systems thinking, and leadership with technology

A discussion of the key questions and principles addressed by this framework can be found on the SETDA Web site, www.setda-peti.org/Framework.html.

While the PETI tools don't assess student technology competency directly, they focus on the Essential Conditions for technology integration as well as its current state. Data can be collected in a pre- and post-research design to examine the progress made following specific interventions or initiatives. The rubric in Figure 17.5 is used for school-level assessment.

FIGURE 17.5

PETI Scoring Rubric

LEVEL OF USE	DESCRIPTION *With reference to the indicator,* the school...
1—AWARENESS	. . . is still highly traditional. Technology is only beginning to make an appearance, and there is little or no change in practice, proficiency, or policy related to or resulting from technology use.
2—ADOPTION	. . . has addressed technology in practice, proficiency, or policy. On the whole, 80% or more of teachers use technology, existing practices are automated, and policies are beginning to emerge that encourage technology use. But outside of the automation, there is very little that is actually different about what and how students, teachers, and administrators approach the work they do.
3—EXPLORATION	. . . has the qualities (i.e., automation; regular use by teachers and students) of the school that is scored at the Adoption level. In addition, however, there are occasional, *effective* innovations in practice, proficiency, or policy related to technology. At least 25% of teachers experiment with uses of technology that **extend** the quality, rigor, or relevance of what they were previously able to do.
4—TRANSFORMATION	. . . has the qualities (i.e., automation; regular use by teachers and students) of the school that is scored at the Adoption level. In addition, however, there are **regularly** *effective* innovations in practice, proficiency, or policy related to technology. At least 50% of teachers experiment with uses of technology that **extend** the quality, rigor, or relevance of what they were previously able to do. Essentially, teaching, learning, administration, and school culture have been transformed in ways that are related to technology use.

LESSONS LEARNED

It's taken time to strengthen the technology capacity of schools. More time is needed, because there's much work that remains to be done. We've learned in the process that identifying what students, teachers, administrators, and other educational leaders need to know and be able to do with technology is merely a first step—and a fleeting one, at that. Work on the NETS Project and the NETS Essential Conditions has taught us lessons in

Persistence. If you keep using technology, and learning about it, you may never be ahead of the game, but at least you can stay *in* the game.

Collaboration. Working together, sharing, and communicating lightens the load for all who participate and deepens the insights for everyone.

Listening. Open your ears to those in the trenches—to students who are always reaching out for what's new; to researchers who validate what really works; and to business and community leaders who are demanding that students be prepared with technology skills they need for the new global workplace.

Openness. Keep an open mind. We have many ways to reach solutions, many languages to use when sharing ideas, and many possibilities for enriching learning.

When not to be open. Sometimes being open is *not* appropriate. We must, at all costs, protect student safety and security.

Identifying possibilities. Technology holds infinite promise for those who have not previously had learning advantages or communications opportunities, or who have not been accepted or valued for their ideas or products.

Humility. Nothing can more quickly destroy a lesson or diminish the value of the many hours of work put into developing an assessment than technology that does NOT work as intended.

Whether we work in the classroom, the school, the principal's office, the district office, the college of education, or the state department of education, we are all involved in meeting the Essential Conditions, and all of us have a part to play in preparing students to use technology to learn, work, communicate, and produce more effectively.

While educators may debate over the utility of statewide standardized testing, there's little debate as to the usefulness of assessment generally. All teachers assess their students in some way, and in the field of technology assessment, testing methods are particularly varied and innovative. Your colleagues in any academic discipline can benefit from understanding the tools education technology advocates and assessment specialists have long used, such as the systematic scoring rubrics included in this book. So, too, can all educators use this book's guidelines for professional test development and implementation to inform decision making and integrate technology assessment into their overall assessment program.

In fact, integration is a term we return to again and again in discussions of education technology. We talk about the curricular integration of technology in the classroom; the integration of assessment and content learning; the integration of classroom, school, and district data-processing systems; and the integration of technology resources, professional development practices, and district policies and goal-setting that together make up the Essential Conditions for implementing the NETS•S.

Technology assessment also makes little sense unless it's addressed in an integrated way. A teacher's course syllabus or a statewide educational standard can have stand-alone value even if that value is greatly enhanced when integrated into a larger educational plan. Testing, on the other hand, is useful only for the information it provides teachers, students, administrators, parents, and the community at large. That information can determine student achievement or advancement and support decision making regarding professional development needs and resource allocation.

Indeed, assessment is the primary vehicle by which we can determine if other elements of the educational process are working, and working well. Assessment in a vacuum tells us little. But assessment informed by the contexts and processes within which it takes place—technology and content area standards, contemporary teaching practices, student learning styles and expectations, and state and national education goals and policies—should be considered an integral part of the education process.

References

Botstein, L. (2000, May 28). The tyranny of standardized testing. *New York Times.*

Dede, C. (2002).Vignettes about the future of learning technologies. In *Visions 2020: Transforming education and training through advanced technologies*, pp. 18–25. Washington, DC: U.S. Department of Commerce. Retrieved June 2005 from http://www.technology.gov/reports/ TechPolicy/2020Visions.pdf

Dede, C., Whitehouse, P., & Brown-L'Bahy, T. (2002). Designing and studying learning experiences that use multiple interactive media to bridge distance and time. In C. Vrasidas & G. V. Glass (Eds.), *Current perspectives on applied information technologies: Distance education and distributed learning*, pp. 1–30. Greenwich, CT: Information Age Press.

Dede, C. (2005). Planning for neomillennial learning styles: Implications for investments in technology and faculty. In D. G. Oblinger & J. L. Oblinger (Eds.), *Educating the Net generation.* Boulder, CO: EDUCAUSE. Retrieved June 2005 from http://www.educause.edu/ educatingthenetgen/

International Society for Technology in Education. (2002). *National educational technology standards for teachers: Preparing teachers to use technology.* Eugene, OR: Author.

Wolf, M. *Assessing technology integration in schools.* Retrieved June 2005 from http://www.thejournal. com/magazine/vault/A5273.cfm

APPENDIX A

Essential Conditions for Implementing the NETS

This appendix provides supplementary materials for the NETS Essential Conditions. These Essential Conditions must be present for the successful implementation of the National Educational Technology Standards for Students, Teachers, and Administrators. For a thorough discussion of the Essential Conditions and how to use these resources, see chapters 1 and 17.

THE NETS•A ESSENTIAL CONDITIONS

Shared Vision. The school board and administrators provide proactive leadership in the development of shared education technology vision among school personnel, parents, and the community.

Equitable Access. Students, teachers, staff, and administrators have equitable access to current technologies, software, and telecommunications resources.

Skilled Personnel. District leaders and support personnel are skilled in the use of technology appropriate for their job responsibilities.

Professional Development. District leaders and support personnel have consistent access to technology-related professional development pertinent to their job assignments.

Technical Assistance. Personnel have technical assistance for maintaining and using technology.

Content Standards and Curriculum Resources. Instructional personnel and school leaders are knowledgeable about content and technology standards, related curriculum resources, teaching methodologies, and the use of technology to support learning.

Student-Centered Teaching. Teaching in all settings includes the use of technology to facilitate student-centered approaches to learning.

Assessment and Accountability. The school district has a system for the continual assessment of the effectiveness of technology to improve student learning.

Community Support. The district maintains partnerships and communications with parents, businesses, and the community to support technology use within the district.

Support Policies. The district has policies, financial plans, and incentive structures to support the use of technology in learning and district operations.

External Conditions. Policies, requirements, and initiatives at the national, regional, and state levels support the district in the effective implementation of technology for achieving national, state, and local curriculum and technology standards.

APPENDIX A TABLES

- **TABLE 1.** Essential Conditions for Implementing the NETS•S, NETS•T, and NETS•A
- **TABLE 2.** NETS•T Essential Conditions Rubric
- **TABLE 3.** NETS•S Essential Conditions Scorecard

TABLE 1
Essential Conditions for Implementing NETS•S, NETS•T, and NETS•A

NETS•S (NETS for Students)	NETS•T (NETS for Teachers)	NETS•A (NETS forAdministrators)
VISION The education system provides support and proactive leadership.	**SHARED VISION** The entire education system provides proactive leadership and support for the implementation of technology in teaching and learning. • **General Preparation.** University leaders share a vision for technology use in all appropriate courses and content areas. • **Professional Preparation.** Professional education administration and faculty share a vision for technology use to support new modes of teaching and learning. • **Student Teaching and Internship.** University personnel and cooperating school site teachers and school administrators share a vision for technology use in the classroom. • **First-Year Teaching.** Schools, districts, and universities share a vision for supporting new teachers in their use of technology in the classroom.	**SHARED VISION** The school board and administrators provide proactive leadership in the development of a shared education technology vision among school personnel, parents, and the community.
ACCESS Students have access to contemporary technologies, software, and telecommunications networks.	**ACCESS** Educators have access to current technologies, software, and telecommunications networks. • **General Preparation.** Access to current technologies, software, and telecommunications networks is provided for all students and faculty both inside and outside the classroom. • **Professional Preparation.** Access to current technologies, software, and telecommunications networks is provided for teacher education faculty, classes, and field sites, including technology-enhanced classrooms that model environments for facilitating a variety of collaborative learning strategies. • **Student Teaching and Internship.** Access to current technologies, software, and telecommunications networks is provided for student teachers and interns and their master teachers, mentors, and supervisors in the classroom and professional work areas. • **First-Year Teaching.** Access to current technologies, software, and telecommunications networks is provided for new teachers for classroom and professional use, including access beyond the school day.	**EQUITABLE ACCESS** Students, teachers, staff, and administrators have equitable access to current technologies, software, and telecommunications resources.

continued

TABLE 1 *continued*

Essential Conditions for Implementing NETS•S, NETS•T, and NETS•A

NETS•S (NETS for Students)	NETS•T (NETS for Teachers)	NETS•A (NETS for Administrators)
SKILLED EDUCATORS Students have access to educators skilled in the use of technology for learning.	**SKILLED EDUCATORS** Educators are skilled in the use of technology for learning. • **General Preparation.** Faculty teaching general education and major courses are knowledgeable about and model appropriate use of technology in their disciplines. • **Professional Preparation.** Teacher education faculty are skilled in using technology systems and software appropriate to their subject area specialty and model effective use as part of the coursework. • **Student Teaching and Internship.** Master (cooperating and supervising) teachers and university supervisors model technology use that helps students meet the National Educational Technology Standards for Students. • **First-Year Teaching.** Peers and administrators are skilled users of technology for teaching and school management.	**SKILLED PERSONNEL** District leaders and support personnel are skilled in the use of technology appropriate for their job responsibilities.
PROFESSIONAL DEVELOPMENT Educators have consistent access to professional development to support technology use in teaching and learning.	**PROFESSIONAL DEVELOPMENT** Educators have consistent access to professional development to support technology use in teaching and learning. • **General Preparation.** University faculty and students are provided opportunities for technology skill development and reward structures that recognize the application of technology in teaching, learning, and faculty collaboration. • **Professional Preparation.** Personnel in teacher education and at field experience sites are provided with ongoing professional development. • **Student Teaching and Internship.** Cooperating teachers, master teachers, and supervisors of student teachers and interns are provided professional development in the use of applications of technology in teaching. • **First-Year Teaching.** Faculty has continual access to a variety of professional development opportunities in several delivery modes, with time to take advantage of the offerings.	**PROFESSIONAL DEVELOPMENT** District leaders and support personnel have consistent access to technology-related professional development pertinent to their job assignments.

continued

TABLE 1 *continued*

Essential Conditions for Implementing NETS•S, NETS•T, and NETS•A

NETS•S (NETS for Students)	NETS•T (NETS for Teachers)	NETS•A (NETS for Administrators)
TECHNICAL ASSISTANCE Technical assistance for maintaining and using technology resources is provided.	**TECHNICAL ASSISTANCE** Educators have technical assistance for maintaining and using technology. • **General Preparation.** Timely technical assistance is available for all faculty to ensure consistent, reliable functioning of technology resources. • **Professional Preparation.** Technical assistance for teacher education faculty and students is readily accessible and includes expertise in the use of technology resources for teaching and learning in PK–12 settings. • **Student Teaching and Internship.** In field-experience settings, technical assistance is on-site to ensure reliability of technology resources. • **First-Year Teaching.** Technical assistance for faculty and staff is timely and on-site and includes mentoring to enhance skills in managing classroom software and hardware resources.	**TECHNICAL ASSISTANCE** Personnel have technical assistance for maintaining and using technology.
CONTENT STANDARDS AND CURRICULUM Content standards and curriculum resources are provided.	**CONTENT STANDARDS AND CURRICULUM RESOURCES** Educators are knowledgeable in their subject matter and current on the content standards and teaching methodologies in their discipline. • **General Preparation.** Prospective teachers have knowledge in the subject area(s) they intend to teach. • **Professional Preparation.** Technology-based curriculum resources that address standards for subject matter content and support teaching, learning, and productivity are available to teacher candidates. • **Student Teaching and Internship.** Technology-based curriculum resources that are appropriate to the content standards in teaching areas and grade ranges are available to teacher candidates at the student and intern site. • **First-Year Teaching.** The school district provides professional development opportunities related to local policies and content standards as well as the technology-based resources to support the new teacher's efforts to address those standards.	**CONTENT STANDARDS AND CURRICULUM RESOURCES** Instructional personnel and school leaders are knowledgeable about content and technology standards, related curriculum resources, teaching methodologies, and the use of technology to support learning.

continued

TABLE 1 *continued*

Essential Conditions for Implementing NETS•S, NETS•T, and NETS•A

NETS•S (NETS for Students)	NETS•T (NETS for Teachers)	NETS•A (NETS for Administrators)
STUDENT-CENTERED LEARNING Student-centered approaches to learning are followed.	**STUDENT-CENTERED TEACHING** Teaching in all settings encompasses student-centered approaches to learning. • **General Preparation.** University faculty incorporate student-centered approaches to learning, for example, active, cooperative, and project-based learning. • **Professional Preparation.** Teacher education faculty and professional teaching staff model student-centered approaches to instruction in education coursework and field experiences. • **Student Teaching and Internship.** Opportunities to implement a variety of technology-enhanced, student-centered learning activities are provided for teacher candidates and interns. • **First-Year Teaching.** Faculty routinely use student-centered approaches to learning to facilitate student use of technology.	**STUDENT-CENTERED TEACHING** Teaching in all settings includes the use of technology to facilitate student-centered approaches to learning.
ASSESSMENT The effectiveness of technology for learning is assessed.	**ASSESSMENT** Assessment of the effectiveness of technology for learning is continual. • **General Preparation.** University faculty and support staff assess the effectiveness of technology for learning both to examine educational outcomes and to inform procurement, policy, and curriculum decisions. • **Professional Preparation.** Teacher education faculty and professional teaching staff model the integration of teaching and assessment used to measure the effectiveness of technology-supported teaching strategies. • **Student Teaching and Internship.** Cooperating and master teachers work with student teachers and interns to assess the effectiveness of student learning, and of technology in supporting that learning. • **First-Year Teaching.** The district and school site support classroom teachers in the assessment of learning outcomes for technology-supported activities to inform planning, teaching, and further assessment.	**ASSESSMENT AND ACCOUNTABILITY** The school district has a system for the continual assessment of the effectiveness of technology to improve student learning.

continued

TABLE 1 *continued*

Essential Conditions for Implementing NETS•S, NETS•T, and NETS•A

NETS•S (NETS for Students)	NETS•T (NETS for Teachers)	NETS•A (NETS for Administrators)
COMMUNITY SUPPORT Community partners provide expertise, support, and real-life interactions.	**COMMUNITY SUPPORT** The community and school partners provide expertise, support, and resources. • **General Preparation.** Prospective teachers experience technology use in real-world settings related to their general education and courses in their majors. • **Professional Preparation.** Teacher preparation programs provide teacher candidates with opportunities to participate in field experiences at partner schools where technology integration is modeled. • **Student Teaching and Internship.** Student teachers and interns teach in partner schools where technology integration is modeled and supported. • **First-Year Teaching.** Schools provide beginning teachers with connections to the community and models of effective use of local and outside resources.	**COMMUNITY SUPPORT** The district maintains partnerships and communications with parents, businesses, and the community to support technology use within the district.
SUPPORT POLICIES 1. Ongoing financial support for sustained technology use is provided. 2. Policies and standards support new learning environments.	**SUPPORT POLICIES** School and university policies, financing, and reward structures are in place to support technology in learning. • **General Preparation.** University faculty are provided with resources for meeting subject area needs and with reward structures that recognize the application of technology in teaching, learning, and faculty collaboration. • **Professional Preparation.** Policies associated with accreditation, standards, budget allocations, and personnel decisions in teacher education programs and at field experience sites support technology integration. Retention, tenure, promotion, and merit policies reward faculty's innovative uses of technology with their students. • **Student Teaching and Internship.** Student teaching and internships are located at sites where administrative policies support and reward the use of technology. • **First-Year Teaching.** School induction-year policies, budget allocations, and mentoring assignments support the first-year teacher's use of technology. Hiring practices include policies regarding technology skills of prospective hires.	**SUPPORT POLICIES** The district has policies, financial plans, and incentive structures to support the use of technology in learning and district operations. **EXTERNAL CONDITIONS** Policies, requirements, and initiatives at the national, regional, and state levels support the district in the effective implementation of technology for achieving national, state, and local curriculum and technology standards.

TABLE 2

NETS•T Essential Conditions Rubric

ESSENTIAL CONDITION	INITIATING (Attempting)	APPROACHING (Working)	MEETS (Achieving)	EXCEEDS (Leading)
SHARED VISION The entire education system provides proactive leadership and support for the implementation of technology in teaching and learning.	Each area within the university and the local school district has an idea of how technology should be implemented and supported. However, there has not been an open consensus built around the vision with a concrete implementation plan.	A collaborative consensus-building process has been used to establish a consistent and well-articulated vision for the implementation of technology to support students, parents, teachers, and faculty in their use of technology in the classroom and home for teaching and learning. However, little evidence of a concrete, thorough implementation plan to support the vision is shown.	University leaders, teacher education program administrators, faculty, school district teachers, and administrators have reached consensus on a shared vision for the PK–18 school community in their use of technology for teaching and learning. A collaboratively designed, well-articulated implementation plan that is proactively supported by the leadership exists.	The PK–18 school community has a dynamic and ongoing consensus-building process for establishing and revising a proactive, shared vision for supporting technology in teaching and learning. The implementation plan reflects not only the shared vision, but also a collaborative atmosphere for the sharing of resources to bring the vision to life.
ACCESS Educators have access to current technologies, software, and telecommunications networks.	Student access to technology is limited to lab settings. Faculty and teacher access to the technology hardware is inconsistently limited to offices or workspaces. Access to technology resources is tightly controlled and creates a negative, competitive environment within the faculty.	Access to technology is available in the classroom to support student learning and faculty teaching and productivity. Access to technology resources is growing to include both classroom and lab settings for student use. Access to telecommunications and network resources is not consistently available.	Access to current technologies, software, and telecommunications networks is provided for PK–18 students, teachers, faculty, and support personnel, both inside and outside the school and during and beyond the school day.	The university and school district jointly support on-demand access to technology resources: hardware and software, telecommunications, and other online resources for students and faculty, including home, community, and global access.
SKILLED EDUCATORS Educators are skilled in the use of technology for learning.	PK–18 faculty and teachers are skilled in the basic professional productivity tools, using technology primarily for their own productivity in relationship to teaching and learning (creating plans and syllabi, writing letters and reports).	PK–18 faculty, teachers, students, and teacher candidates are skilled in the uses of technology for teaching and learning.(Both teachers and students are using the technology with limited productivity tools and basic Web-based resources.)	All PK–18 faculty, teachers, supervising personnel (cooperating teachers, supervisors, and administrators), and teacher candidates are skilled users of technology to improve teaching, learning, and school management.	Because stakeholders define educators as all who participate in the education of students, everyone who comes in contact with students is a skilled user of technology to support teaching and learning. The circle is expanded to include all staff, parents, and supportive community members.

continued

TABLE 2 *continued*
NETS Essential Conditions Rubric

ESSENTIAL CONDITION	INITIATING (Attempting)	APPROACHING (Working)	MEETS (Achieving)	EXCEEDS (Leading)
PROFESSIONAL DEVELOPMENT Educators have consistent access to professional development to support technology use in teaching and learning.	Professional development in technology focuses only on technology skills and is limited in offering. The university and school districts do not communicate to the larger community about professional development opportunities that occur online or elsewhere in the vicinity.	Professional development is provided for all but not based on a needs assessment of the faculty, teachers, students, or teacher candidates. The professional development may also not be based on a comprehensive technology plan. The modes of delivery are limited.	PK–18 faculty and students are provided with timely, ongoing, needs-based professional development opportunities for technology skill development and application of technology in teaching and learning, with the time and equipment to be successful. Professional development opportunities provided use various modes of delivery and are evaluated for effectiveness and satisfaction. Professional development is based on a comprehensive technology plan.	PK–18 faculty, teachers, students, and teacher candidates have access to professional development on-demand and in a mode suitable to various learning styles. Professional development is financially supported by the educational agency, with necessary resources provided. Professional development opportunities are regularly evaluated and revised, with innovative input from participants encouraged to design new opportunities.
TECHNICAL ASSISTANCE Educators have technical assistance for maintaining and using technology.	Technical assistance for PK–18 faculty, teachers, teacher candidates, and students is viewed as inconsistent or inadequate by faculty, teachers, teacher candidates, and students. Issues of access and quality are unresolved.	Technical assistance for PK–18 faculty, teachers, teacher candidates, and students is readily available but is limited to troubleshooting hardware. Technical assistance for supporting teaching and learning is not a clearly defined role or is understaffed and, therefore, not useful.	Technical assistance for PK–18 faculty, teachers, teacher candidates, students, staff, and administrators is readily accessible. It includes mentoring to enhance skills in managing classroom hardware and software resources as well as instructional strategies to support teaching and learning.	Technical assistance for PK–18 faculty, teachers, teacher candidates, students, staff, and administrators is available 24/7. The technical assistance includes paid staff, identified peer and student mentors, and content and pedagogy specialists for supporting the use of technology in teaching and learning.
CONTENT STANDARDS AND CURRICULUM RESOURCES Educators are knowledgeable in their subject matter and current on the content standards and teaching methodologies in their discipline.	Educators are beginning to feel comfortable in implementing the content area standards and understand which teaching methodologies are most appropriate. Knowledge of the NETS is limited. NETS is viewed as a separate subject from content area standards. The use of technology-based content area resources in teaching and learning is unclear.	Educators are comfortable with how to meet content area standards and teaching methodologies in their discipline. Although aware of technology use and integration, access to technology-based resources and supporting methodologies and knowledge about how to use them are limited, inconsistent, and somewhat disconnected to the objective of the lessons.	PK–18 faculty, teachers, and teacher candidates are knowledgeable in the subject areas they teach. Technology-based curriculum resources appropriate in meeting content standards are readily accessible and appropriately applied.	PK–18 administrators, faculty, teachers, and teacher candidates are knowledgeable about the subject areas they teach and the technology-based resources appropriate to support student learning. Faculty and teachers regularly share innovative ideas for use of technology resources to support standards-based instruction.

continued

TABLE 2 *continued*
NETS Essential Conditions Rubric

ESSENTIAL CONDITION	INITIATING (Attempting)	APPROACHING (Working)	MEETS (Achieving)	EXCEEDS (Leading)
STUDENT-CENTERED TEACHING Teaching in all settings encompasses student-centered approaches to learning.	Teacher- and faculty-directed instruction is the predominant mode of instruction. The teacher is "on stage" in teaching and in using technology, with little student interaction in the classroom. When technology is used, students usually work alone. The tasks chosen have few options for student interaction, cooperative learning, or project-based learning.	PK–18 faculty, teachers, and teacher candidates attempt to implement student-centered approaches to learning, but insufficient time, inappropriate technology-based resources, and incomplete directions are given to students for successful completion of the activity.	PK–18 faculty, teachers, and teacher candidates routinely use student-centered approaches to learning (meaningful, active, cooperative, and project-based learning) that facilitate appropriate student use of technology.	PK–18 faculty, teachers, and teacher candidates routinely use student-centered approaches to learning. They include constructivist pedagogy (allowing students to create, identify, and construct their own problems, scenarios, or innovative solutions to complex problems) that facilitates appropriate student use of technology-based resources.
ASSESSMENT Assessment of the effectiveness of technology for learning is continual.	Technology is periodically assessed in terms of presence of hardware or resources and teacher and faculty use of it, but not in terms of the effects on instruction and student learning. Simple grade-book packages may be used for examining student learning data.	The use of technology in some curriculum areas is assessed in terms of teacher use and student outcomes. Technology is used for aggregating student performance data to make curriculum decisions.	With administrative support, PK–18 faculty and teachers model integration of technology and assessment to measure the effectiveness of technology-supported teaching strategies. Results are used to examine student outcomes, inform future planning and teaching, and drive further assessment. Results also inform procurement, policy, and curriculum decisions.	Institutional commitment to comprehensive use of technology in assessment for informing teaching, learning, policy, and budgetary decisions exists. How technology resources are assessed, upgraded, and retired is a shared vision indicating a support of instruction at all levels of PK–18.

continued

TABLE 2 *continued*

NETS Essential Conditions Rubric

ESSENTIAL CONDITION	INITIATING (Attempting)	APPROACHING (Working)	MEETS (Achieving)	EXCEEDS (Leading)
COMMUNITY SUPPORT The community and school partners provide expertise, support, and resources.	The university, schools, and community are inconsistently connected, causing unnecessary duplication of efforts and resources. Although an awareness of real-world uses of technology exists, teaching and learning experiences show little connection.	In an effort to make connections with the use of technology in real-world settings, many experiences are contrived. Teaching and learning are often one-dimensional, with either the school or community carrying the burden.	Students, teacher candidates, teachers, and faculty experience technology in real-world settings, making connections to models of technology use in the community.	The school and the community are integral to the mission and vision of each other. A feeling of reciprocity in teaching and learning is evident. They assist and inform each other. Faculty, teachers, and teacher candidates actively involve technology-rich, real-world experiences in the process of learning subject matter content.
SUPPORT POLICIES School and university policies, financing, and reward structures are in place to support technology in teaching and learning.	The incentive and reward structures are perceived to limit faculty, teacher, and teacher candidate willingness to be innovative in the use of technology to teach and learn. Resources for technology are not designated in the budget but are pulled from other budget lines to support technology needs.	Some policies appear to support the integration of technology in teaching and learning, while others continue to obstruct progress. Inconsistency in the application of policies leads to confusion about the goals for technology resources.	Personnel and resource-acquisition policies, budgets for programs, technology-based resources, and incentive and reward structures for PK–18 faculty, teachers, and teacher candidates support the use of technology in teaching, learning, and professional collaboration.	Administrative support policies, including budgeting, personnel, incentive and reward structures, are consistent and supportive of a shared, proactive, dynamic vision for the use of technology in teaching and learning.

TABLE 3
NETS•S Essential Conditions Scorecard

Name _____ School _____

Essential Conditions for Implementing the NETS for Students

Directions: Place an X on the continuum to indicate your school or classroom level of progress in each area.

	INITIATING	APPROACHING	MEETS	EXCEEDS
SHARED VISION				
EQUITABLE ACCESS				
SKILLED PERSONNEL				
PROFESSIONAL DEVELOPMENT				
TECHNICAL ASSISTANCE				
CONTENT STANDARDS AND CURRICULUM RESOURCES				
STUDENT-CENTERED TEACHING				
ASSESSMENT AND ACCOUNTABILITY				
COMMUNITY SUPPORT				
SUPPORT POLICIES (INCLUDING EXTERNAL CONDITIONS)				

NETS•S Assessement Rubrics

The following rubrics are based on the NETS•S Assessment Model introduced in chapter 2 (Figure 2.1). Table 1 is the NETS•S Developmental Rubric for Grades PK–12, which appears in chapter 2 as Figure 2.2. Tables 2 through 5 identify technology literacy benchmarks and expectations for the four grade ranges: K–2, 3–5, 6–8, and 9–12. These rubrics are designed to be used to develop assessments to measure student proficiency in the National Educational Technology Standards for Students (NETS•S).

Learning Point Associates (LPA), a nonprofit educational organization and owner of the North Central Regional Educational Laboratory, partnered with ISTE to develop these rubrics. LPA is also collaborating with ISTE to develop an empirically based assessment model using these NETS•S assessment rubrics. For the assessment model, LPA is working with measurement experts at the University of Illinois at Chicago to gather evidence of construct validity, and with an ISTE NETS project leadership team to gather evidence of content validity.

Surveys of school-level factors that affect student technology literacy, teacher technology integration, and administrator technology leadership have also been completed and are available for use. Together, the assessment and survey battery provide a cost-effective method for school districts to provide evidence that students and teachers are meeting the technology literacy and technology integration goals set out by Title II, Part D, of the No Child Left Behind Act of 2001 (NCLB). The assessments and surveys are delivered via the the Web and require only an Internet connection and updated browsers. Contact LPA at 1-800-252-0283 or visit www.learningpt.org for more information.

APPENDIX B TABLES

- **TABLE 1.** NETS•S Developmental Rubric for Grades PK–12
- **TABLE 2.** NETS•S Assessment Rubric for Grades PK–2 (Primary Level)
- **TABLE 3.** NETS•S Assessment Rubrics for Grades 3–5 (Intermediate Level)
- **TABLE 4.** NETS•S Assessment Rubric for Grades 6–8 (Middle School Level)
- **TABLE 5.** NETS•S Assessment Rubric for Grades 9–12 (High School Level)

TABLE 1

NETS•S Developmental Rubric for Grades PK–12

NETS•S	PROFICIENCY			
	By End of Grade 2	By End of Grade 5	By End of Grade 8	By End of Grade 12
1. BASIC OPERATIONS AND CONCEPTS				
• Students demonstrate a sound understanding of the nature and operation of technology systems.	Students describe how to use basic input devices (e.g., keyboard fingering, mouse/track pad), output devices (e.g., monitor, printer), and software resources (e.g., MP3 player, DVD). Students name common technology found in homes (e.g., DVRs, tape or digital recorders, CD players, digital still and video cameras, tele-phones, radios). Students identify functions represented by symbols and icons commonly found in applications (e.g., font name, font size, bold, underline, alignment, color of type). Students know how to use correct sitting, hand, arm, and fingering posi-tions to type complete sentences (including Shift for capital letters, the Space Bar for spacing, and punctuation keys). Students discuss how to properly care for and use software media (e.g., mini DV tapes, CDs, DVDs, memory cards, USB memory sticks).	Students know how to use basic input and output devices (including adaptive devices as needed); how to access network resources (e.g., printers, file servers); and how to use common peripherals (e.g., scanners, digital probes, digital cameras, video projectors). Students recognize, discuss, and visually represent ways tech-nology has changed life and work at school and in the home, community, business, industry, and government during the past three decades. Students identify and know how to use Menu options in applications to develop text, graphics, spreadsheets, and Web documents; to save, print, format, add multi-media features; to store, access, and manage files; and to use dictionary, thesaurus, and spelling and grammar tools. Students know proper keyboarding position and technique to touch-type using the correct hands for alphabetic, numeric, and special-purpose keys (e.g., arrows, Escape, Backspace, Delete, Caps Lock, Control) and how to use these keys and the Edit Menu items to correct errors in a document.	Students recognize hardware and software components used to provide access to network resources and know how common peripherals (e.g., scanners, digital cameras, video projectors) are accessed, controlled, connected, and used effectively and efficiently. Students know how to evaluate, select, and use appropriate technology tools and information resources to plan, design, develop, and communi-cate content information, appropriately addressing the target audience and providing accurate cita-tions for sources. Students know how to identify appropriate file formats for a variety of applications and apply utility programs to convert formats (as necessary) for effec-tive use in Web, video, audio, graphic, presenta-tion, word-processing, database, publication, and spreadsheet applica-tions. Students continue touch-typing techniques, increasing keyboarding facility, and improving accuracy, speed, and general efficiency in computer operation.	Students evaluate new and/or advanced technology resources for information-dissemina-tion options (e.g., video servers, webcasting, com-pressed video delivery, online file sharing, graphing calculators, multifunction commu-nications devices, global positioning software) and technology-career opportunities. Students assess the capabilities and limita-tions of contemporary and emerging technology resources as well as the potential of these systems and services to address personal lifelong learning and workplace needs. In teams, students collaborate to illustrate content-related concepts integrating a variety of media (e.g., print, audio, video, graphic, probes, simulations, models) with presentation, word-processing, publishing, database, graphics design software, or spreadsheet applications. Students routinely exhibit touch-typing techniques with advanced facility, accuracy, speed, and effi-ciency as they complete their assignments.

 continued

TABLE 1 *continued*

NETS•S Developmental Rubric for Grades PK–12

NETS•S	PROFICIENCY			
	By End of Grade 2	By End of Grade 5	By End of Grade 8	By End of Grade 12
1. BASIC OPERATIONS AND CONCEPTS				
• Students demonstrate a sound understanding of the nature and operation of technology systems.		Students identify characteristics suggesting that the computer needs upgraded system or application software, virus-detection software, or spam-defense software to protect the information and functioning of the technology system.	Students examine changes in hardware and software systems over time and identify how changes affect businesses, industry, government, education, and individual users.	In teams, students collaborate to evaluate software, hardware, and networking systems to inform the development of a technology plan for a specific real-world business, educational entity, industry, organization, or other group.
• Students are proficient in the use of technology.	Students recognize functions of basic File Menu commands (e.g., New, Open, Close, Save, Save As, Print) and folders to manage and maintain computer files on a hard drive or other storage medium (e.g., CD, DVD). Students recognize accurate terminology to describe hardware, software, multimedia devices, storage media, and peripherals as well as to identify the basic functions of technology resources (hardware and software) commonly used in early elementary classrooms.	Students identify basic software commands used to manage and maintain computer files on a hard drive, CD, or DVD; manage and maintain their files on a network; and know how to exchange files with other students and the teacher through network file sharing and e-mail attachments. Students identify the used to describe basic hardware, software, and networking functions as well as to discuss the functions, processes, and/or procedures applied in common use of these technology resources.	Students identify strategies and procedures for efficient and effective management and maintenance of computer files in a variety of different media and formats on a hard drive and network. Students know how to solve basic hardware, software, and network problems occurring every day; protect computers, networks, and information from viruses, vandalism,and unauthorized use; and access online help and user documentation to solve common hardware, software, and network problems.	Students know how to use advanced utilities (e.g., compression, antivirus) with computer files in a variety of media and formats. Students know how to identify, assess, and solve advanced hardware, software, and network problems by using online help and other user documentation and support.
2. SOCIAL, ETHICAL, AND HUMAN ISSUES				
• Students understand the ethical, cultural, and societal issues related to technology.	Students identify common uses of information and communication technology in the community and in daily life.	Students identify issues related to how information and communication technology supports collaboration, personal productivity, lifelong learning, and assistance for students with disabilities.	Students identify legal and ethical issues related to using information and communication technology, recognize consequences of its misuse, and predict possible long-range effects of ethical and unethical uses of technology on culture and society.	Students analyze current trends in information and communication technology and assess the potential of emerging technologies for ethical and unethical uses in culture and society.

continued

TABLE 1 *continued*
NETS•S Developmental Rubric for Grades PK–12

NETS•S	PROFICIENCY			
	By End of Grade 2	By End of Grade 5	By End of Grade 8	By End of Grade 12
2. SOCIAL, ETHICAL, AND HUMAN ISSUES				
• Students practice responsible use of technology systems, information, and software.	Students recognize that copyright affects how one can use technology systems, information, and software resources.	Students discuss basic issues related to the responsible use of technology and information, identify scenarios describing acceptable and unacceptable computer use, and describe personal consequences of inappropriate use.	Students discuss issues related to acceptable and responsible use of information and communication technology (e.g., privacy, security, copyright, file sharing, plagiarism), analyze the consequences and costs of unethical use of information and computer technology (e.g., hacking, spamming, consumer fraud, virus setting, intrusion), and identify methods for addressing these risks.	Students analyze the consequences and costs of unethical use of information and computer technology and identify how individuals can protect their technology systems from the unethical and unscrupulous user.
• Students develop positive attitudes toward technology uses that support lifelong learning, collaboration, personal pursuits, and productivity.	Students describe acceptable and unacceptable computer etiquette and how to work cooperatively with peers, family members, and others when using technology in the classroom or at home.	Students identify software or technology-delivered access valuable to them and describe how it improves their ability to communicate, be productive, or achieve personal goals.	Students examine issues related to computer etiquette and discuss means for encouraging more effective use of technology to support effective communication, collaboration, personal productivity, lifelong learning, and assistance for individuals with disabilities.	Students analyze current trends in information and communication technology and discuss how emerging technologies could affect collaboration, enhance personal productivity, meet the diverse needs of learners, and promote opportunities for lifelong learning among local and global communities.
3. TECHNOLOGY PRODUCTIVITY TOOLS				
• Students use technology tools to enhance learning, increase productivity, and promote creativity.	Students know how to use word processors, drawing tools, presentation software, concept-mapping software, graphing software, and other productivity software to illustrate concepts and convey ideas.	Students identify and apply common productivity software features such as menus and toolbars to plan, create, and edit word-processing documents, spreadsheets, and presentations.	Students describe and apply common software features (e.g., spelling and grammar checkers, editing options, dictionary, thesaurus) to maximize accuracy in development of word-processing documents; sorting, formulas, and chart generation in spreadsheets; and insertion of pictures, movies, sound, and charts into presentation software to enhance communication to an audience, promote productivity, and support creativity.	Students understand and apply advanced software features, such as templates and styles to improve the appearance of word-processing documents, spreadsheets, and presentations and to provide evidence of learning, productivity, and creativity.

 continued

TABLE 1 *continued*
NETS•S Developmental Rubric for Grades PK–12

NETS•S	PROFICIENCY			
	By End of Grade 2	By End of Grade 5	By End of Grade 8	By End of Grade 12
3. TECHNOLOGY PRODUCTIVITY TOOLS				
• Students use productivity tools to collaborate in constructing technology-enhanced models, preparing publications, and producing other creative works.	Students know how to work together to collect and create pictures, images, and charts for development of word-processed reports and electronic presentations.	Students know procedures for importing and manipulating pictures, images, and charts in word-processing documents, spreadsheets, presentations, and creative works.	Students describe how to use online environments or other collaborative tools to facilitate design and development of materials, models, publications, and presentations; and how to apply utilities for editing pictures, images, and charts.	Students analyze a plan and procedures for development of a multimedia product (e.g., model, presentation, webcast, publication, creative work) and identify authoring tools, other hardware and software resources, research, and team personnel needed to plan, create, and edit the product.
4. TECHNOLOGY COMMUNICATIONS TOOLS				
• Students use telecommunications to collaborate, publish, and interact with peers, experts, and other audiences.	Students—with assistance from teacher, parents, or student partners—identify procedures for safely and securely using telecommunications tools (e.g., e-mail, message boards, blogs) to read, send, or post electronic messages for peers, experts, and other audiences.	Students identify telecommunications tools (e.g., e-mail, message boards, blogs) and online resources for collaborative projects with other students inside and outside the classroom who are studying similar curriculum-related content.	Students know how to use telecommunications tools (e.g., e-mail, message boards, blogs, online collaborative environments) to exchange data collected and learn curricular concepts by communicating with peers, experts, and other audiences.	Students plan and implement collaborative projects (with peers, experts, or other audiences) using advanced telecommunications tools (e.g., groupware, interactive Web sites, simulations, joint data collection, videoconferencing) to support curriculum concepts or benefit the local, regional, or global community.
• Students use a variety of media and formats to communicate information and ideas effectively to multiple audiences.	Students know how to use a variety of developmentally appropriate media (e.g., presentation software; newsletter templates; Web sites as resources for clip art, music, and information resources) to communicate ideas relevant to the curriculum to their classmates, families, and others.	Students identify a variety of media and formats to create and edit products (e.g., presentations, newsletters, Web sites, PDFs) to synthesize and communicate information and ideas from the curriculum to multiple audiences.	Students know how to use a variety of media and formats to design, develop, publish, and present products (e.g., presentations, newsletters, Web sites) that effectively communicate information and ideas about the curriculum to multiple audiences.	Students know how to use a variety of media and formats to design, develop, publish, and present products (e.g., presentations, newsletters, Web sites) that incorporate information from the curriculum and communicate original ideas to multiple audiences.

continued

TABLE 1 *continued*

NETS•S Developmental Rubric for Grades PK–12

NETS•S	PROFICIENCY			
	By End of Grade 2	By End of Grade 5	By End of Grade 8	By End of Grade 12
5. TECHNOLOGY RESEARCH TOOLS				
• Students use technology to locate, evaluate, and collect information from a variety of sources.	Students—with assistance from teachers, parents, or student partners—identify steps for using technology resources such as CDs (e.g., reference or educational software) and Web-based search engines to locate information on assigned topics in the curriculum.	Students describe steps for using common Web search engines and basic search functions of other technology resources to locate information, as well as guidelines for evaluating information from a variety of sources for its relevance to the curriculum.	Students know how to conduct an advanced search using Boolean logic and other sophisticated search functions; and know how to evaluate information from a variety of sources for accuracy, bias, appropriateness, and comprehensiveness.	Students know how to locate, select, and use advanced technology resources (e.g., expert systems, intelligent agents, real-world models and simulations) to enhance their learning of curriculum topics selected.
• Students use technology tools to process data and report results.	Students, with assistance from the teacher, know how to use existing common databases (e.g., library catalogs, online archives, electronic dictionaries, encyclopedias) to locate, sort, and interpret information on assigned topics in the curriculum.	Students describe how to perform basic queries designed to process data and report results on assigned topics in the curriculum.	Students know how to identify and implement procedures for designing, creating, and populating a database; and in performing queries they know how to process data and report results relevant to an assigned hypothesis or research question.	Students formulate a hypothesis or research question on a curriculum topic they choose, and design, create, and populate a database to process data and report results.
• Students evaluate and select new information resources and technological innovations based on the appropriateness to specific tasks.	Students identify technology resources (e.g., concept-mapping software, drawing software) to show steps in a sequence; to demonstrate likenesses and differences; and to recognize, record, and organize information related to assigned curricular topics.	Students identify, record, and organize information on assigned topics in the curriculum by selecting and using appropriate information and communication technology tools and resources (e.g., slideshow, timeline software, database, conceptual mapping).	Students know how to select and use information and communication technology tools and resources to collect and analyze information and report results on an assigned hypothesis or research question.	Students formulate a hypothesis or research question and select and use appropriate information and communication technology tools and resources for collecting and analyzing information and reporting results to multiple audiences.

continued

TABLE 1 *continued*

NETS•S Developmental Rubric for Grades PK–12

NETS•S	PROFICIENCY			
	By End of Grade 2	By End of Grade 5	By End of Grade 8	By End of Grade 12
6. TECHNOLOGY PROBLEM-SOLVING AND DECISION-MAKING TOOLS				
• Students use technology resources for solving problems and making informed decisions.	Students know how to select information and communication technology tools and resources that can be used to solve particular problems (e.g., concept-mapping software to generate and organize ideas for a report, illustrate same/different, or illustrate the sequence of a story; drawing program to make a picture; presentation software to communicate and illustrate ideas; graph program to organize and display data; a Web browser and search engine to locate needed information).	Students know how to apply their knowledge of problem-solving tools to select appropriate technology tools and resources to solve a specific problem or make a decision.	Students identify two or more types of information and communication technology tools or resources that can be used for informing and solving a specific problem and presenting results or for identifying and presenting an informed rationale for a decision.	Students describe integration of two or more information and communication technology tools and resources to collaborate with peers, community members, experts, and others to solve a problem and present results or to present an informed rationale for a decision.
• Students employ technology in the development of strategies for solving problems in the real world.	Students identify ways technology has been used to address real-world problems.	Students know how to select and use information and communication technology tools and resources to collect, organize, and evaluate information relevant to a real-world problem.	Students describe the information and communication technology tools they might use to compare information from different sources, to analyze findings, to determine the need for additional information, and to draw conclusions for addressing real-world problems.	Students integrate information and communication technology to analyze a real-world problem, design and implement procedures to monitor information, to set timelines, and to evaluate progress toward the solution of a real-world problem.

TABLE 2

NETS•S Assessment Rubric for Grades PK–2 (Primary Level)

NETS•S	NOVICE	BASIC	PROFICIENT	ADVANCED
	By End of Kindergarten	By End of Grade 1	By End of Grade 2	
1. BASIC OPERATIONS AND CONCEPTS				
• Students demonstrate a sound understanding of the nature and operation of technology systems.	Students recognize the major hardware components in a computer system and identify the functions and care of them (e.g., computer, monitor, mouse or track pad, keyboard). Students know how to use the mouse or track pad to access an application, indicate a choice, or activate a hyperlink. Students recognize symbols and icons used to identify common hardware and software functions within prepared materials (e.g., arrows for proceeding to the next page of curriculum-related software, underlined and colored text to represent a link). Students know how to use the keyboard to type letters and numbers and how to use special key functions (e.g., Enter/Return, Backspace, Delete, arrows, Shift, Space Bar). Students identify basic care of the computer, monitor, keyboard, mouse or track pad.	Students name and label the main parts of a computer system (CPU [central processing unit], monitor, keyboard, disk drive, printer, mouse, track pad, joystick) and identify the functions of each. Students know how to start up the computer; locate applications; choose icons to select, open, save, print, close files; and shut down the computer, monitor, and printer. Students recognize symbols and icons commonly used in curriculum-related software to identify options (e.g., printer icon represents printing option, diskette icon represents saving a file, musical notes icon represents a music link, movie camera icon represents a movie file, speaker icon indicates that sound or audio is available. The students know how to use correct sitting, hand, arm, and fingering positions to type words and phrases. Students discuss how to properly care for and use software media (CD, DVD, diskette, zip disk).	Students describe how to use basic input devices (e.g., keyboard, and mouse or track pad), output devices (e.g., monitor, printer), and software resources (e.g., diskette, CD-ROM). Students name common technology found in homes (e.g., VCRs, tape or digital recorder, CD player, digital still and video cameras, telephones, radios). Students identify functions represented by symbols and icons commonly found in application programs (e.g., font, size, bold, underline, alignment, color of type). Students know how to use correct sitting, hand, arm, and fingering positions to type complete sentences (including Shift for capital letters, the Space Bar for spacing, and punctuation keys). Students discuss how to properly care for and use software media (e.g., mini DV tapes, videotapes, audiotapes).	Students identify characteristics that describe input devices and output devices as well as name some devices that can provide input and output. Students accurately identify common uses of technology found in daily life (at home and in the community). Students recognize functions represented by symbols and icons commonly found in the drawing toolbars of application programs (e.g., arrange, select, rotate, text box, Word Art, insert clip art, insert picture, line, rectangle, shapes, lines, line style, font color, line color, fill color). Students know how to use correct sitting, hand, arm, and fingering positions to type and edit a brief story or message employing the full alphabetic keyboard. Students describe how to properly care for and use the computer system hardware, software, peripherals, and storage media.

   continued

TABLE 2 *continued*

NETS•S Assessment Rubric for Grades PK–2 (Primary Level)

NETS•S	NOVICE By End of Kindergarten	BASIC By End of Grade 1	PROFICIENT By End of Grade 2	ADVANCED
1. BASIC OPERATIONS AND CONCEPTS				
• **Students are proficient in the use of technology.**	Students know how to select applications and curriculum-related software by associating icons with resources they wish to access (e.g., students understand that clicking on icons or hyperlinks may allow them to access applications or Internet resources).	Students understand and know how to use basic commands for saving and printing their work, and they understand that file names and folders are used to identify and organize stored information and programs.	Students recognize functions of basic File Menu commands (New, Open, Close, Save, Save As, Print) and folders to manage and maintain computer files on a hard drive or other storage medium (e.g., diskette, CD-ROM).	Students identify software for graphing as a way to gather, organize, and display numerical information; multimedia as a way to organize information and/or illustrate it in a presentation (e.g., draw and label a picture, type and illustrate a story or report, create a simple slideshow); and access age-appropriate multimedia dictionaries and encyclopedias as resources for gathering information.
• **Students are proficient in the use of technology.**	Students correctly identify technology terminology by labeling major technology hardware components (e.g., computer, monitor, keyboard, mouse or track pad, printer).	Students identify technology hardware peripherals (e.g., speakers, earphones, projector) and storage components (e.g., disk drive, hard drive, CD-RW drive); and can name software used for typing, drawing, and electronic slide presentations.	Students recognize accurate terminology to describe hardware, software, multimedia devices, storage media, and peripherals as well as identify the basic functions of technology resources (hardware and software) commonly used in early elementary classrooms.	Students identify characteristics of computers that support multimedia (e.g., letters, sound, pictures, video) and the technology through which these are produced and displayed.
2. SOCIAL, ETHICAL, AND HUMAN ISSUES				
• **Students understand the ethical, cultural, and societal issues related to technology.**	Students identify a computer as a machine that helps people work, learn, communicate, and play.	Students identify ways that the computer is used at home and in school.	Students identify common uses of information and communication technology in the community and in daily life.	Students discuss the advantages and disadvantages of using technology and how the lack of access to technology can affect a person's access to information, learning opportunities, and future job prospects.
• **Students practice responsible use of technology systems, information, and software.**	Students recognize that using a password protects privacy of information.	Students recognize that passwords protect the security of technology systems.	Students recognize that copyright affects how one can use technology systems, information, and software resources.	Students describe the consequences of irresponsible use of technology resources at home and at school.

continued

TABLE 2 *continued*

NETS•S Assessment Rubric for Grades PK–2 (Primary Level)

NETS•S	NOVICE By End of Kindergarten	BASIC By End of Grade 1	PROFICIENT By End of Grade 2	ADVANCED
2. SOCIAL, ETHICAL, AND HUMAN ISSUES				
• Students develop positive attitudes toward technology uses that support lifelong learning, collaboration, personal pursuits, and productivity.	Students recognize technology as a source of information, learning, and entertainment.	Students understand appropriate uses of computers in the classroom and identify a variety of learning and communications opportunities available through the use of technology resources.	Students describe acceptable and unacceptable computer etiquette and how to work cooperatively with peers, family members, and others when using technology in the classroom or at home.	Students identify places in the community where one can access technology.
3. TECHNOLOGY PRODUCTIVITY TOOLS				
• Students use technology tools to enhance learning, increase productivity, and promote creativity.	Students know how to navigate developmentally appropriate multimedia resources (e.g., interactive books, educational software, drawing and presentation programs) to support learning, productivity, and creativity.	Students create, edit, move, and save multimedia resources (e.g., word processors, concept-mapping software, writing tools, drawing tools, graphing software) to communicate and illustrate thoughts, ideas, and stories.	Students know how to use word processors, drawing tools, presentation software, concept-mapping software, graphing software, and other productivity software to illustrate concepts and convey ideas.	Students identify the best type of productivity software to use for a certain task.
• Students use productivity tools to collaborate in constructing technology-enhanced models, preparing publications, and producing other creative works.	Students—with assistance from teacher, parents, or student partners—know how to use developmentally appropriate technology tools to produce creative works.	Students know how to collaborate to develop, print, and present a document using a word processor and/or drawing software.	Students know how to work together to collect and create pictures, images, and charts for development of word-processed reports and electronic presentations.	Students know how to collaborate to plan, organize, develop, and orchestrate a presentation of a multimedia slideshow that communicates information and ideas to classmates (and possibly to family members and others).
4. TECHNOLOGY COMMUNICATIONS TOOLS				
• Students use telecommunications to collaborate, publish, and interact with peers, experts, and other audiences.	Students—with assistance from teachers, parents, or student partners—recognize and respond to bulletin board (or e-mail) postings projected on large screen by their teacher.	Students—with assistance from teacher, parents, or student partners—know how to use telecommunications resources (e.g., electronic bulletin boards, e-mail, teacher-selected Web sites) to gather information, share ideas, and respond to questions posed by the teacher and other classmates.	Students—with assistance from teachers, parents, or student partners—identify procedures for safely and securely using telecommunications tools (e.g., e-mail, bulletin boards, newsgroups) to read, send, or post electronic messages for peers, experts, and other audiences.	Students know how to use telecommunications tools safely and securely to read, send, or post electronic messages to peers, experts, and family members.

continued

TABLE 2 *continued*

NETS•S Assessment Rubric for Grades PK–2 (Primary Level)

NETS•S	NOVICE By End of Kindergarten	BASIC By End of Grade 1	PROFICIENT By End of Grade 2	ADVANCED
4. TECHNOLOGY COMMUNICATIONS TOOLS				
• Students use a variety of media and formats to communicate information and ideas effectively to multiple audiences.	Students identify media formats demonstrated by their teacher that are used to communicate ideas (e.g., text, clip art, photos, video, Web pages, newsletters).	Students—with assistance from teachers, parents, or student partners—know how to select media formats (e.g., text, clip art, photos, video, Web pages, newsletters) to communicate and share ideas with students in other classrooms.	Students know how to use a variety of developmentally appropriate media (e.g., presentation software; newsletter templates; and Web pages as resources for clip art, music, and information resources) to communicate ideas relevant to the curriculum to their classmates, families, and others.	Students know how to independently use a variety of media to gather information and ideas relevant to curriculum, accurately summarize and illustrate the material, and effectively present the final information using a variety of media.
5. TECHNOLOGY RESEARCH TOOLS				
• Students use technology to locate, evaluate, and collect information from a variety of sources.	Students—with assistance from teachers, parents, or student partners—know how to access developmentally appropriate Web resources pre-identified (as a hyperlink) by their teacher or parents.	Students know how to recognize the Web browser and associate it with accessing linked resources on the Internet.	Students—with assistance from teachers, parents, or student partners—identify steps for using technology resources such as CD-ROMs (reference or educational software) and Web-based search engines to locate information on assigned topics in the curriculum.	Students know how to apply appropriate steps independently to access technology resources such as CD-ROMs (reference or educational software) and Web-based search engines to locate information on assigned topics in the curriculum.
• Students use technology tools to process data and report results.	There are no expectations with regard to using databases or other data-processing and report-generating software for this level.	There are no expectations with regard to using databases or other data-processing and report-generating software for this level.	Students—with assistance from the teacher—know how to use existing common databases (e.g., library catalogs, online archives, electronic dictionaries, encyclopedias) to locate, sort, and interpret information on assigned topics in the curriculum.	Students independently know how to use existing common databases (e.g., library catalogs, online archives, electronic dictionaries, encyclopedias) to locate, sort, and interpret information on assigned topics in the curriculum.
• Students evaluate and select new information resources and technological innovations based on the appropriateness to specific tasks.	Students identify uses of common hardware components (e.g., monitor for viewing, keyboard for typing or selecting, earphones for hearing privately, drives for inserting storage diskette or CD).	Students choose software appropriate for the task they are completing (e.g., word processor to write a story or paragraph, drawing program to make a picture, developmentally appropriate graphing program to make a graph).	Students identify technology resources (e.g., simple conceptual-mapping software, drawing software) to show steps in a sequence; to demonstrate likenesses and differences; and to recognize, record, and organize information related to assigned curricular topics.	Students provide a logical rationale for choosing one type of hardware or software instead of another for completing a specific assigned task.

continued

TABLE 2 *continued*

NETS•S Assessment Rubric for Grades PK–2 (Primary Level)

NETS•S	NOVICE By End of Kindergarten	BASIC By End of Grade 1	PROFICIENT By End of Grade 2	ADVANCED
6. TECHNOLOGY PROBLEM-SOLVING AND DECISION-MAKING TOOLS				
• Students use technology resources for solving problems and making informed decisions.	Students know how to use developmentally appropriate software focused on early-learning problem-solving skills (e.g., matching, counting, ordering and sequencing, patterns, sorting by shape or color, classification, hidden items, measurement, directional words, critical thinking, logic and prediction, identify likenesses and differences).	Students know how to use developmentally appropriate software to collect classroom data, create a graph, identify questions that could be answered by the information in the graph, and interpret the results from the graph.	Students know how to select information and communication technology tools and resources that can be used to solve particular problems (e.g., concept-mapping software to generate and organize ideas for a report or to illustrate likenesses and differences or the sequence of a story; drawing program to make a picture; presentation software to communicate and illustrate ideas; graph program to organize and display data; Web browser and search engine to locate needed information).	Students know how to use technology resources to access information that can assist them in making informed decisions about everyday matters (e.g., which movie to see and the time and location of the entertainment, what product to buy, how to build a kite).
• Students employ technology in the development of strategies for solving problems in the real world.	Students recognize how technology is used in their home or at school for learning and entertainment.	Students identify how technology is used in their community to support different types of jobs.	Students identify ways technology has been used to address real-world problems.	Students identify a strategy for solving a problem or completing a task by applying information generated using technology tools and resources.

TABLE 3
NETS•S Assessment Rubric for Grades 3–5 (Intermediate Level)

NETS•S	NOVICE	BASIC	PROFICIENT	ADVANCED
	By End of Grade 3	By End of Grade 4	By End of Grade 5	
1. BASIC OPERATIONS AND CONCEPTS				
• **Students demonstrate a sound understanding of the nature and operation of technology systems.**	Students identify characteristics that describe input devices and output devices and name some devices that can provide input and output. Students accurately identify common uses of technology found in daily life (at home and in the community). Students recognize functions represented by symbols and icons commonly found in the drawing toolbars of application programs (e.g., arrange, select, rotate, text box, Word Art, insert clip art, insert picture, line, rectangle, shapes, lines, line style, font color, line color, fill color). Students know how to use the correct sitting, hand, arm, and fingering positions to type and edit a brief story or message employing the full alphabetic keyboard. Students describe how to properly care for and use the computer system hardware, software, peripherals, and storage media.	Students describe the purposes of specific input and output devices (e.g., digital cameras, scanners, video projectors, printers, file servers) and know how to use keyboarding and mouse-pad manipulation efficiently and effectively. Students describe common purposes of technology use in daily life at home, at school, and in the community (e.g., for learning, finding information, work, entertainment). Students associate words, symbols, and icons commonly found in the menus and toolbars of application programs (e.g., arrange, select, rotate, text box, Word Art, insert clip art, insert picture, line, rectangle, shapes, lines, line style, font color, line color, fill color) with their functions. Students know how to use both alphabetic and numeric keys (above the alphabetic keys) by touch, using the correct fingers of the correct hands to compose and edit a letter or brief report. Students demonstrate proper care in the use of the computer system hardware, software, peripherals, and storage media.	Students know how to use basic input and output devices (including adaptive devices as needed), access network resources (e.g., printers, file servers), and use common peripherals (e.g., scanners, digital probes, digital cameras, video projectors). Students recognize, discuss, and visually represent ways technology has changed life at school, at home, and in the community, business, industry, and government during the past three decades. Students identify and know how to use Menu options in application programs to develop text, graphics, spreadsheets, and Web documents; to save, print, format, and add multimedia features; to store, access, and manage files; and to use the dictionary, thesaurus, and spelling and grammar tools. Students know proper keyboarding position and technique to touch-type using the correct hands for alphabetic, numeric, and special-purpose keys (e.g., arrows, Escape, Backspace, Delete, Caps Lock, Control) and how to use these keys and the Edit Menu items to correct errors in a document.	Students know how to connect and use a wide variety of input and output devices and common peripherals (e.g., scanners, digital probes, digital cameras, video projectors); and how to access networked resources. Students know how to explore, identify, and develop presentations describing types of occupations or careers that rely on computer-based technology. Students know how to insert photos, graphics, graphs, spreadsheets, sound, and video clips into word-processor, presentation, and Web documents. Students know the functions of all alphabetic, numeric, special-purpose, and symbol keys; can touch-type with the correct fingers of the correct hands using the full keyboard; and know how to use a word processor to compose, type, proofread, and edit a document. Students know how to locate and use system- and application-upgrade, virus-protection, and spam-defense software to keep a technology system working properly.

continued

TABLE 3 *continued*

NETS•S Assessment Rubric for Grades 3–5 (Intermediate Level)

NETS•S	NOVICE	BASIC	PROFICIENT	ADVANCED
	By End of Grade 3	By End of Grade 4	By End of Grade 5	
1. BASIC OPERATIONS AND CONCEPTS				
• Students demonstrate a sound understanding of the nature and operation of technology systems.			Students identify characteristics suggesting that the computer needs upgraded system or application software, virus-detection software, or spam-defense software to protect the information and functioning of the technology system.	
• Students are proficient in the use of technology.	Students identify software for graphing as a way to gather, organize, and display numerical information; multimedia as a way to organize information and/or illustrate it in a presentation (e.g., draw and label a picture, type and illustrate a story or report, create a simple slideshow); and age-appropriate multimedia dictionaries and encyclopedias as resources for gathering information.	Students know how to identify types of files by their icons and extensions; understand that particular file types are accessed through specific applications; and know how to use system menus to access particular files located in different folders and on a variety of internal and external media.	Students identify basic software commands used to manage and maintain computer files on a hard drive, diskette, CD-ROM, or network as well as know how to exchange files with other students and the teacher via network file sharing and e-mail attachments.	Students identify software used for information management and know which types of software can be used most effectively for different types of data and information needs as well as for conveying results to different audiences.
• Students are proficient in the use of technology.	Students identify characteristics of computers that support multimedia (e.g., letters, sound, pictures, video) and the technology through which these are produced and displayed.	Students identify the correct terminology used to describe basic hardware, software, and networking functions and to discuss the functions, processes, and/or procedures applied in common use of these technology resources.	Students identify the correct terminology used to describe basic hardware, software, and networking functions and to discuss the functions, processes, and/or procedures applied in common use of these technology resources.	Students identify search strategies for locating needed information and resources that contribute to solving a particular problem, organize information, and communicate solution strategies and conclusions using appropriate terminology.
2. SOCIAL, ETHICAL, AND HUMAN ISSUES				
• Students understand the ethical, cultural, and societal issues related to technology.	Students discuss the advantages and disadvantages of using technology and how the lack of access to technology can affect a person's access to information, learning opportunities, and future job prospects.	Students identify cultural and societal issues related to technology.	Students identify issues related to how information and communication technology supports collaboration, personal productivity, lifelong learning, and assistance for students with disabilities.	Students evaluate the accuracy, relevance, appropriateness, comprehensiveness, and bias of electronic information sources.

continued

TABLE 3 *continued*

NETS•S Assessment Rubric for Grades 3–5 (Intermediate Level)

NETS•S	NOVICE By End of Grade 3	BASIC By End of Grade 4	PROFICIENT By End of Grade 5	ADVANCED
2. SOCIAL, ETHICAL, AND HUMAN ISSUES				
• Students practice responsible use of technology systems, information, and software.	Students describe consequences of irresponsible use of technology resources at home and at school.	Students identify uses for information and communication technology in daily life and discuss implications of ethical and unethical use of current technologies at school and in society.	Students discuss basic issues related to the responsible use of technology and information, identify scenarios describing acceptable and unacceptable computer use, and describe personal consequences of inappropriate use.	Students identify a broad range of issues related to the use and misuse of information and communication technology resources (e.g., privacy, security, copyright, file sharing, plagiarism) and discuss laws relating to each.
• Students develop positive attitudes toward technology uses that support lifelong learning, collaboration, personal pursuits, and productivity.	Students identify places in the community where one can access technology.	Students discuss the types of skills that can be developed, information that can be located, and collaborations that can be initiated through use of technology.	Students identify software- or technology-delivered access that is valuable to them and describe how it improves their ability to communicate, be productive, or achieve personal goals.	Students identify their personal goals or pursuits and explore technology resources that may assist them in identifying paths leading to their goals or pursuits.
3. TECHNOLOGY PRODUCTIVITY TOOLS				
• Students use technology tools to enhance learning, increase productivity, and promote creativity.	Students identify the best type of productivity software to use for a certain task.	Students name general productivity tools and software features (e.g., dictionary, thesaurus, spelling and grammar checkers) and identify how the tools and features are most frequently used in their schoolwork and at home.	Students identify and apply common productivity software features (e.g., menus, toolbars) to plan, create, and edit word-processing documents, spreadsheets, and presentations.	Students describe how specific productivity tools and software features (e.g., spelling checker, dictionary, editing options) support personal productivity, remediation of skill deficits, and their capacity for learning in different subjects.
• Students use productivity tools to collaborate in constructing technology-enhanced models, preparing publications, and producing other creative works.	Students know how to collaborate to plan, organize, develop, and orchestrate a presentation of a multimedia slideshow that communicates information and ideas to classmates (and possibly to family members and others).	Students identify technology resources (e.g., multimedia authoring, presentation software, Web tools, digital cameras, scanners) used in developing individual and collaborative writing as well as published knowledge products for audiences inside and outside the classroom.	Students know the procedures for importing and manipulating pictures, images, and charts in word-processing documents, spreadsheets, presentations, and other creative works.	Students understand the basic principles for collaborative product development and identify common roles for group members, typical rules governing individual group-member responsibilities, and cooperative attitudes that facilitate successful teamwork.

continued

TABLE 3 *continued*

NETS•S Assessment Rubric for Grades 3–5 (Intermediate Level)

NETS•S	NOVICE	BASIC	PROFICIENT	ADVANCED
	By End of Grade 3	By End of Grade 4	By End of Grade 5	
4. TECHNOLOGY COMMUNICATIONS TOOLS				
• Students use tele-communications to collaborate, publish, and interact with peers, experts, and other audiences.	Students know how to safely and securely use telecommunications tools to read, send, or post electronic messages to peers, experts, and family members.	Students know how to use telecommunications to access remote information, communicate with others in support of direct and independent learning, and pursue personal interests.	Students identify telecommunications tools (e.g., e-mail, online discussions, Web environments) and online resources for collaborative projects with other students inside and outside the classroom who are studying similar curriculum-related content.	Students know how to develop Web-based telecommunications projects (e.g., WebQuest) that identify content; challenge other students who access the site to answer questions, add to the content, or give opinions; and provide the opportunity to evaluate responses or submissions for currency and accuracy.
• Students use a variety of media and formats to communicate information and ideas effectively to multiple audiences.	Students know how to independently use a variety of media to gather information and ideas relevant to curriculum, accurately summarize and illustrate the material, and effectively present the final information using a variety of media.	Students identify, discuss, and use multimedia terms, software tools, and design strategies (e.g., multimedia authoring, Web tools) to develop and communicate curriculum content.	Students identify a variety of media and formats to create and edit products (e.g., presentations, newsletters, Web pages, PDFs) that communicate syntheses of information and ideas from the curriculum to multiple audiences.	Students identify how different forms of media can be used within one presentation to communicate effectively with a wide variety of audience participants.
5. TECHNOLOGY RESEARCH TOOLS				
• Students use technology to locate, evaluate, and collect information from a variety of sources.	Students independently know how to apply appropriate steps to access technology resources such as CD-ROMs (reference or educational software) and Web-based search engines to locate information on assigned topics in the curriculum.	Students use and identify correct terminology to describe technology resources and search strategies for locating information in prepared content-area databases.	Students describe steps for using common Web search engines and basic search functions of other technology resources to locate information as well as guidelines for evaluating information from a variety of sources for its relevance to the curriculum.	Students know how to apply Boolean strategies to narrow the focus of the search for online information.
• Students use technology tools to process data and report results.	Students independently know how to use existing common databases (e.g., library catalogs, online archives, electronic dictionaries, encyclopedias) to locate, sort, and interpret information on assigned topics in the curriculum.	Students identify, discuss, and visually represent how and why databases are used widely to collect and organize information in schools, government, business, and sciences.	Students identify, record, and organize information on assigned topics in the curriculum by selecting and using appropriate information and communication technology tools and resources (e.g., slide-show, timeline software, database, conceptual mapping).	Students compare and contrast the functions and capabilities of a database, spreadsheet, and word processor for processing data, calculating data, and reporting results.

continued

TABLE 3 *continued*
NETS•S Assessment Rubric for Grades 3–5 (Intermediate Level)

NETS•S	NOVICE By End of Grade 3	BASIC By End of Grade 4	PROFICIENT By End of Grade 5	ADVANCED
5. TECHNOLOGY RESEARCH TOOLS				
• Students evaluate and select new information resources and technological innovations based on the appropriateness to specific tasks.	Students provide a logical rationale for choosing one type of hardware or software instead of another for completing a specific assigned task.	Students know how to select appropriate technology tools and resources evaluating the accuracy, relevance, appropriateness, comprehensiveness, and bias of electronic information resources.	Students identify, record, and organize information on assigned topics in the curriculum by selecting and using appropriate information and communication technology tools and resources (e.g., slideshow, timeline software, database, conceptual mapping).	Students compare and contrast the functions and capabilities of a database, spreadsheet, and word processor for processing data, calculating data, and reporting results.
6. TECHNOLOGY PROBLEM-SOLVING AND DECISION-MAKING TOOLS				
• Students use technology resources for solving problems and making informed decisions.	Students know how to use technology resources to access information that can assist them in making informed decisions about everyday matters (e.g., which movie to see and the time and location of entertainment, what product to buy, how to build a kite).	Students know how to use spreadsheet software to examine, sort, and graph data as well as apply functions and formulas to calculate the data.	Students know how to apply their knowledge of problem-solving tools to select appropriate technology tools and resources to solve a specific problem or make a decision.	Students know how to use spreadsheet data and simulations to make predictions, strategize solutions, and evaluate decisions regarding steps to take in solving problems.
• Students employ technology in the development of strategies for solving problems in the real world.	Students identify a strategy for solving a problem or completing a task by applying information generated using technology tools and resources.	Students know how to use technology resources (e.g., calculators, data-collection probes, videos, educational software) for problem solving, self-directed learning, and extended learning activities.	Students know how to select and use information and communication technology tools and resources to collect, organize, and evaluate information relevant to a real-world problem.	Students recognize and discuss how spreadsheets are used to calculate, graph, and represent data in a variety of settings (e.g., schools, government, business, industry, mathematics, sciences).

TABLE 4

NETS•S Assessment Rubric for Grades 6–8 (Middle School Level)

NETS•S	NOVICE	BASIC	PROFICIENT	ADVANCED
	By End of Grade 6	By End of Grade 7	By End of Grade 8	
1. BASIC OPERATIONS AND CONCEPTS				
• Students demonstrate a sound understanding of the nature and operation of technology systems.	Students know how to connect and use a wide variety of input and output devices and common peripherals (e.g., scanners, digital probes, digital cameras, video projectors) as well as how to access networked resources. Students know how to explore, identify, and develop presentations describing types of occupations and careers that rely on computer-based technology. Students know how to insert photos, graphics, graphs, spreadsheets, and sound and video clips into word-processor, presentation, and Web documents. Students know functions of all alphabetic, numeric, special-purpose and symbol keys; how to touch-type with the correct fingers of the correct hands, using the full keyboard; and how to use a word processor to compose type, proofread, and edit a document. Students know how to locate and use system- and application-upgrade, virus-protection, and spam-defense software to keep a technology system working properly.	Students discuss common hardware and software problems and identify strategies for trouble-shooting and solving minor hardware and software problems. Students know how to apply search engines, word processors, databases, spread-sheets, timelines, charts and graphs, surveys, communications, and other technology-based research, analysis, and communications tools to organize, synthesize, interpret, and commu-nicate results from data collected on techno-logical advances over time and the effects of the changes on business, industry, and education. Students know how to use application features such as columns, tables, headers and footers, borders, the drawing menu, and a variety of other toolbars to format and publish content projects and products. Students know how to use proper keyboarding posture, hand and finger positions, and touch-typing techniques to improve accuracy, speed, and general efficiency in computer operation. Students research and compare features of different virus-protec-tion, spam-defense, and firewall software and present features of each.	Students recognize hardware and software components that provide access to network resources and know how common peripherals (e.g., scanners, digital cameras, video projectors) are accessed, controlled, connected, and used effectively and efficiently. Students know how to evaluate, select, and use appropriate technology tools and information resources to plan, design, develop, and communi-cate content information, appropriately addressing the target audience and providing accurate cita-tions for sources. Students know how to identify appropriate file formats for a variety of applications and apply utility programs to convert formats, as necessary, for effective use in Web, video, audio, graphic, presenta-tion, word-processing, database, publication, and spreadsheet applica-tions. Students continue touch-typing techniques, increasing keyboarding facility and improving accuracy, speed, and general efficiency in computer operation. Students examine changes in hardware and software systems through time and identify how changes affect business, industry, government, education, and individual users.	Students describe strategies for identifying, solving, and preventing routine hardware and software problems that occur during everyday technology use. Students know how to research and evaluate the accuracy, relevance, appropriateness, compre-hensiveness, and bias of electronic information sources concerning real-world problems. Students demonstrate an understanding of concepts underlying hardware, software, and connectivity; how information and tech-nology resources can be combined to develop and promote understanding; and the value of visual and auditory features to convey accurate and convincing information. Students manipulate the keyboard and other input devices by touch with speed, accuracy, and efficiency. Students know how to make informed choices among technology systems, resources, and services.

continued

TABLE 4 *continued*

NETS•S Assessment Rubric for Grades 6–8 (Middle School Level)

NETS•S	NOVICE	BASIC	PROFICIENT	ADVANCED
	By End of Grade 6	By End of Grade 7	By End of Grade 8	
1. BASIC OPERATIONS AND CONCEPTS				
• Students are proficient in the use of technology.	Students identify software used for information management and know which types of software can be used most effectively for different types of data, for different information needs, and for conveying results to different audiences.	Students know how to organize materials in files and folders, sort files and e-mail lists (e.g., by file name and date) and sort data within application programs (e.g., word-processor tables, spreadsheets, and databases.	Students identify strategies and procedures for efficient and effective management and maintenance of computer files in a variety of different media and formats on a hard drive and network.	Students identify information storage devices and strategies used most efficiently and effectively for storing different types of data, for different purposes, for portability, and for very large files.
• Students are proficient in the use of technology.	Students identify search strategies for locating needed information, identify resources that contribute to solving a particular problem, organize information, and communicate solution strategies and conclusions using appropriate terminology.	Students select correct terminology and concepts associated with hardware, software, computer systems, networks, Internet connectivity, and technology applications (e.g., word-processor, database, spreadsheet, multimedia, telecommunications, drawing, concept-mapping, simulation) as well as other digital resources.	Students know how to solve basic hardware, software, and network problems that occur during everyday use; protect computers, networks, and information from viruses, vandalism, and unauthorized use; and access online help and user documentation to solve common hardware, software, and network problems.	Students use accurate terminology and select appropriate tools and technology resources to accomplish a variety of tasks and solve problems.
2. SOCIAL, ETHICAL, AND HUMAN ISSUES				
• Students understand the ethical, cultural, and societal issues related to technology.	Students evaluate the accuracy, relevance, appropriateness, comprehensiveness, and bias of electronic information sources.	Students recognize, discuss, and visually represent current changes in information technologies and the effect those changes have on the workplace and society.	Students identify legal and ethical issues related to use of information and communication technology, recognize consequences of its misuse, and predict possible long-range effects of ethical and unethical use of technology on culture and society.	Students identify capabilities and limitations of contemporary and emerging technology resources.

continued

TABLE 4 *continued*

NETS•S Assessment Rubric for Grades 6–8 (Middle School Level)

NETS•S	NOVICE By End of Grade 6	BASIC By End of Grade 7	PROFICIENT By End of Grade 8	ADVANCED
2. SOCIAL, ETHICAL, AND HUMAN ISSUES				
• Students practice responsible use of technology systems, information, and software.	Students identify a broad range of issues related to use and misuse (e.g., privacy, security, copyright, file sharing, plagiarism) of information and communication technology resources and discuss laws relating to each.	Students identify and develop scenarios or examples that illustrate ethical behaviors for use of personal copyrighted media (e.g., images, music, video, content, language, correctly formatted citations for the copyrighted materials).	Students discuss issues related to acceptable and responsible use (e.g., privacy, security, copyright, file sharing, plagiarism) of information and communication technology, analyze the consequences and costs of unethical use (e.g., hacking, spamming, consumer fraud, virus setting, intrusion) of information and computer technology, and identify methods for addressing these risks.	Students identify and discuss terms and concepts associated with safe, effective, and efficient use of the Internet and telecommunications resources (e.g., password, firewall, spam, security, fair use, acceptable use policy, release form) and recognize strategies that demonstrate ethical, legal, and socially responsible uses of technology and electronic resources.
• Students develop positive attitudes toward technology uses that support lifelong learning, collaboration, personal pursuits, and productivity.	Students identify their personal goals or pursuits and explore technology resources that may assist them in identifying paths leading to their goals or pursuits.	Students identify how they currently use technology and predict how they may use and benefit from its use in the future.	Students examine issues related to computer etiquette and discuss how to encourage more effective use of technology to support effective communication, collaboration, personal productivity, lifelong learning, and assistance for individuals with disabilities.	Students identify and present a strategy they would use for preparing for a job interview in a career for which they have had little or no training.
3. TECHNOLOGY PRODUCTIVITY TOOLS				
• Students use technology tools to enhance learning, increase productivity, and promote creativity.	Students describe how specific productivity tools and software features (e.g., spelling checker, dictionary, editing options) support personal productivity, remediation of skill deficits, and their capacities for learning in different subjects.	Students know how to use content-specific hardware and software (e.g., environmental probes, graphing calculators, exploratory environments, simulations, Web tools) to support learning, research, productivity, and creative thinking.	Students describe and apply common software features (e.g., spelling and grammar checkers, editing options, dictionary, thesaurus) to maximize accuracy in development of word-processing documents; sorting, formulas, and chart generation in spreadsheets; and insertion of pictures, movies, sound, and charts into presentation software to enhance communication to an audience, promote productivity, and support creativity.	Students know how to use technology tools and resources for managing and communicating personal, professional, and educational information (e.g., finances, schedules, addresses, purchases, correspondence, URLs, e-mail addresses, online references, citations).

continued

TABLE 4 *continued*

NETS•S Assessment Rubric for Grades 6–8 (Middle School Level)

NETS•S	NOVICE By End of Grade 6	BASIC By End of Grade 7	PROFICIENT By End of Grade 8	ADVANCED
3. TECHNOLOGY PRODUCTIVITY TOOLS				
• **Students use productivity tools to collaborate in constructing technology-enhanced models, preparing publications, and producing other creative works.**	Students understand basic principles for collaborative product development and identify common roles for group members, typical rules governing individual group-member responsi-bilities, and cooperative attitudes that facilitate successful teamwork.	Students know how to work in teams to use hardware and software tools (e.g., concept-mapping, word-processor, database, spreadsheet, publishing, Web publishing, drawing, puzzle-development, and timeline-develop-ment software; digital still and video cameras; probes, motion detectors, light detectors, digital microscopes) to support learning, research, pro-ductivity, and creativity.	Students describe how to use online environments or other collaborative tools to facilitate design and development of materials, models, publications, and presentations as well as apply utilities for editing pictures, images, and charts.	Students know how to work collaboratively to design, develop content for, and construct a Web-based publication.
4. TECHNOLOGY COMMUNICATIONS TOOLS				
• **Students use tele-communications to collaborate, publish, and interact with peers, experts, and other audiences.**	Students know how to develop Web-based tele-communications projects (e.g., WebQuest) that identify content; chal-lenge other students who access the site to answer questions, add to the content, or give opinions; and provide opportunity to evaluate responses or submissions for currency and accuracy.	Students know how to identify, evaluate, select, and use collaborative tools to survey, collect, share, and communicate information within and outside the school com-munity.	Students know how to use telecommunica-tions tools (e.g., e-mail, discussion groups, online collaborative environ-ments) to exchange data collected and learn curricular concepts by communicating with peers, experts, and other audiences.	Students know how to develop evaluation criteria for use in judging the quality of published (e.g., print, digital, video) materials for group projects; plan, develop, and present content-based group projects based on the criteria; and conduct peer reviews of the group projects using the criteria.
• **Students use a variety of media and formats to communicate information and ideas effectively to multiple audiences.**	Students identify how different forms of media can be used within one presentation to commu-nicate effectively with a wide variety of audience participants.	Students demonstrate knowledge of multimedia tools and concepts used by the media industry (e.g., music, games, video, radio, TV, Web sites) to entertain, sell, and influ-ence ideas and opinions.	Students know how to use a variety of media and formats (e.g., presen-tations, newsletters, Web pages) to design, develop, publish, and present products that effectively communicate informa-tion and ideas about the curriculum to multiple audiences.	Students know how to plan, design, and develop a multimedia product using data (e.g., graphs, charts, database reports) to present content information.

continued

TABLE 4 *continued*

NETS•S Assessment Rubric for Grades 6–8 (Middle School Level)

NETS•S	NOVICE	BASIC	PROFICIENT	ADVANCED
	By End of Grade 6	By End of Grade 7	By End of Grade 8	
5. TECHNOLOGY RESEARCH TOOLS				
• Students use technology to locate, evaluate, and collect information from a variety of sources.	Students know how to apply Boolean strategies to narrow the focus of the search for online information.	Students know how to search, collect, and evaluate resources from a variety of locations online and construct a linked list of resources (e.g., information, research, data, photos, video clips, illustrations, graphics) to support content learning and project development.	Students know how to conduct an advanced search using Boolean logic and other sophisticated search functions as well as evaluate information from a variety of sources for accuracy, bias, appropriateness, and comprehensiveness.	Students know how to research and evaluate the accuracy, relevance, appropriateness, comprehensiveness, and bias of electronic information sources concerning real-world problems.
• Students use technology tools to process data and report results.	Students know how to plan and develop database reports to organize, display, and explain findings in content areas.	Students know how to search for and sort information in an electronic database using multiple criteria, add and delete records, and identify strategies for finding specific information.	Students know how to identify and implement procedures for designing, creating, and populating a database; and, in performing queries, to process data and report results relevant to an assigned hypothesis or research question.	Students know how to create, edit, and modify a database report and identify trends reflecting analysis of the data.
• Students evaluate and select new information resources and technological innovations based on the appropriateness to specific tasks.	Students compare and contrast the functions and capabilities of the database, spreadsheet, and word processor for processing data, calculating, and reporting results.	Students know how to select information and technological resources based on the appropriateness and efficiency for completing tasks, providing the desired information, or addressing the identified objectives.	Students know how to select and use information and communication technology tools and resources to collect and analyze information and report results on an assigned hypothesis or research question.	Students know how to select and use technology tools to efficiently collect, analyze, and display data for class assignments, projects, and presentations.

continued

TABLE 4 *continued*
NETS•S Assessment Rubric for Grades 6–8 (Middle School Level)

NETS•S	NOVICE	BASIC	PROFICIENT	ADVANCED
	By End of Grade 6	By End of Grade 7	By End of Grade 8	
6. TECHNOLOGY PROBLEM-SOLVING AND DECISION-MAKING TOOLS				
• Students use technology resources for solving problems and making informed decisions.	Students know how to use spreadsheet data and simulations to make predictions, strategize solutions, and evaluate decisions regarding steps to take in solving problems.	Students know how to integrate data-gathering instruments (e.g., probes, electronic calculators, handheld devices) with spreadsheets, use data-analysis tools within the spreadsheet to analyze the data, graph results, and inform conclusions drawn from the data.	Students identify two or more types of information and communication technology tools or resources that can be used for informing and solving a specific problem and presenting results or for identifying and presenting an informed rationale for a decision.	Students develop strategies for use of data analyses, models, and simulations to make specific decisions regarding a course of action for solving real-world problems.
• Students employ technology in the development of strategies for solving problems in the real world.	Students recognize and discuss how spreadsheets are used to calculate, graph, and represent data in a variety of settings (e.g., schools, government, business, industry, mathematics, science).	Students know how to apply formulas, functions, and "what if" statements in spreadsheets and graphs or charts to analyze and interpret data for content assignments.	Students describe the information and communication technology tools they might use to compare information from different sources, analyze findings, determine the need for additional information, and draw conclusions for addressing real-world problems.	Students know how to identify a problem; develop a solution strategy; collect data on the effectiveness of the strategy; and analyze, interpret, publish, and present the data and conclusions based on real-world data.

TABLE 5
NETS•S Assessment Rubric for Grades 9–12 (High School Level)

NETS•S	NOVICE By End of Grade 9	BASIC By End of Grade 10	PROFICIENT By End of Grade 11	ADVANCED By End of Grade 12
1. BASIC OPERATIONS AND CONCEPTS				
• Students demonstrate a sound understanding of the nature and operation of technology systems.	Students describe strategies for identifying, solving, and preventing routine hardware and software problems that occur during everyday technology use. Students know how to research and evaluate the accuracy, relevance, appropriateness, comprehensiveness, and bias of electronic information sources concerning real-world problems. Students demonstrate an understanding of concepts underlying hardware, software, and connectivity; how a variety of information and technology resources can be combined to develop and promote understanding; and the value of visual and auditory features to convey accurate and convincing information. Students manipulate the keyboard and other input devices by touch with speed, accuracy, and efficiency. Students know how to make informed choices among technology systems, resources, and services.	Students apply their knowledge of the nature and operation of technology systems to anticipate, manage, and solve hardware, software, networking, and communications problems that occur in everyday technology use. Students apply strategies for authenticating information, challenging conclusions, and accurately citing online resources. Students select and apply hardware, software, information resources, and presentation hardware to research, analyze, compile, and communicate specific critical concepts from subject-area content. Students accurately and efficiently select, set up, and use a variety of input and output devices (e.g., keyboard, mouse, graphing calculators, cameras, video projectors, distance-learning hardware, microphones, electronic microscopes, sensors, drawing palates, earphones). Students discriminate among software applications according to their usefulness for solving particular analytical, informational, relational, or quantitative problems.	Students evaluate technology-based options, including distance and distributed education for lifelong learning. Students identify and analyze the advantages and disadvantages of widespread use and reliance on technology in the workplace and society as a whole. Students investigate and apply expert systems, intelligent agents, and simulations to explore real-world concepts and situations. Students exhibit facility, speed, and accurate hand position and fingering when using the keyboard as well as work with confidence in manipulating a variety of technology-based devices. Students collaborate in researching new and emerging technologies and their effects on current technology; effects on the types of resources, services, and educational opportunities available; and impact on health, business, and industry.	Students evaluate new and advanced technology resources (e.g., video servers, webcasting, compressed video delivery, online file sharing, graphing calculators, multifunction communications devices, global-positioning software) for information-dissemination options and technology career opportunities. Students assess capabilities and limitations of contemporary and emerging technology resources and the potential of these systems and services to address personal, lifelong learning, and workplace needs. Students collaborate in teams to illustrate content-related concepts integrating a variety of media (e.g., print, audio, video, graphic, probes, simulations, models) with presentation, word-processing, publishing, database, graphics-design software, or spreadsheet applications. Students routinely exhibit use of touch-typing techniques with advanced facility, accuracy, and speed, as they complete their assignments. Students collaborate in teams to evaluate software, hardware, and networking systems to inform the development of a technology plan for a specific real-world business, educational entity, industry, organization, or other group.

continued

TABLE 5 *continued*

NETS•S Assessment Rubric for Grades 9–12 (High School Level)

NETS•S	NOVICE By End of Grade 9	BASIC By End of Grade 10	PROFICIENT By End of Grade 11	ADVANCED By End of Grade 12
1. BASIC OPERATIONS AND CONCEPTS				
• **Students are proficient in the use of technology.**	Students identify information storage devices and strategies used most efficiently and effectively for storing different types of data, for different purposes, for portability, and for very large files.	Students know how to use a variety of internal and external devices, management strategies, and software resources for storage and manipulation of media and information.	Students compare a variety of file types according to their uses, characteristics, and relationships to specific software or utility applications.	Students know how to use advanced utilities (e.g., compression, antivirus, filters) with computer files in a variety of different media and formats.
• **Students are proficient in the use of technology.**	Students use accurate terminology and select appropriate tools and technology resources to accomplish a variety of tasks and to solve problems.	Students compare a variety of technology-based tools to determine the most effective and efficient hardware and software resources to accomplish specific tasks.	Students locate and accurately interpret help features to aid them in solving hardware, software, communications, programming, or other common technology-related problems.	Students know how to identify, assess, and solve advanced hardware, software, and network problems by using online help and other user documentation and support.
2. SOCIAL, ETHICAL, AND HUMAN ISSUES				
• **Students understand the ethical, cultural, and societal issues related to technology.**	Students identify capabilities and limitations of contemporary and emerging technology resources.	Students present research on consequences to society for failure to adhere to ethical and legal issues related to technology and advances in assistive technology resources and medical applications.	Students explore and report the effects of digital technology on current society, economies, and cultures across the globe as well as predict possible future implications.	Students analyze current trends in information and communication technology and assess the potential of emerging technologies for ethical and unethical uses in culture and society.
• **Students practice responsible use of technology systems, information, and software.**	Students identify and discuss terms and concepts associated with safe, effective, and efficient use of the Internet and telecommunications resources (e.g., password, firewall, spam, security, fair use, acceptable-use policy, release form) and recognize strategies that demonstrate ethical, legal, and socially responsible use of technology and electronic resources.	Students develop and present scenarios illustrating dilemmas that individuals may face regarding safe, effective, ethical, and legal use of technology resources as well as generate examples of appropriate and inappropriate solutions to these dilemmas.	Students provide accurate citations and bibliographical references for both traditional and electronic resources used in development of reports, projects, and papers in subject-related research, according to fair use and copyright guidelines.	Students analyze the consequences and costs of unethical use of information and computer technology and identify how individuals can protect their technology systems from the unethical and unscrupulous user.

continued

TABLE 5 *continued*

NETS•S Assessment Rubric for Grades 9–12 (High School Level)

NETS•S	NOVICE	BASIC	PROFICIENT	ADVANCED
	By End of Grade 9	By End of Grade 10	By End of Grade 11	By End of Grade 12
2. SOCIAL, ETHICAL, AND HUMAN ISSUES				
• Students develop positive attitudes toward technology uses that support lifelong learning, collaboration, personal pursuits, and productivity.	Students identify and present a strategy they would use for preparing for a job interview in a career for which they have had little or no training.	Students research job opportunities, interview an individual working in a specific profession, and report how technology is used in that particular profession.	Students evaluate a variety of sites aimed at lifelong learning and specific personal or professional pursuits by comparing the design, delivery, accessibility, and additional qualities that facilitate interest and ease of use.	Students analyze current trends in information and communication technology and discuss how emerging technologies could affect collaboration, enhance personal productivity, meet the diverse needs of learners, and promote opportunities for lifelong learning among local and global communities.
3. TECHNOLOGY PRODUCTIVITY TOOLS				
• Students use technology tools to enhance learning, increase productivity, and promote creativity.	Students know how to use technology tools and resources for managing and communicating personal, professional, and educational information (e.g., finances, schedules, addresses, purchases, correspondence, URLs, e-mail addresses, online references, citations).	Students know how to select and use appropriate technology tools to collect, analyze, store, and display data efficiently as well as communicate, illustrate, and present information.	Students compare features of productivity tools and develop a rationale for use of a particular set of tools for developing a specific product, or creative work.	Students understand and apply advanced software features (e.g., templates and styles) to improve the appearance of word-processing documents, spreadsheets, and presentations and provide evidence of learning, productivity, and creativity.
• Students use productivity tools to collaborate in constructing technology-enhanced models, preparing publications, and producing other creative works.	Students know how to work collaboratively to design, develop content for, and construct a Web-based publication.	Students use technology collaboratively to illustrate, demonstrate, and explain scientific, conceptual, and mathematical models.	Students collaborate with peers, experts, and others to develop a content-related knowledge base by using technology to compile, synthesize, produce, and disseminate information, models, and other creative works.	Students analyze a plan and procedures for development of a multimedia product (e.g., model, presentation, webcast, publication, or other creative work) and identify authoring tools; other hardware and software resources; research; and team personnel needed to plan, create, and edit the product.

continued

TABLE 5 *continued*

NETS•S Assessment Rubric for Grades 9–12 (High School Level)

NETS•S	NOVICE By End of Grade 9	BASIC By End of Grade 10	PROFICIENT By End of Grade 11	ADVANCED By End of Grade 12
4. TECHNOLOGY COMMUNICATIONS TOOLS				
• Students use tele-communications to collaborate, publish, and interact with peers, experts, and other audiences.	Students know how to develop evaluation criteria for use in judging the quality of published materials (e.g., print, digital, video) for group projects; plan, develop, and present content-based group projects based on the criteria; and conduct peer reviews of the group projects using the criteria.	Students identify, explore, and participate in sites hosting collab-orative study, publica-tion-development, creative-development, dialogue, discussion, expert-mentoring, data-sharing, model-develop-ment, or codevelopment opportunities.	Students routinely and efficiently use online information resources to meet needs for collabo-ration, research, publica-tions, higher education, or employment informa-tion, communications, and productivity.	Students plan, imple-ment, and evaluate collaborative projects (with peers, experts, or other audiences) using advanced telecom-munications tools (e.g., groupware, interactive Web sites, simulations, joint data collection, videoconferencing) to support curriculum concepts or benefit the local, regional, or global community.
• Students use a variety of media and formats to communicate information and ideas effectively to multiple audiences.	Students know how to plan, design, and develop a multimedia product including data (e.g., graphs, charts, database reports) to present content information.	Students develop multimedia presentations and/or video to illustrate conceptual, scientific, mathematical, or proce-dural models.	Students collaborate to develop multimedia presentations appropriate for a variety of purposes: to demonstrate; convince; advertise; provide concise or in-depth information; illustrate a hierarchy or sequence; and model scientific principles, mathematical process, properties, or concepts.	Students know how to use a variety of media and formats to design, develop, publish, and present products (e.g., presentations, newsletters, Web sites, video) that incorporate information from the curriculum and com-municate original ideas to multiple audiences.
5. TECHNOLOGY RESEARCH TOOLS				
• Students use technology to locate, evaluate, and collect information from a variety of sources.	Students know how to research and evaluate the accuracy, relevance, appropriateness, compre-hensiveness, and bias of electronic information sources concerning real-world problems.	Students identify and apply strategies for veri-fying results of research from technology-based resources.	Students collaborate to locate, evaluate, and collect information from a variety of sources and develop a report on the topic that compares and analyzes the differences found in specific facts, details, and interpreta-tions gleaned from different sources.	Students know how to locate, select, and use advanced technology resources (e.g., expert systems, intelligent agents, real-world models and simulations) to enhance their learning of curriculum topics selected.

continued

TABLE 5 *continued*

NETS•S Assessment Rubric for Grades 9–12 (High School Level)

NETS•S	NOVICE	BASIC	PROFICIENT	ADVANCED
	By End of Grade 9	By End of Grade 10	By End of Grade 11	By End of Grade 12
5. TECHNOLOGY RESEARCH TOOLS				
• Students use technology tools to process data and report results.	Students know how to create, edit, and modify a database report and identify trends reflecting analysis of the data.	Students apply spreadsheet and database tools to compile, sort, and chart data as well as analyze results.	Students develop spreadsheet templates designed to provide ongoing results immediately as new data is entered.	Students formulate a hypothesis or research question on a curriculum topic they choose, and then design, create, and populate a database to process data and report results.
• Students evaluate and select new information resources and technological innovations based on the appropriateness to specific tasks.	Students know how to select and use technology tools to efficiently collect, analyze, and display data for class assignments, projects, and presentations.	Students determine criteria for selection of a technology tool or resource to accomplish a specific task.	Students explore and report on technology innovations and how the use of them may affect jobs, education, leisure, or the global economy.	Students formulate a hypothesis or research question, and then select and use appropriate information and communication technology tools and resources for collecting and analyzing information and reporting results to multiple audiences.
6. TECHNOLOGY PROBLEM-SOLVING AND DECISION-MAKING TOOLS				
• Students use technology resources for solving problems and making informed decisions.	Students develop strategies for using data analysis, models, and simulations to make specific decisions regarding a course of action for solving real-world problems.	Students apply technology resources to identify, research, test, and affirm solutions that address problem-based scenarios.	Students know how to use technology tools that electronically collect, present, compile, and illustrate results of group data to support problem solving and decision making.	Students describe the integration of two or more information and communication technology tools and resources to collaborate with peers, community members, experts, and others to solve a problem and present results or an informed rationale for a decision.
• Students employ technology in the development of strategies for solving problems in the real world.	Students know how to identify a problem, develop a solution strategy, collect data on the effectiveness of the strategy, and analyze, interpret, publish, and present the data and conclusions based on real-world data.	Students research a community problem; use technology communications tools to solicit input on ideas for addressing the problem from a variety of individuals (e.g., peers, experts, community members); and compile, analyze, and report the results.	Students analyze results of problem-based simulations, identifying problem areas and developing strategies for change that can be predicted from the simulation to result in positive outcomes.	Students integrate information and communication technology to analyze a real-world problem, design and implement procedures to monitor information, set timelines, and evaluate progress toward the solution of a real-world problem.

The National Educational Technology Standards

Below are the National Educational Technology Standards for Teachers (NETS•T) and Administrators (NETS•A). The **NETS for Students (NETS•S)** appear on page 13, and the accompanying performance indicators for each grade range appear on pages 14–15.

NETS FOR TEACHERS (NETS•T)

All classroom teachers should be prepared to meet the following standards and performance indicators.

I. **Technology Operations and Concepts**
    Teachers demonstrate a sound understanding of technology operations and concepts. Teachers:

    A. demonstrate introductory knowledge, skills, and understanding of concepts related to technology (as described in the ISTE National Educational Technology Standards for Students).

    B. demonstrate continual growth in technology knowledge and skills to stay abreast of current and emerging technologies.

II. **Planning and Designing Learning Environments and Experiences**
    Teachers plan and design effective learning environments and experiences supported by technology. Teachers:

    A. design developmentally appropriate learning opportunities that apply technology-enhanced instructional strategies to support the diverse needs of learners.

    B. apply current research on teaching and learning with technology when planning learning environments and experiences.

    C. identify and locate technology resources and evaluate them for accuracy and suitability.

    D. plan for the management of technology resources within the context of learning activities.

    E. plan strategies to manage student learning in a technology-enhanced environment.

III. **Teaching, Learning, and the Curriculum**
    Teachers implement curriculum plans that include methods and strategies for applying technology to maximize student learning. Teachers:

    A. facilitate technology-enhanced experiences that address content standards and student technology standards.

    B. use technology to support learner-centered strategies that address the diverse needs of students.

    C. apply technology to develop students' higher-order skills and creativity.

    D. manage student learning activities in a technology-enhanced environment.

IV. **Assessment and Evaluation**
Teachers apply technology to facilitate a variety of effective assessment and evaluation strategies. Teachers:

A. apply technology in assessing student learning of subject matter using a variety of assessment techniques.

B. use technology resources to collect and analyze data, interpret results, and communicate findings to improve instructional practice and maximize student learning.

C. apply multiple methods of evaluation to determine students' appropriate use of technology resources for learning, communication, and productivity.

V. **Productivity and Professional Practice**
Teachers use technology to enhance their productivity and professional practice. Teachers:

A. use technology resources to engage in ongoing professional development and lifelong learning.

B. continually evaluate and reflect on professional practice to make informed decisions regarding the use of technology in support of student learning.

C. apply technology to increase productivity.

D. use technology to communicate and collaborate with peers, parents, and the larger community in order to nurture student learning.

VI. **Social, Ethical, Legal, and Human Issues**
Teachers understand the social, ethical, legal, and human issues surrounding the use of technology in PK–12 schools and apply that understanding in practice. Teachers:

A. model and teach legal and ethical practice related to technology use.

B. apply technology resources to enable and empower learners with diverse backgrounds, characteristics, and abilities.

C. identify and use technology resources that affirm diversity.

D. promote safe and healthy use of technology resources.

E. facilitate equitable access to technology resources for all students.

NETS FOR ADMINISTRATORS (NETS•A)

All school administrators should be prepared to meet the following standards and performance indicators. These standards are a national consensus among educational stakeholders regarding what best indicates effective school leadership for comprehensive and appropriate use of technology in schools.

I. **Leadership and Vision**—Educational leaders inspire a shared vision for comprehensive integration of technology and foster an environment and culture conducive to the realization of that vision. Educational leaders:

A. facilitate the shared development by all stakeholders of a vision for technology use and widely communicate that vision.

B. maintain an inclusive and cohesive process to develop, implement, and monitor a dynamic, long-range, and systemic technology plan to achieve the vision.

C. foster and nurture a culture of responsible risk taking and advocate policies promoting continuous innovation with technology.

D. use data in making leadership decisions.

E. advocate for research-based effective practices in use of technology.

F. advocate, on the state and national levels, for policies, programs, and funding opportunities that support implementation of the district technology plan.

II. **Learning and Teaching**—Educational leaders ensure that curricular design, instructional strategies, and learning environments integrate appropriate technologies to maximize learning and teaching. Educational leaders:

A. identify, use, evaluate, and promote appropriate technologies to enhance and support instruction and standards-based curriculum leading to high levels of student achievement.

B. facilitate and support collaborative technology-enriched learning environments conducive to innovation for improved learning.

C. provide for learner-centered environments that use technology to meet the individual and diverse needs of learners.

D. facilitate the use of technologies to support and enhance instructional methods that develop higher-level thinking, decision-making, and problem-solving skills.

E. provide for and ensure that faculty and staff take advantage of quality professional learning opportunities for improved learning and teaching with technology.

III. **Productivity and Professional Practice**—Educational leaders apply technology to enhance their professional practice and to increase their own productivity and that of others. Educational leaders:

A. model the routine, intentional, and effective use of technology.

B. employ technology for communication and collaboration among colleagues, staff, parents, students, and the larger community.

C. create and participate in learning communities that stimulate, nurture, and support faculty and staff in using technology for improved productivity.

D. engage in sustained, job-related professional learning using technology resources.

E. maintain awareness of emerging technologies and their potential uses in education.

F. use technology to advance organizational improvement.

IV. **Support, Management, and Operations**—Educational leaders ensure the integration of technology to support productive systems for learning and administration. Educational leaders:

A. develop, implement, and monitor policies and guidelines to ensure compatibility of technologies.

B. implement and use integrated technology-based management and operations systems.

C. allocate financial and human resources to ensure complete and sustained implementation of the technology plan.

D. integrate strategic plans, technology plans, and other improvement plans and policies to align efforts and leverage resources.

E. implement procedures to drive continuous improvements of technology systems and to support technology-replacement cycles.

V. **Assessment and Evaluation**—Educational leaders use technology to plan and implement comprehensive systems of effective assessment and evaluation. Educational leaders:

A. use multiple methods to assess and evaluate appropriate uses of technology resources for learning, communication, and productivity.

B. use technology to collect and analyze data, interpret results, and communicate findings to improve instructional practice and student learning.

C. assess staff knowledge, skills, and performance in using technology and use results to facilitate quality professional development and to inform personnel decisions.

D. use technology to assess, evaluate, and manage administrative and operational systems.

VI. **Social, Legal, and Ethical Issues**—Educational leaders understand the social, legal, and ethical issues related to technology and model responsible decision making related to these issues. Educational leaders:

A. ensure equity of access to technology resources that enable and empower all learners and educators.

B. identify, communicate, model, and enforce social, legal, and ethical practices to promote responsible use of technology.

C. promote and enforce privacy, security, and online safety related to the use of technology.

D. promote and enforce environmentally safe and healthy practices in the use of technology.

E. participate in the development of policies that clearly enforce copyright law and assign ownership of intellectual property developed with district resources.

This material was originally produced as a project of the Technology Standards for School Administrators Collaborative.

DATE DUE